Lingít G̲unéi Sh Tóo Dultóow X'úx'

Workbook for Beginning to Study Lingít

2nd edition

X̲'unei Lance Twitchell

Based on *Beginning Tlingit*
by Nora Marks Dauenhauer and Richard Dauenhauer

Lingít G̲unéi Sh Tóo Dultóow X'úx'
Workbook for Beginning to Study Lingít

The publication of the 2nd Edition Tlingit Workbook was made possible by the work of Dr. X̲'unei Lance Twitchell with sponsorship from Sealaska Heritage Institute.

This text is not intended to show the only way to speak Lingít. No single text can document a language and its many dialects and variations.

© 2017, 2022 Sealaska Heritage Institute and X̲'unei Lance Twichell

Cover images: "Dictionary Birds" by X̲'unei.
"Documenting Fluent Elders at a Language Camp in Yakutat" photo by X̲'unei.

Images in text: Public domain use photos from U.S. Fish and Wildlife, National Oceanic and Atmospheric Administration, National Park Service, Wikimedia, Pexels, and goodfreephotos.com. Stock images from Adobe Stock and Alamy Stock Photos. Additional photos by Kaasteen Jill Meserve, Sue Shotridge, Shuwuteen Karenza Bott, and Alaska Seafood Marketing Institute.

Printed in the United States of America.
All rights reserved.

Library of Congress Control Number: 2016962443
ISBN: 978-1-946019-46-2

First edition published 2017. Second edition 2020.

Address correspondence to:

Sealaska Heritage Institute
105 S. Seward St.
Suite 201
Juneau, AK 99801

X̲'unei Lance Twitchell
(907) 796-6114
latwitchell@alaska.edu

K̲eiwxnéi k̲a Xwaayeenák̲ jiyís áyá.
Tlax̲ wáa sá yee x̲six̲án.

For Nora and Richard Dauenhauer.
I love you both so very much.

Ách áwé tsu héide shugax̱tootáan
héi yaa ḵusgé daakeit.
Haa jeex' a náḵ has kawdik'éet'
haa káak hás ḵa haa léelk'u hás.

— Kichnáalx̱

That is why we will open again
this container of wisdom.
Our grandparents and our uncles
left it behind in our hands.

– George Davis, Deisheetaan
(*Because We Cherish You*, Dauenhauer and Dauenhauer 1981)

ách	á-wé	tsu	héi-dei	∅-shu-<ga-u-g̱a>--tu-∅-√táan
because	focus-there	again	here-toward	it(3.O)-end-<future>-we.(1p.S)-cl.(∅)-√carry-(wooden.object)

hé	yaa=ḵu-s-√gé	daaka-át
here	mentally=areal-cl.(d,s)-√understand	surrounding.surface-thing

haa=	jee-x'	a=	náḵ	has=	ka-<ÿu>-∅-di-√k'éet'
our.(1p.O)=	possession-at.(residing)	it.(3nh.O)=	leave.behind	3ph=	surface-<perfective>-they.(3.S)-cl.(d,∅,i)-√move.in.mass

haa=	káak	=hás	ḵa	haa=	léelk'u	=hás
our.(1p.O)=	maternal.uncle	=plural.kinship	and	our.(1p.O)=	grandparent	=plural.kinship

Contents

Foreword:
Voices of Our Ancestors Through the Voices of Our Children

We have made significant progress since 1998 when our Board of Trustees first declared the revitalization of Native languages to be Sealaska Heritage Institute's highest priority. At that time, language programs were non-existent and Native languages were described as "moribund." We refused to accept that our languages were "death bound" and made the vow that the voices of our ancestors would always be heard in our land.

Today, thanks to the efforts of many, and notably the "language learners," as the teachers who were learning Native languages and simultaneously teaching in the classroom called themselves, the Voices of Our Ancestors are now heard through the Voices of Our Children!

It was not an easy challenge, as we had to launch language revitalization efforts on multiple fronts—securing legislative action and funding, training teachers in updated approaches to language learning, developing curricula, and convincing schools to integrate language into the classroom.

I will continue to repeat this message until it is ingrained in the consciousness of the public, that Native languages contain intellectual wealth accumulated through thousands of years. They convey how Native people see and use the land, and they provide knowledge about our environment and land in Southeast Alaska. Language is a uniquely human gift central to our experience as people and as Alaska Natives. This knowledge and the differing world views among our Native societies are worthy of protection and transmittal to future generations. Linguistic and cultural diversity is a benefit to society.

Public policy makers must also come to accept what our evaluations demonstrate, that the integration of language and culture into our schools results in improved academic success that benefits students and ultimately our society.

The language learners, who are now the masters in language revitalization, continue to teach and to develop material such as this *Beginning Tlingit Workbook*. We are confident that this text will become another essential tool in our language restoration effort.

Our deepest gratitude to the author, X̱'unei Lance Twitchell, for yet another successful language effort. He has made a significant difference in ensuring the survival of our Native languages.

Rosita Ḵaaháni Worl, Ph.D.
President, Sealaska Heritage Institute

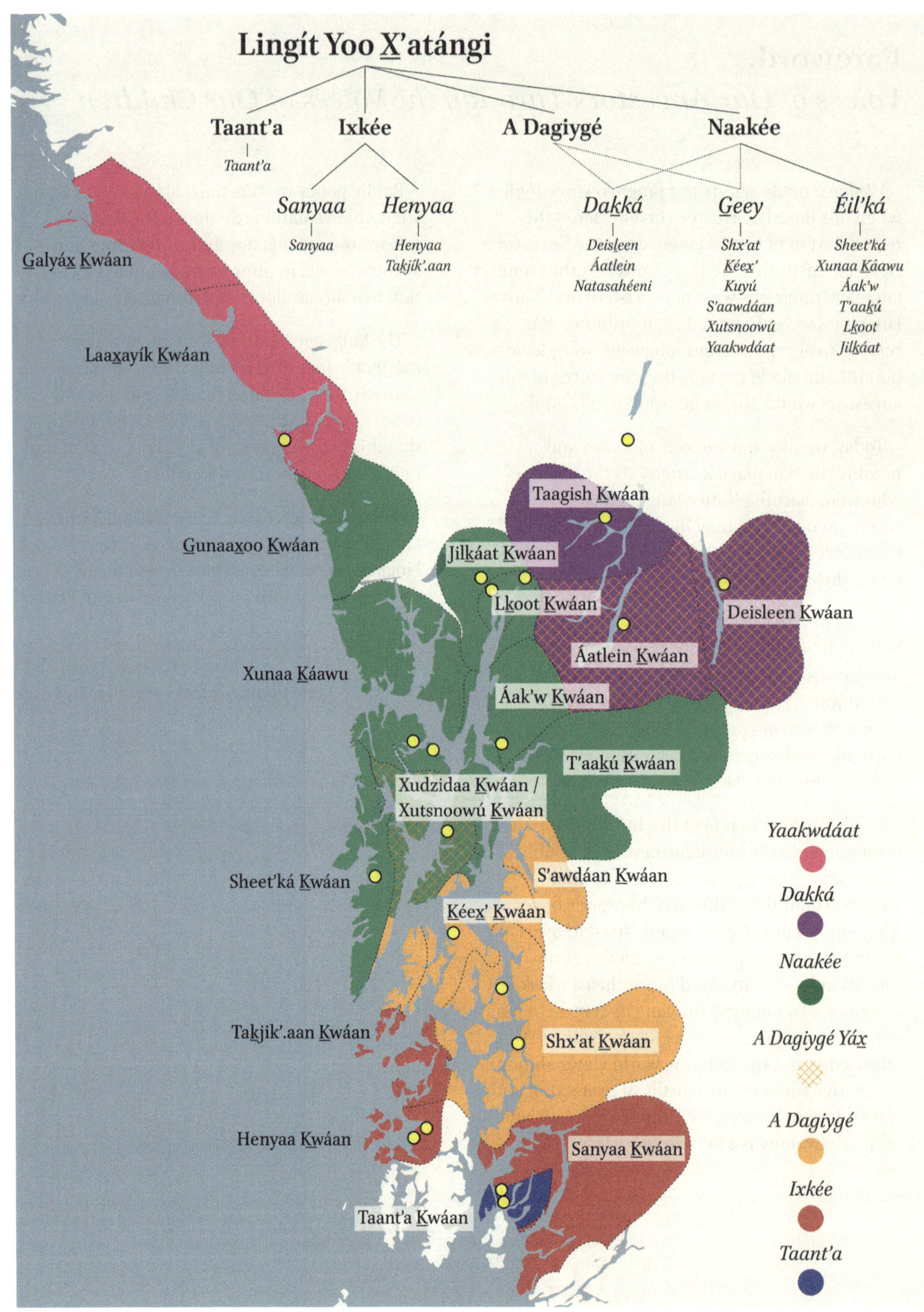
Lingít Yoo X̲'atángi
Taant'a
Taant'a
Ixkée
Sanyaa
Sanyaa
Henyaa
Henyaa
Tak̲jík'.aan
A Dagiygé
Naakée
Dak̲k̲á
Deisl̲een
Áatlein
Natasahéeni
Geey
Shx'at
K̲éex̲'
Kuyú
S'aawdáan
Xutsnoowú
Yaakwdáat
Éil'ká
Sheet'ká
Xunaa K̲áawu
Áak'w
T'aak̲ú
L̲koot
Jilk̲áat
Galyáx̲ K̲wáan
Laax̲ayík K̲wáan
Gunaax̲oo K̲wáan
Taagish K̲wáan
Jilk̲áat K̲wáan
L̲koot K̲wáan
Deisleen K̲wáan
Áatlein K̲wáan
Xunaa K̲áawu
Áak'w K̲wáan
T'aak̲ú K̲wáan
Xudzidaa K̲wáan / Xutsnoowú K̲wáan
Sheet'ká K̲wáan
S'awdáan K̲wáan
K̲éex̲' K̲wáan
Tak̲jik'.aan K̲wáan
Shx'at K̲wáan
Henyaa K̲wáan
Sanyaa K̲wáan
Taant'a K̲wáan
Yaakwdáat
Dak̲k̲á
Naakée
A Dagiygé Yáx̲
A Dagiygé
Ixkée
Taant'a

RICHARD and NORA DAUENHAUER
PHOTO BY BRIAN WALLACE, COURTESY OF SEALASKA HERITAGE INSTITUTE

Tlax̱ ḵúnáx̱ yee eedáx̱ sh tóog̱aa haa ditee, haa jiyís yan yéi jiyeeynei.

We really appreciate what you all have done for us.

Introduction

Anyone who does work in the Lingít language is blessed with an incredible collection of recordings, grammar documentation, dictionaries, inspirational speeches, and much more. *Beginning Tlingit* has gone through many updates through the incredible work of Nora and Richard Dauenhauer and the team of language advocates at the Sealaska Heritage Institute over the years. Generations of teachers have been taking what they know or were learning into classrooms over the past thirty years, and the result of their feedback and ideas is this current edition of the *Beginning Tlingit Workbook*.

The goal of creating this workbook is to transition towards image-based language learning to encourage word-image association instead of Lingít-word to English-word association. Additions have been made, and some optional grammatical explanations have been added through a number of different sections, but the basic philosophy remains the same: learn nouns that start off with sounds familiar to English speakers and begin introducing nouns with more challenging sounds. Phrases are introduced through substitution drills, where students can learn something basic and then make it more dynamic by adding other elements they are learning.

I think the oldest image I started using for this project was from 2002, when I began teaching Lingít in Skagway. I had been a huge fan of *Beginning Tlingit* since I discovered it in 1995 and started studying Lingít seriously with my grandfather Gooshdehéen Silas Dennis, Sr. After looking into the troubled state of Indigenous languages in North America while studying at the University of Minnesota, my commitment to the Lingít language intensified. The more I learned, the more I had the desire to teach, and the first time I was introduced to the language community working with Nora and Richard Dauenhauer was at a sponsored immersion gathering at Glacier Bay in 2004. It was amazing to see how many people were invested in our language, but at the same time we could see that the number of speakers was in great decline.

Several of us formed a network of learners, and many of us became teachers. It seemed like we learned something and then turned right around and taught it to someone else. I had limited resources in Skagway at the time, with only one fully fluent speaker and little access to the materials that were being developed in Juneau. While teaching the language, it became clear that associating Lingít with images instead of English might make a clearer connection between the object and the Lingít name for it. Out of that idea, and after interacting with fluent speakers, teachers, and learners, the project began to take off.

Florence Sheakley came to Skagway to help us with classes, and one time she brought her mother, Emma Marks. It was a special moment for us to see the fluency in the Marks family, and additional language camps in Haines and Carcross helped contribute to the ideas behind the workbook. It is based entirely on the teaching methods and steps developed by Nora and Richard, as well as many other contributors over the years, but it also incorporates some of the ways we are documenting and teaching various parts of Lingít grammar today, especially verbs.

Any piece of curriculum is something that builds upon the wonderful body of work before it and merely contributes to the materials that are available to the speakers, teachers, and learners. The moment of power comes when that material is brought to life in the exchange of knowledge where new speakers are made. After working in Lingít for over two decades now, I am greatly encouraged to see the number of learners coming to the language, determined to become speakers and to be a part of a language movement that restores the stability of our language. My overall hope is that this is done with love, kindness, and humility, and that its members acknowledge all of the hard and wonderful work that took place over the years.

From the elders who suffered as children when people were trying to kill off our language, to the generation who never had a chance to learn, to the generation that shifted their lives to create space for our language, to the children who are now being raised with our language, we watch this journey come around to a place of hope. The next steps are ensuring that our languages are fully functional and respectable parts of curriculum across all educational levels, doing the hard work of bringing the languages back into the home, and continuing to focus on healing and recovering from a great and horrible attempted genocide.

The Lingít language contains an endless ocean of complexity, metaphor, and spirituality. It unlocks a relationship between people, place, and other living beings that stretches back into time immemorial. Our work, which continues upon the path that was made for us, is to ensure that it exists forever. As I work late into the days and nights on projects like this, I am encouraged by all the speakers and teachers who have walked on into the forest, leaving their gifts behind to shape into the next thing. It is an absolute honor to be a part of that exchange, and to watch speakers, teachers, and learners interact through a language that is both our inheritance and the intellectual property that we must protect for future generations.

The material presented here can be supplemented by a number of different activities and games to help students engage in the language. There is no single technique that teaches language, but instead there are a variety of things a teacher should employ to engage students, create opportunities for repetition and practice, and to stress cultural relevance and proper language use. Many of the patterns here encourage using whole language, which may sound unnatural to the fluent speaker. For example, in a natural speaking environment one might ask, "what do you have?" and you might respond with "a bracelet." In language exercises, however, you would be encouraged to say "I have a bracelet." As we begin our adventures in Lingít language learning, we start with an artificial language, but it opens the door to create fluency in the future through careful listening, self-monitoring, feedback from the language community, and gaining confidence.

Language learning is a journey. It is not a race against others; it is a race against time and circumstance. High levels of fluency can be attained, but the journey is long and requires tremendous amounts of effort and motivation. Through it all, the learner is encouraged to stay positive and productive, and to take all feedback in but also be aware of unhealthy actions that might stunt language learning.

You are involved in undoing generations of attempted genocide of the Lingít language and people. This is no small miracle but is actually one of the most inspirational parts of being human. It takes courage to sit in the chair and study a language that has become foreign to most of its own people. In 2021, there are an estimated 40 speakers of Lingít at various levels, and that includes all second language speakers at an intermediate level or higher. Out of that 100, 40 are highly fluent and perhaps 10 could be considered fully fluent and able to perform highly complex language tasks such as classical oratory, advanced verb modes, and translations.

But the sun is not setting on our language. A classic Lingít greeting is *tsu haa káa ḵeiwa.aa* (it has dawned on us again) and that summarizes the attitude of the Lingít language movement. The work that we do is carried out with the energy of all of the speakers who made words for their little grandchildren, for the teachers who spent countless hours developing materials and activities that help give learners the language in manageable chunks that follow a path to being able to speak and listen. There are many people who have supported language efforts by securing and managing grants and developing whole programs to help the cause.

Indigenous languages did not put themselves in danger. The people did not outgrow a use for them. The reality is that we see today the result of a massive attempted genocide that was executed by American governments and religious institutions that targeted languages to assimilate the people. Many of our elders have shared stories of themselves and children they grew up with who experienced the horrors of American genocide. Kaséix̱ Selina Everson spoke often of our dearly departed Ḵaalḵáawu Cyril George talking about the times when our language was forbidden, and how he would still cry about it as an elder. Shakshháani Marge Dutson courageously shared her life experience: when she first started school a teacher grabbed her by the hair, picked her up off the ground, and shook her violently in front of the class to force her to stop speaking Lingít.

These realities are often overlooked today, as Alaskan education systems operate ignorant of their deviant history. We can see some of this from the words of teachers who came to Alaska in the late 1800s and early 1900s to implement education systems, as in the following passage that seems to gloat about torture methods developed to annihilate Indigenous languages:

> In order, that the children might the more rapidly acquire the English language, they were expected to speak nothing but English in the home. Of course, this was hard for many of them who only knew two or three words, knowing none at all when they came, and naturally they would among themselves talk Indian. This made their pronunciation of English very bad, and interfered with their construction of sentences; so we required them to speak nothing but English except by permission; but they often would get into the washroom or in the wood shed, and having set a watch, they would indulge in a good Indian talk. A few cases of this kind, and we applied a heroic remedy to stop it. We obtained a bottle of myrrh and capsicum: myrrh is bitter as gall and capsicum hot like fire. We prepared a little sponge; saturated it with this solution, and everyone that talked Indian had his mouth washed to take away the taint of the Indian language! One application usually was sufficient; but one or two cases had to receive a second application. From that time on, progress in their studies was almost doubly rapid, for they

> dared not talk their own language, and talking English, helped them the better, to comprehend the language; but like all children, they were not always good in everything else.[1]

To help balance this, we look back towards our cultural teachings and philosophies. Kaxwaan Éesh George Davis, T'ak̲deintaan k̲a Tsaagweidí Yádi, talks about what his mother used to always tell him. Within these words we find some useful learning and life philosophies:

Hél i yáx̲
lingit'aaní k̲áa
néekwdéin daayeek̲áak̲
k̲a néekwdéin k̲udaa.eenéik̲!
Ch'as tula.aan
k̲a k̲usax̲án k̲wá i téix̲' tóo yéi na.oo!
Yaa nalgwátl yáa lingit'aaní.
A kagéide gux̲lagwáatl áx' ux̲ kei kg̲wateeyí
 i k̲usteeyí.
Gwál néekw tsú i kaadé kg̲wagóot.
Ách áwé ch'as k̲usax̲án
k̲a tula.aan i téix̲' tóo yéi na.oo!
Ch'a wáa sá yéi ux̲ kei igatéeni
yá aan ituwli.aani k̲u.oo
gwál i éede has gux̲dashée.

Do not speak
or act with ill will
to the people of the world,
who are like yourself!
Only love and kindness,
put that in your heart!
The world is spinning around.
It's going to roll up to the place where your life will
 be going out of control.
Maybe illness, too, will come your way.
That is why, only love and kindness,
put that in your heart!
However your life gets out of control,
these people you have been kind with,
maybe they will help you.[2]

This information is shared with you to create inspiration. We need all the courage and unity we can muster to create a world where we have more than 10,000 speakers and our language is relatively safe. Sometimes this requires thinking about the big picture and developing strategies to counter cultural hegemonies that dominate educational systems and organizations.

But more than anything, you need to know that the biggest changes often occur at the individual level, where you shift your life patterns to bring more and more language into your daily existence. Listen. Speak. Build vocabulary. Internalize grammar. Allow the Lingít worldview—Lingít Tundatáani—to take root in your consciousness to a point that you become multilingual.

As advocates of our languages, we commit to hard work and persistence to honor all those who have suffered to keep our language alive in times of peril. We do so in order to protect the gifts our ancient ones envisioned for their little grandchildren. We do this for our own mental health, and to undo a century of genocidal tendencies and we do so in love, unity, and strength of purpose.

I am grateful to all those who helped prepare this text, from the elders who visited classrooms and talked with me to help understand concepts to the many students at the University of Alaska Southeast and language camps in Carcross, Teslin, Atlin, and Skagway who endured pile after pile of loose-leaf drafts of this work. Many of those students were particularly helpful in spotting errors and providing valuable feedback of what helps the learner. We are blessed with wonderful elders and tireless workers who helped develop the core concepts here, which this workbook does not seek to replace but instead to complement.

This workbook attempts to incorporate known dialect differences. If you hear things said differently by fluent speakers in your area, then adjust your language learning to honor your own dialect. The map in this section shows the known Lingít dialects.

This second edition corrected errors and revisions to the presentation of some content. The weather section was split and the more complex verbs were moved to the end at the suggestion of K̲aayák'w Kyle Worl. G̲uneiwtí Marsha Hotch provided additional vocabluary and structural ideas. A chapter was also added to practice object pronouns, and additional explanations were given throughout the text. Gunalchéesh to a team of exceptional proofreaders:

1 Replogle, Charles. *Among the Indians of Alaska.* Headley Brothers, 1904.
2 Davis, George Kaxwaan Éesh. Recorded Language Session, 2015.

Ch'eet Wú Joe Binger, Yéilt'ooch' Tláa Collyne Bunn, Koolyéik Roby Littlefield, Aandax̱ltín Teik Stephanie Tripp, and Éedaa Heather Burge.

In addition to proofreaders, students, and teachers who helped with editing, the second edition received a thorough review and incredibly helpful edits and additions from Yeilkunéiyi Jeff Leer and Chalyee Will Geiger. Their careful reading and depth of knowledge of our language combined with a commitment to improve curriculum development, and for that I am grateful.

With Indigenous languages, there are often dialogues on spelling conventions, methods to teach up to more complex concepts, and the terms used to describe the phenomena of a language. The decisions made in the updates of this text are not meant to displace the ideas that others have, but do attempt to further document some aspects of Lingít in ways that provide building blocks to allow learners to push themselves towards understanding some of the more complex and nuanced parts of Lingít.

Lingít is incredibly complex and speakers will often find themselves searching for ways to imitate our ancestors. As Kaatyé David Kadashan once said:

Ch'a a kayaa áyá yéi gax̱tusanéi.
We will only imitate (our ancestors).

While visiting Ḵeixwnéi at her home, I was talking to her about this phrase in regards to a potential name for a dance group. She was very excited to hear this phrase, and said, "Yes! That's true!"

To those who are exploring the upper realms of our language, who are trying to understand the depths of the ocean of knowledge our ancestors waded into, I am thankful. My work contains many mistakes as I try to understand more and more and attempt to help students reach a higher level of fluency.

Our language has been blessed by incredible speakers, who left us with pieces of language that challenge our abilities to understand how to create meaning and connection, and to understand more of what we hear and to speak in ways that honor the powerful voices that still echo on this land today.

Lastly, as this final update is made, credit must be given to Kingeestí David Katzeek, who regularly engaged in teaching, speech making, storytelling, and contributions to conversations on how to teach Lingít. His voice is especially present in my commitments to working in our language with love, respect, and kindness. He had an intense curiosity in how to help learners build bridges from English thought modes to Lingít tundatáani. He helped to develop some of the concepts that are presented here, as did conversations with Keiyishí Bessie Cooley and Ḵaaḵal.aat Florence Sheakley, who were present at many workshops and classes where this material was created and field tested.

Finally, although this workbooks creates some additional content and adds images, the original text *Beginning Tlingit* is the place where it all started. My first teacher was my grandfather, Gooshdehéen Si Dennis Sr. He passed away before I learned to speak, but he put me on the path, and when I first found *Beginning Tlingit* and the tapes that came with it, the work of Ḵeixwnéi and Xwaayeenáḵ, along with the voice of G̱unáak'w Fred White and the behind the scenes work of many others, kept me connected to my grandpa. I started learning from *Beginning Tlingit* in 1997 while living in Saxman, and then for the next few years while in Minneapolis.

Then in 2000 I attended a *Haa Ḵusteeyí* summer session at the University of Alaska, and started teaching it to others informally. That put my on a path of working on curriculum and trying to learn and create content at the same time. I continue to make mistakes, but I learn from those mistakes and am not trying to pursue perfection. Instead, I am trying to do my part to maintain safe spaces for language use and learning, to document speakers, and to help our language have power and use in more and more places.

Wherever you are in your language journey, I hope that you know that language use and learning is a place of respect and love, and that you are cherished by the language community and by all those who dreamt of a time when we were gaining more speakers than we were losing. That is the direction we are seeking as we imitate them, and search for the path they cleared for us.

Yee gu.aa yáx̱ x'wán!
X̱'unei Lance Twitchell, Ph.D.

Haa jiyís wududliyéx̱ haa yoo x̱'atángi.
Has du jeedé gax̱tootée,
haa dachx̱ánx̱ siteeyi aa.

Our language was made for us.
We will hand it to those
who are our grandchildren.

0

Lingít X̲'ayéigi

Sounds of Human Speech

Aax̱ áwé
has du x̱'wáal'i áwé a kaadéi
has akooldánch
wé eeshandéin tuwateeyi ḵáa.

—Naa Tláa

Then they
would let their down fall
like snow
over the person who is feeling grief.

– Jessie Dalton, T'aḵdeintaan

(*Haa Tuwunáagu Yís*, Dauenhauer and Dauenhauer 1990)

á-dáx̱	á-wé	has du=	x̱'wáal'-i
there-from	focus-that	them.all's(3p.P)	down.feathers-relational

á-wé	a=	ká-de	has=	a-ka-<ÿu>-∅-la-√dán-ch
focus-that	it.(3nh.P)	surface-toward	3ph=	it.(3.O)-surface-<perfective>-they.(3.S)-cl.(l)-√snow.fall.heavily-habitual

wé	eesháan-déin	∅-tu-ÿa-√tee-ÿi=	ḵáa
that	pitiful-ly.(adverb)	they.(3.O)-inside-cl.(∅,i)-√be-relational=	person.(4h.i)

Lingít x̲'éinák̲ du.áx̲ji

Lingít is full of sounds that you do not hear in the English language, and some that may be unique to Lingít (x', x'w x̲', x̲'w). English is a language heavily situated towards the front of your mouth, while Lingít consonants are produced from the tooth ridge on back. This means a lot of guttural sounds that will challenge your muscle control within your mouth. A great practice technique to warm yourself up is to look up, relax your throat, and make noises like a raven, or just make the dangly guy in the back of your throat (your uvula) rattle around. This may feel like you are gurgling or clearing your throat, but in later lessons you will need to control this part of your body, and the best way to do that is through exercise

Practice sounds that are unfamiliar; pay close attention to what is going on inside your mouth, and use your hands and body language to help locate sounds and enunciate tones. Chances are, you will be using different areas than you have used for much of your life, so you will have to wake them up through exercise and gain command over them to improve your pronunciation. Have patience. Sounds are introduced gradually in our lessons, more complex ones come later.

When looking at Lingít vowels, it is important to remember two things. First, vowels can be either long or short, meaning that in some cases a syllable will be pronounced either long or short depending on the situation. The vowels of verb stems regularly shift between long and short with predictable frequency. Equally as important, Lingít has two tones: high and low. This can greatly affect meaning, so you need to be conscious of tone, which is marked with an accent (á, áa) when high, and unmarked (a, aa) when low. Try to use body movements, such as holding your hand out when speaking and raising it when you see a tone mark. Let this be your cue to raise the pitch of your name.

Lingít has vowels that have sonorant endings. They end in a consonant that speakers of English are used to making at the beginning of words. The examples of sonorant endings in English are "wow" and "eeew!" Exaggerate the differences between vowel sounds, length, and tone while learning them.

The «o̱o» and «ó̱o» vowels are part of the Dak̲ká dialect, and are made when an uvular consonant is before or after the vowel. It is the same sound as the coastal «o» heard in «ho ho!»

Vowels

SHORT		LONG	
LOW	HIGH	LOW	HIGH
a	á	aa	áa
e	é	ei	éi
i	í	ee	ée
u	ú	oo / o̱o	óo / ó̱o

Vowels With Sonorant Ending

VOWELS PLUS SEMIVOWEL PAIRS			
SHORT	LONG	SHORT	LONG
ay	aay	aw	aaw
ey	eiy	ew	eiw
iy	eey	iw	eew
(uy) *	—	uw	oow

* found only in rare interjection úy, attested in noblewoman's wedding song: "Hei-yoo-waa. Hei-lg̲ei-waa. Uy, uy! Uy, uy, uy!"

Consonant locations and sound practice

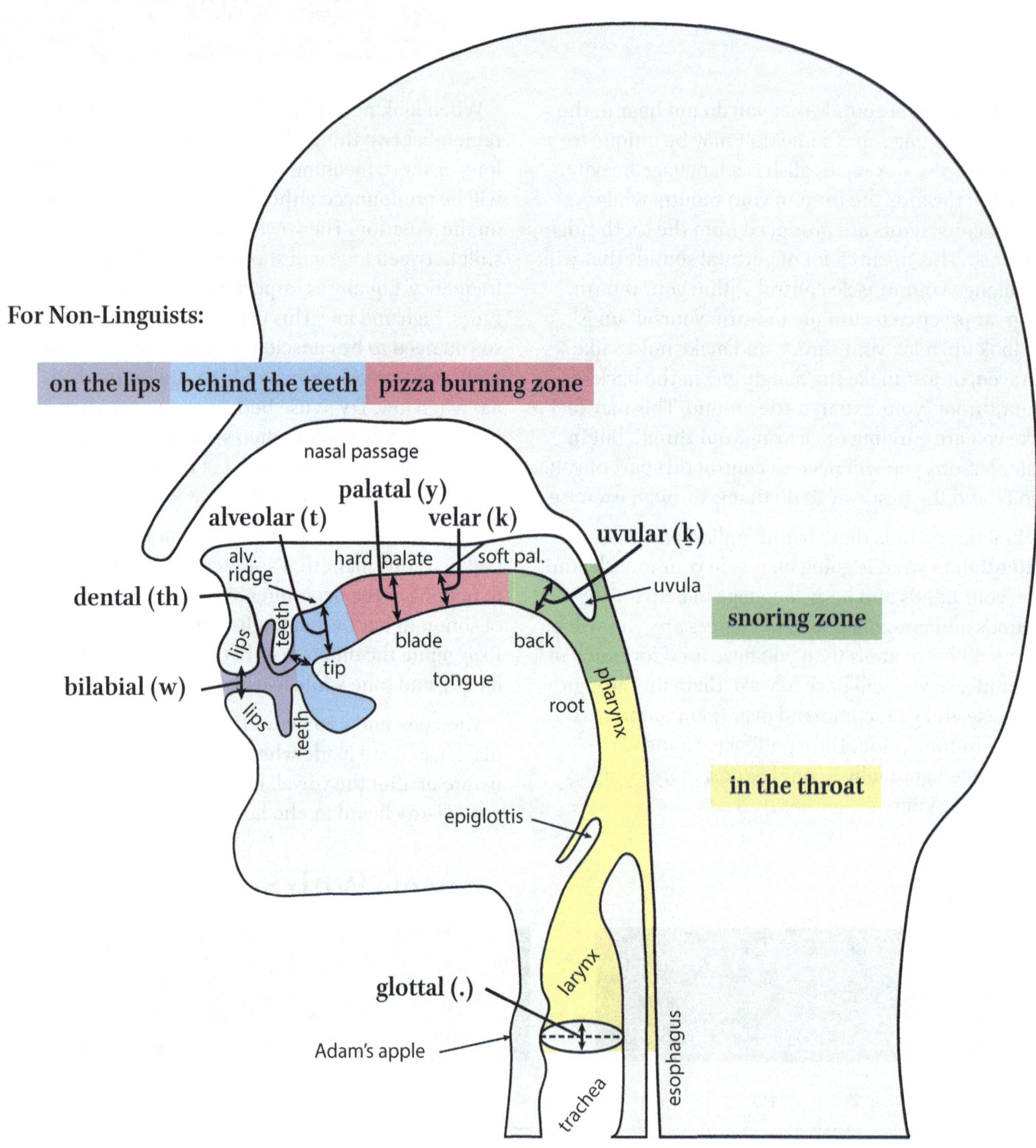

based on the work of Jeff Leer (2001) and James Crippen (2013)

	labial lips	alveolar tongue behind teeth				velar middle of tongue against roof of mouth		uvular back of tongue touches uvula at back of throat		glottal vocal chords	
stops (stop of breath)							rounded		rounded		rounded (rare)
plain		dáa weasel	dleit snow	dzánti flounder	jánwu mountain goat	gán firewood	gwéil bag	g̱ooch wolf	g̱wéinaa towel	naa.át clothing	yéi ana.weich [1] wears it (every time)
aspirated followed by a puff of air		tá sleep	tleilóo butterfly	tsáats bear root	chál cache	káast barrel	kwéiy marker	ḵákw basket	–ḵwáan people of -		
glottalized followed by a pop		t'á king salmon	tl'átk earth; ground	ts'ats'ée bird	ch'áak' eagle	k'ínk' fermented fish heads	k'wát' egg	ḵ'ateil pitcher	ḵ'wátl cooking pot		
fricatives (breath flows through narrow opening, creating friction)											
plain			lóol fireweed	séek belt	shaa mountain	xáshaa saw	xwaasdáa canvas; tarp	x̱áat fish	x̱waagoot i went	hít house	
glottalized raised vocal chords			l'ook coho	s'eek black bear		x'áax' apple	x'wán boots	x̱'aan fire	x̱'wáat' dolly varden trout		
sonorants (softer, you can sing them continuously)											
nasal air through nose	máa sá? [2] how	nóoskw wolverine									
non-nasal	–waaḵ eye		dan̲eiyí lake trout		yaakw boat	ÿóow [3] lunch					

[1] also yéi ana.eich

[2] in Teslin and Carcross, elsewhere wáa sá

[3] in Carcross, elsewhere wóow

Vowels

A			
a	á	aa	áa

E			
e	é	ei	éi

I			
i	í	ee	ée

U			
u	ú	oo / o̱o	óo / ó̱o

Labial

w	m
wasóos	másh (T)

Dialects are important in Lingít, and when variations are known to the author and editors, they are marked with (T) for Teslin, (C) for Carcross, and (Y) for Yakutat.

Alveolar

ch	ch’	d
cheech	ch’eet	dáa
	(murrelet)	
dl	**dz**	**j**
dleit	dzeit	jánwu / jínwu (Y)
(snow)		

Alveolar (cont'd)

Alveolar (cont'd)

tl'	ts	ts'
tl'eex	tsaa	ts'ats'ée
y		
yaak		

Velar

Velar Labial (rounded)

Uvular

g̱	ḵ	ḵ’
g̱ooch / g̱oo̱ch	ḵákw	ḵ’ateil

x̱	x̱’
x̱áat	x̱’aan
(fish)	

Uvular Labial (rounded)

g̱w	ḵw	-ḵw
g̱wéinaa *	–ḵwáan	náaḵw
	(people of; person of; traditional territoy of)	

* this word most often appears with a prefix, such as jig̱wéinaa (hand towel) or lug̱wéinaa (handkercheif)

Uvular Labial (rounded)

ḵ'w	-ḵ'w	x̱w
ḵ'wátl 	léiḵ'w 	shanax̱wáayi 
-x̱w	x̱'w	-x̱'w
–húnx̱w	x̱'wáat'	néx̱'w
 (male's older brother)	 (Dolly Varden trout)	 (cloudberry)

Glottal

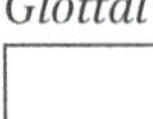

.	h	hw
yaana.eit	hít	yaa nahwéin

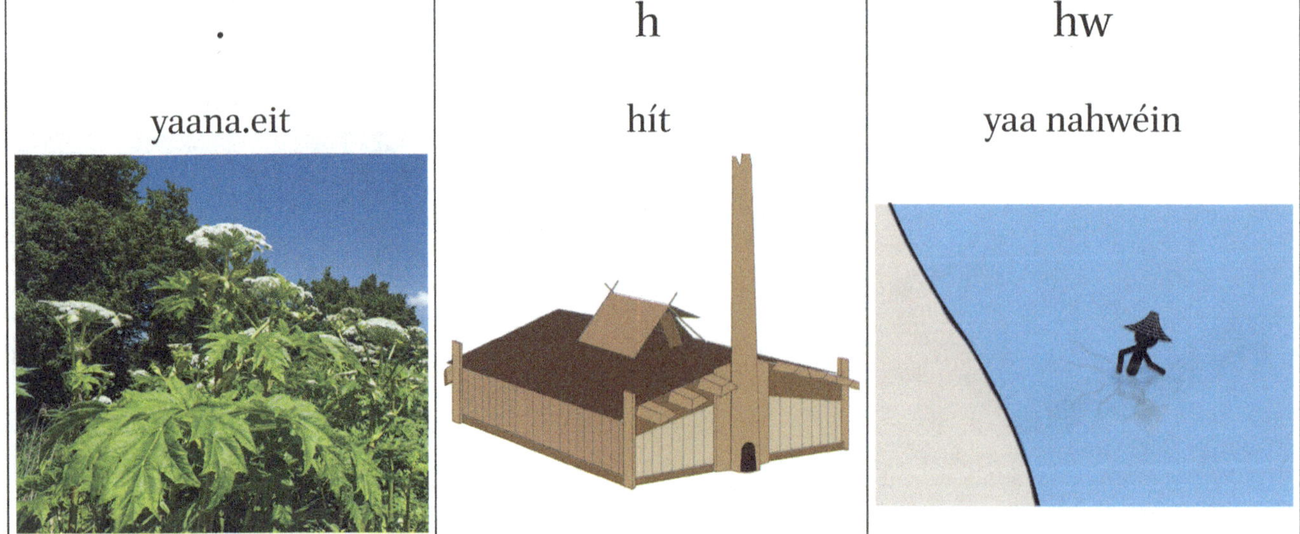

1A

Daa sáyá?

What is this?

Yee gu.aa yáx̱ x'wán.
Yee leelk'u hás x̱á yee x̱'éit has wusi.áx̱ yeedát.

Yee gu.aa yáx̱ x'wán.
G̱unéi x̱too.aadí tsú.

Yee gu.aa yáx̱ x'wán.
Huháan áyá, Haa Leelk'u Hás, has du ítx̱ yaa ntoo.át

Yee gu.aa yáx̱ x'wán,
Ldakát yeehwáan.

— Shgaté

Have strength and courage, all of you.
Your grandparents are really listening to you now.

Have strength and courage, all of you.
Let's start walking, too.

Have strength and courage, all of you.
It is us, we are following Our Ancestors.

Have strength and courage, all of you.
Every one of you.

– Jessie Johnnie, Chookansháa

ÿee=	gu.aa	yáx̱	x'wán
you.all's.(2p.P)=	best.effort	like	be.sure.to

ÿee=	léelk'w	=hás	x̱á	ÿee	x̱'é-t	has=	<ÿu>-Ø-si-√.áx̱	yeedát
you.all's.(2p.P)=	grandparent	=kinship.plural	you.see	you.all's.(2p.P)	mouth-at.(arrived)	3ph=	<perfective>-they.(3.S)-cl.(s,i)-√hear	now

g̱unaÿéi=	<Ø-g̱a>-tu-Ø-√.aat-í	tsú
begin=	<hortative>-we.(1p.S)-cl.(Ø)-√go.(plural)-relational	also

uháan	á-yá	haa=	léelk'w-u	=hás
us.(1p.i)	focus-here	our.(1p.P)=	grandparent	=kinship.plural

has du=	ít-x̱	<ÿaa=	na>-tu-Ø-√.át
them.all's.(3p.P)=	following-at.(repeatedly)	<prog=	progessive>-we.(1p.S)-cl.(Ø)-√go.(plural)

ldakát	ÿeehwáan
every	you.all.(2p.i)

Daa sáyá?

Now we will begin our first lesson. In this section, you will be introduced to a letter in the Lingít alphabet, beginning with vowel sounds. There are two things here that are important to remember: these vowels have tone, which means the pitch of your voice helps determine meaning. High toned vowels also receive more emphasis, and they are marked with an accent (á é í ú ó). Also, vowels can be long or short—like the differences between the first vowel in *amazing* and the vowel in *Saab*—and this also affects meaning. You will learn later that there are shifts with both tone and length of vowels, but for now, focus on exaggerating the difference between high tone and low tone, long vowel and short vowel.

As you say the word, focus your eyes on the image because doing so is better than thinking of the English word for the same object. Our goal is to create a Lingít way of thinking and seeing the world, and that means beginning to transition from the modern world to that of the traditional. After introducing the basic sounds of this chapter, we will practice some phrases where we can fill in the blanks with the nouns we are learning. After that, we will break down a little of the grammar. Remember to drill and repeat, practice with other speakers and learners, and to just keep trying.

Vocabulary	a	
	at daayí	birch (lit. thing's bark)
á		
	tás	thread

aa		
	shaawát	woman
áa		
	áa	lake
e		
	ín	flint
é		
	té	rock, stone

ei		
	seit	necklace
éi		
	shéiyi	spruce
i		
	dagatgiyáa / digitgiyáa	hummingbird
í		
	hít	house

ee		
	ayawditee / ayamditee (T)	windy weather
ée		
	kées	bracelet
u		
	nukshiyáan / lukshiyáan	mink
ú		
	gút	dime

<table>
<tr><td colspan="3">oo</td></tr>
<tr><td></td><td>woosh yaayí</td><td>pair</td></tr>
<tr><td colspan="3">óo</td></tr>
<tr><td></td><td>óonaa</td><td>rifle
(lit. thing that shoots)</td></tr>
<tr><td colspan="3">aay</td></tr>
<tr><td></td><td>yáay</td><td>whale</td></tr>
<tr><td colspan="3">aaw</td></tr>
<tr><td></td><td>yaaw</td><td>herring</td></tr>
</table>

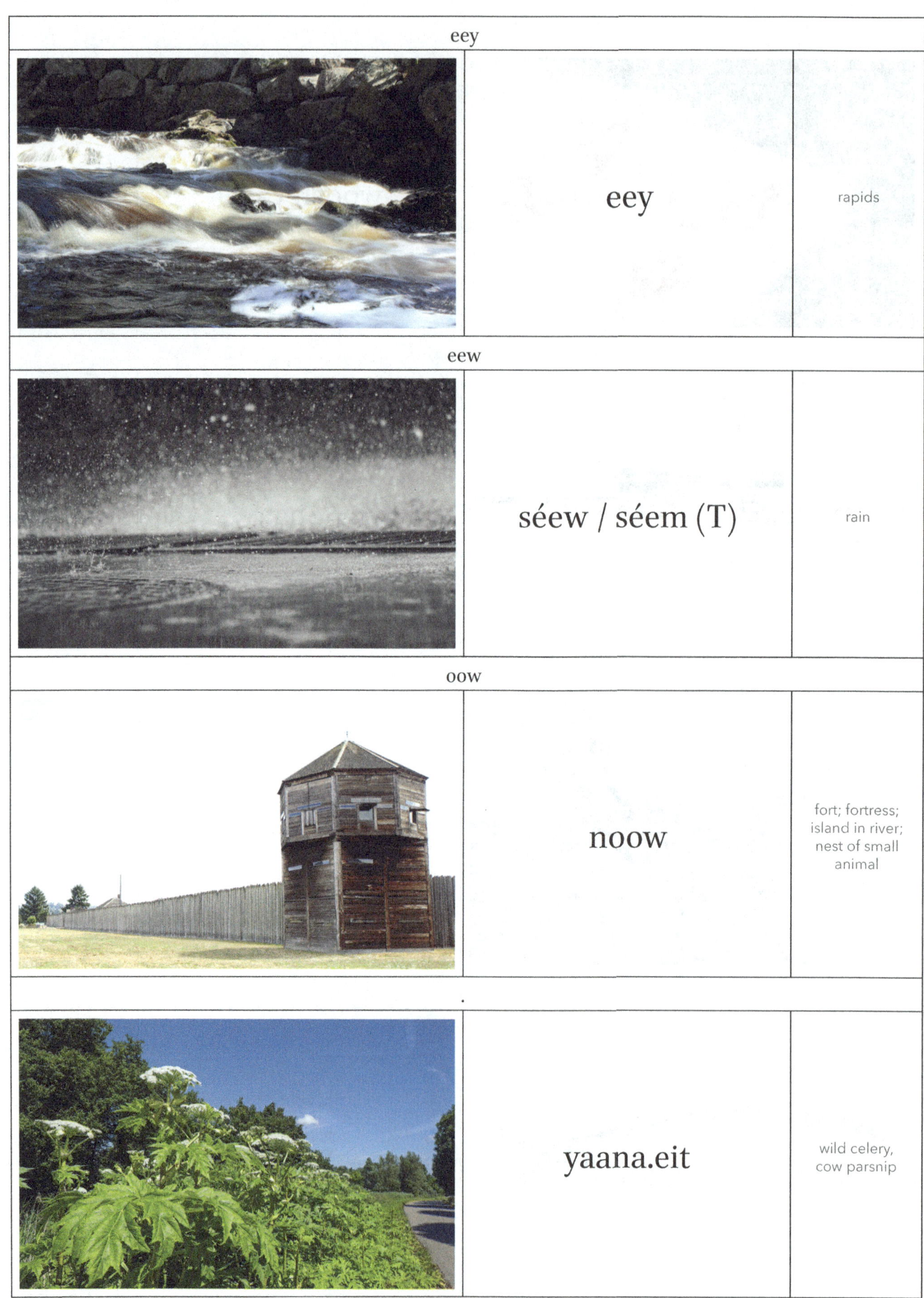

eey		
	eey	rapids
eew		
	séew / séem (T)	rain
oow		
	noow	fort; fortress; island in river; nest of small animal
.		
	yaana.eit	wild celery, cow parsnip

-kw		
	yaakw	canoe; boat
-kw-		
	sakwnéin	bread
ch		
	cheech	porpoise
d		
	dáa	weasel

g		
	gaaw / gaam (T)	drum; clock; bell; time
h		
	héen	water; river; creek
j		
	jánwu / jánu (T) / ján (C) / jínwu (Y)	mountain goat
k		
	kakéin	yarn

n		
	nóoskw	wolverine
s		
	saak	eulachon, hooligan, candlefish
sh		
	shaa	mountain
t		
	tíyaa	chisel (lit. thing that chisels)

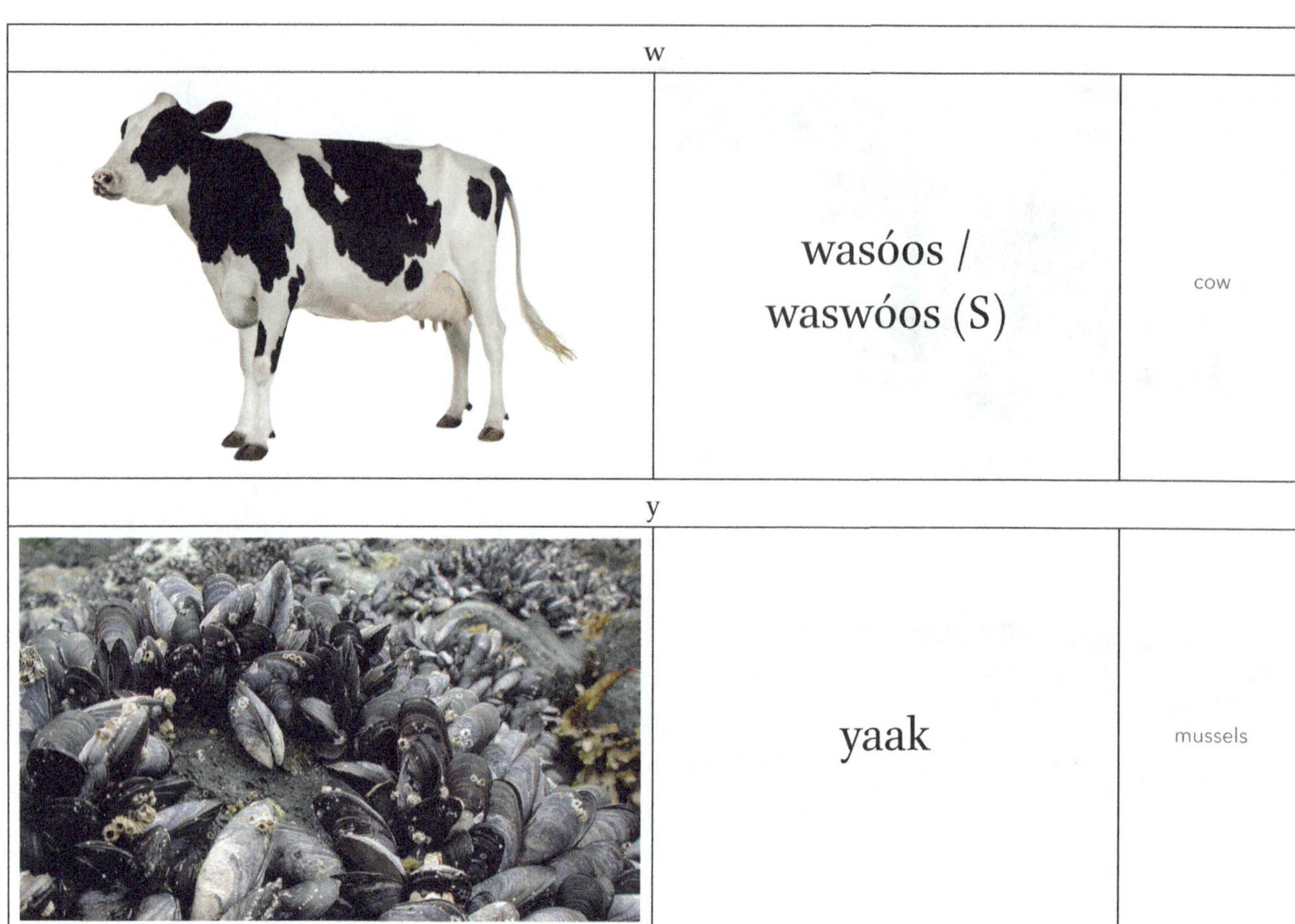

w		
	wasóos / waswóos (S)	cow
y		
	yaak	mussels

Particles & questions

As you build vocabulary in Lingít, the names we start with in this chapter contain sounds that are also in the English language. In the following chapters, we will look at some of the sneakier sounds (as Nora and Richard liked to call them) which will require some more practice and explanation. The sounds in the language are made up of sixteen vowels, which are actually four sets of vowels that each have four variations. Those variations involve vowel length, which are called short and long, and vowel tone which are called low and high. These are marked with the number of letters and a tone marker (v, v́, vv, v́v). There are forty four consonants and a glottal stop. A vowel is made using your vocal chords without anything impeding the airflow through your mouth, and a consonant involves changes to airflow that create sounds, and some of the most challenging ones in Lingít turn off the airflow from your lungs.

Next we will learn some basic phrases that will help us with conversation and will also allow us to use the nouns we just covered in basic sentences. While we will be moving on with material, you must discipline yourself to drill the words above using the pictures until you have a good idea of the sounds and the meaning of the words; in doing so, challenge yourself to think of the object itself, and not the English word for it.

The following pages take a look at particles that combine to form basic questions and answers. It is important to keep in mind that even though particles have meaning, they do not appear on their own. Instead, they combine with other parts of speech to create communication. Whenever we break language into its smaller pieces, we have to remember that it is done to help us build up the ability to communicate in the language by learning how to use these parts.

PARTICLES	
sá	name it! This is the imperative form of the verb O-S-∅-√saa ² (∅ event verb – transitive) | for S to name O; for S to nominate O. It combines with question particles to form questions and phrases.
á	[focus particle] Used to draw attention to a particular word or concept within speech. Can add emphasis, show what part of the utterance is important, or slightly shift meaning.

Lingít sense of space

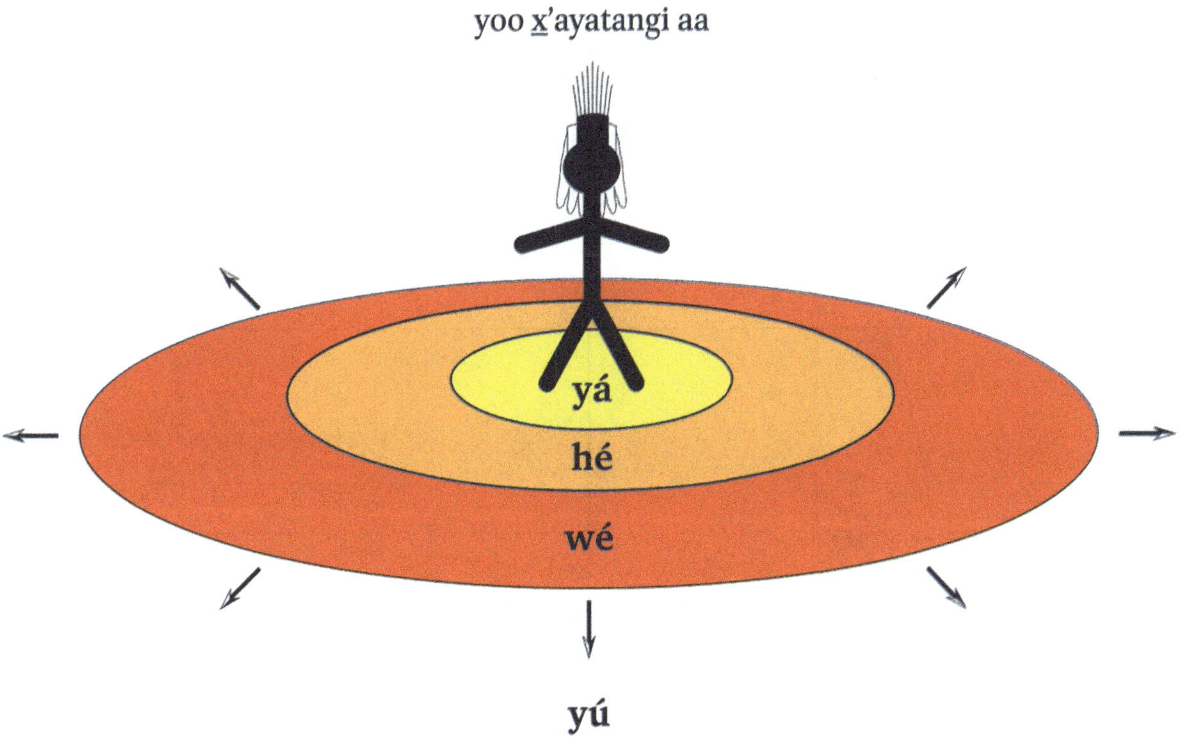

yoo x̲'ayatangi aa

yá

hé

wé

yú

yá ~ yáa	this (right here)	Refers to something that is touchable or in hand.
hé ~ héi	this (here)	Refers to something closer to the speaker than the listener, or right behind the speaker; can also refer to a nearby but unknown location.
wé ~ wéi	that (over there)	Refers to something out of reach but usually within the same basic space.
yú ~ yóo	that (over yonder)	Refers to something far away, including distant areas that cannot be seen.

daa sáyá?

what is this?

daa =sá-yá
what =name-right.here

Asks about something that is touchable or in hand.

___ áwé.

that is ___.

á-wé
focus-there

Refers to something out of reach but usually within the same basic space · used in oratory as a pause, like "well, um, etc." or to signal shifts in subject or scene.

daa sáwé?

what is that?

daa =sá-wé
what =name-there

Asks about something out of reach but usually within the same basic space.

___ áyá.

this is ___.

á-yá
focus-right.here

Refers to something that is touchable or in hand.

goosóo __?	where is __?
	goo-sá-wu ___ where-name-is.at {noun} Some speakers will use «Goosóo wé __?» which refers to a known object, such as "where is that drum?"
yáadu __.	right here is __.
	yáat-u ___ this.place-is.at {noun} It is touchable or in hand.
héidu __.	here is __.
	héit-u ___ this.place-is.at {noun} It is closer to the speaker than the listener, or right behind the speaker; can also refer to a nearby but unknown location, or in the general vicinity.
wéidu __.	there is __.
	wéit-u ___ that.place-is.at {noun} It is out of reach but usually within the same basic space.

yóodu ___.	there is ___.
	yóot-u ___ that.place-is.at {noun} It is far away, over yonder, including distant areas that cannot be seen.
gé / gí (T, C)	yes/no?
	This particle turns statements into a yes/no question, and often appears with the focus particle *á* as in *ágé*.
aaa	yes
	Can have many variations on tone. Used in oratory as a pause, such as "well, um, etc." or to signal shifts in subject or scene.
tléik' / tláayk'	no

__ ákyá?	is this __?
	á-gé-yá focus-yes/no?-right.here The particle *gé* turns the phrase into a yes/no question. Answer "yes" or "no" and then follow with the phrase.
aaa/tléik', __ áwé.	yes/no, that is __.
	For this drill, remember to use the complete answer, which includes saying what the object is, regardless of yes or no.
__ ák.wé?	is that __?
	á-gí-wé focus-yes/no?-there
aaa/tléik', __ áyá.	yes/no, this is __.
	For this drill, remember to use the complete answer, which includes saying what the object is, regardless of yes or no.

Vocabulary

	séek	belt
	dáanaa	silver; money; silver (color)
	kawóot	beads
	dís	moon; month

keishísh	alnus alder (beach or mountain alder)
aan	town; village; settlement; inhabited or owned land
neech	beach
geesh	bull kelp

	gán	firewood; wood
	káast	barrel
	shayeit	pillow (lit. thing below the head)
	kéet	killer whale, orca

	taan	sea lion
	yéin	sea cucumber
	gooch	hill
	nadáakw	table

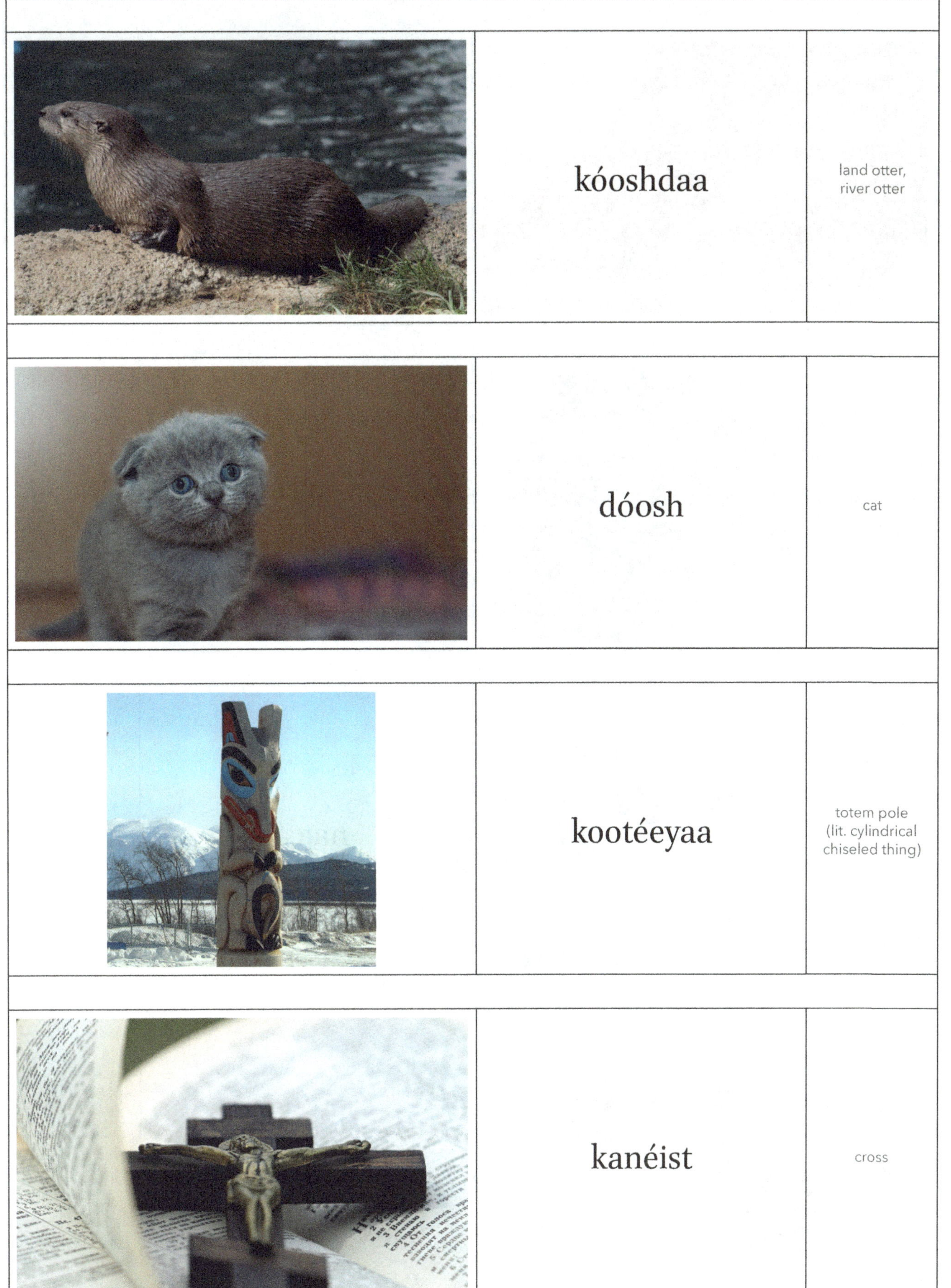

	kóoshdaa	land otter, river otter
	dóosh	cat
	kootéeyaa	totem pole (lit. cylindrical chiseled thing)
	kanéist	cross

kaháakw	salmon eggs
shakee.át	headress (lit. thing on top of head)
naa.át	clothing (lit. torso thing)
jáaji / jáajee	snowshoes

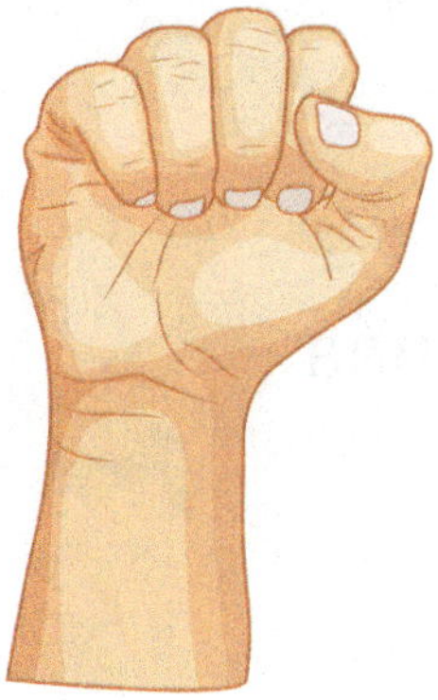	keijín / keejín	five (lit. up-hand)
	shaaw	gumboot; chiton
	shayéinaa	anchor (lit. thing that anchors)
	tawéi	mountain sheep; Dall sheep

	tináa	copper shield
	yaka.óot' / yooka.óot' / ḵaayaku.óot'i (At) / ḵaayuka.óot'i (T)	button

Forming Lingít questions

The chart on the following page shows how to begin forming questions in Lingít. There are three basic components involved. The first is a particle—which is a small function word—that establishes what type of question is being asked. The dotted line in the chart shows what the question type would translate to in English. The second part is the particle *sá* which translates to 'name it!' There is a body part with a similar name (*–sá*) where the base of the neck meets the front of the chest (jugular notch or suprasternal notch). The third part is optional and is one of the determiners, as in the following examples:

daa sá?	what?
daa sáyá	what is this (right here)?
daa sáwé?	what is that?
daa sáhé	what is this (in the area)?
daa sáyú?	what is that (way over there)?

While these do form questions, they can also become statements, as in the following examples:

wáa sáwé?	how is that?
wáa sá iyatee?	how are you doing?
wáa sá yak'éi áwé.	how very good that is.

As you see and hear more Lingít, pay attention to these question particles and how they are being used. As you begin learning more and more phrases, you will see them and use them more dynamically. The particle *goo* ("where") generally requires a suffix, and we will learn more about these later, but here are some common combinations:

goosóo?	where?
goodé sá?	to where?
goodáx̱ sá?	from where?

Types of Lingít questions

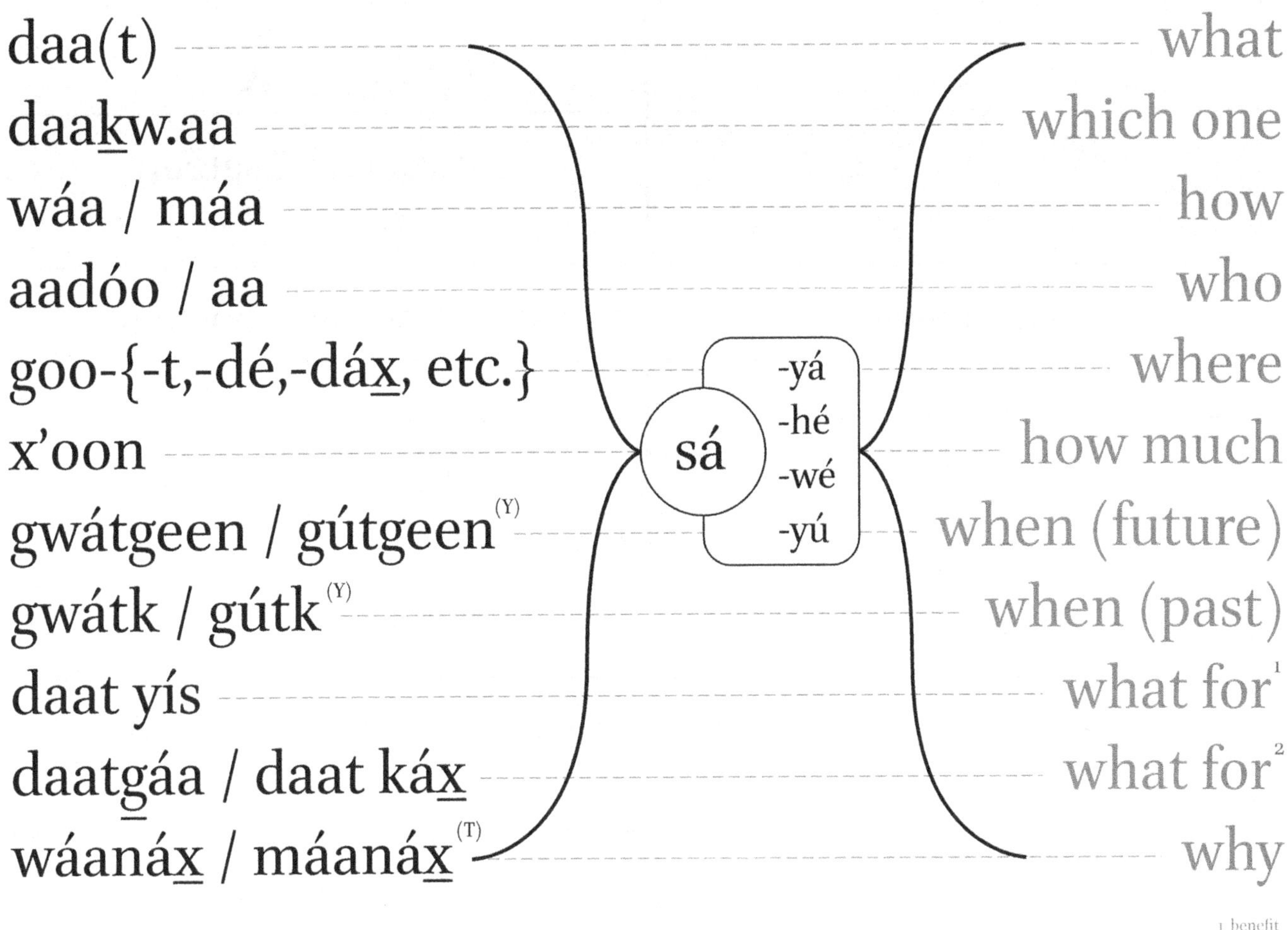

Lingít interjections

gunalchéesh	eesháan!	óosk'! / óosk'i! / óoshk'!
thank you	poor thing!	tiny; cute!
éitsk'!	xwéi!	shk'é
yum!	phew!	let's see
ha.é	hachgwá'!	atsganée!
my goodness!; can't even!	that's what you get!	scary!

Basic conversational phrases

(arriving)	(leaving)
yak'éi ix̲wsateení	tsu yei ikk̲wasatéen
it's good to see you	i'll see you again
wa.é ák.wé?	yei woosh gax̲toostéen
is that you?	we will see each other
tsu haa káa k̲eiwa.aa / k̲eewa.aa	dziyáagin / dziyáageen
it has dawned on us again	later

wáa sá iyatee / máa sá iyatee (T)		
how are you doing?		
yak'éi	tlél wáa sá (x̲at utí)	tlél ushk'é
they are good; it is good	it's okay (i'm okay)	it's bad; it's evil
ax̲ toowú yak'éi	ch'a x̲át áyá	tlél x̲at tooshk'é
i feel good	i'm just me	i feel awful
ax̲ toowú sigóo	ch'u shóogu	tlél ax̲ tooshgú
i feel happy	the same	i'm unhappy
sh tóogaa x̲at ditee	ch'a wáas	x̲at wudixwétl
i'm grateful	okay; just getting by	i'm tired

1B

K̲aa X̲'akaneek Kawdu.aag̲ú 1

Translation Exercises 1

Lingít → English

Daa sáyá?	
Daa sáwé?	
Té áwé.	
Seit áyá. *	
Goosóo óonaa?	
Goosóo wé gaaw?	
Yak'éi ix̲wsateení.	

* this combination (seit áyá) will often be pronounced as seidáyá

English → Lingít

That is a house.	
This is a dime.	
Is that a boat?	
There's a bracelet.	
Is this money?	
How are you?	

Please note that capitalization is used in written Lingít at the beginning of sentences and with proper nouns. In many language learning exercises, words and phrases are written lowercase to avoid confusion between an uppercase letter I (i) and a lowercase letter l (L). Capitalization is encouraged when writing in complete sentences.

2A

Daa sáwé iyatéen?

What do you see?

Aag̱áa áwé k'idéin gax̱tulatéen
haa tl'átgi ḵa Haa Ḵusteeyí
haa ítx̱ yaa has na.ádi aa has du jiyís.

So that too, we may protect
our land and Our Culture for
those yet to come

("Traditional Lingít Prayer," Sealaska Heritage Institute)

á-g̱aa	á-wé	k'é-déin	<ga-u-g̱a>-tu-la-√téen
then/there.(3nh.i)-going.after	focus-that	good-ly.(adverb)	<future>-we.(1p.S)-cl.(l)-√watch

haa=	tl'átk-i	ḵa	haa=	ḵu-s-tee-ÿí
our.(1p.P)=	land-relational	and	our.(1p.P)=	areal-cl.(d,s)-√be-relational

haa=	ít-x̱	<ÿaa=	has=	na>-∅-∅-√.at	aa
our.(1p.P)=	following-contact.with	<prog=	3ph=	progressive>-they.(3.S)-cl.(∅)-√go.(plural)	ones.(part.i)

has du=	ji-yís
them.all's(3p.P)=	hand-for

Daa sáwé iyatéen?

Dialogue Practice			
A	1	Wáa sá iyatee?	How are you? wáa =sá i-ÿa-√tee how =name you.(2s.O)-cl.(∅,i)-√be
B	2	X̲at yak'éi.	I'm good. x̲at= ÿa-√k'éi me.(1s.O)= cl.(∅,i)-√good
	3	Lingít gé x̲'eeya.áx̲ch?	Do you understand Tlingít? Lingít =gé x̲'a-i-ÿa-√.áx̲-ch Lingít =y/n? mouth-you.(2s.S)-cl.(∅,i)-√hear/noise.habitual
A	4	Aaa, sgóonx' k̲aa ée dultóow.	Yes, it is being taught at school. aaa sgóon-x' k̲aa ée ∅-du-l-√tóow yes school-at.(rest) people's.(4h.P) emptybase it(3.O)-people(4h.S)-cl.(d,l)-√read/count/teach
	5	Tsu yei ikk̲wasatéen.	I'll see you again. tsu ÿei= i-<ga-u-g̲a>-x̲a-sa-√téen again down.(conj)= you.(2s.O)-<future>-i(1s.S)-cl.(s)-√see
B	6	Gu.aal kwshé yéi wuteek̲.	I hope that's how it is. gu.aal kwshé yéi= ∅-u-∅-√tee-k̲ hopefully i.guess thus= it(3.O)-irr-cl.(∅)-√be-opt
	7	Haandé i jín!	Give me your hand (for a handshake)! / "Put 'er there!" haan-dé i jín here-toward your(2s.P) hand
A	8	Gunalchéesh.	Thank you. [tlél] <ga-u-na>-l-√chéesh [not] <?>-cl.(l)-√possible

Intermediate and advanced sounds

Our second lesson introduces intermediate and advanced sounds. These are what Nora and Richard Dauehnauer sometimes called 'sneaky sounds.' You might want to look at the sound location chart from page four (daax'oon) and practice over and over again. Remember to have patience! You may be asking things of your mouth, muscles, and vocal chords that they are not used to, but it will come in time. Just as the Lingít people learned to make sounds that are not in Lingít (English letters *b*, *f*, *l*, *p*, *r* and *v*), you can teach yourself to do the same.

The first sounds we practice in this chapter are consonant combinations and ejective consonants—which are made without using air from your lungs, only the bit of air and muscles in your mouth and throat. The sounds come from the same place, but your neck acts as a piston and pushes sound out louder and faster. Next is the Lingít *x*, which is a scraping sound * from the same location as *k*, *k'*, and *g*. Make sure you have some saliva on your tongue, and make a sound like the wind. After this is the Lingít *l*, which is a voiceless consonant that is made by pressing the tip of your tongue on the roof of your mouth and blowing out the sides. Then there are ejective versions of these and combinations with other consonants. Then come the gutturals, so prepare to sound like a raven and to immerse yourself in *Lingít x̱'ayéigi* (sounds of human speech). *I gu.aa yáx̱ x'wán!* (be of brave heart!)

The general idea here is that attempting to speak and sticking with it is more important than being perfect. The only way you will fail here is if you do not do it, so try not to worry about sounding funny or being uncertain how to make certain sounds. Keep speaking and keep listening, and your body will find a way to make these sounds.

Vocabulary	dz	
	dzeit	ladder; dock; stairs
	ts	
	tsaa	hair seal

<table>
<tr><td colspan="3">kw</td></tr>
<tr><td></td><td>aan kwéiyi</td><td>flag</td></tr>
<tr><td colspan="3">ch’</td></tr>
<tr><td></td><td>ch’eet</td><td>murrelet</td></tr>
<tr><td colspan="3">k’</td></tr>
<tr><td></td><td>k’inchéiyi</td><td>rose</td></tr>
<tr><td colspan="3">s’</td></tr>
<tr><td></td><td>s’eek</td><td>black bear</td></tr>
</table>

t’		
	t’á	king salmon, chinook
ts’		
	ts’ítsk’w / ts’ats’ée	bird
k’w		
	k’wát’	egg
-k’w		
	dzísk’w / tsísk’w (Kl)	moose

x		
	xóots	brown bear
xw		
	xwaasdáa	canvas; tarp
-xw		
	gáaxw	duck

Lingít pronouns

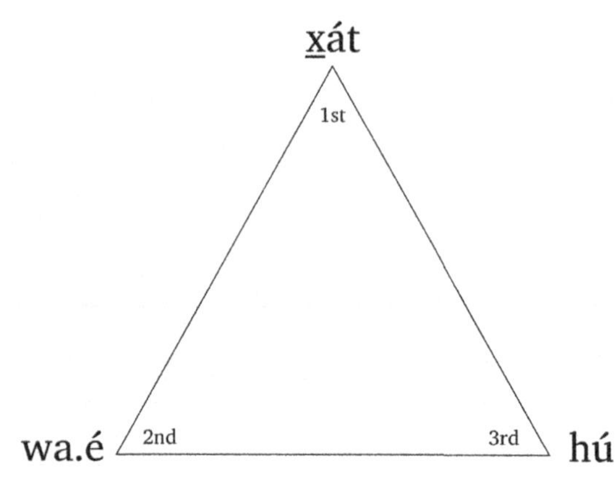

independent

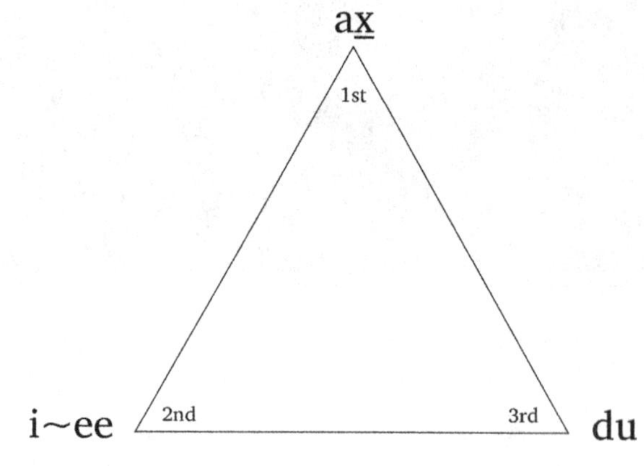

possessive

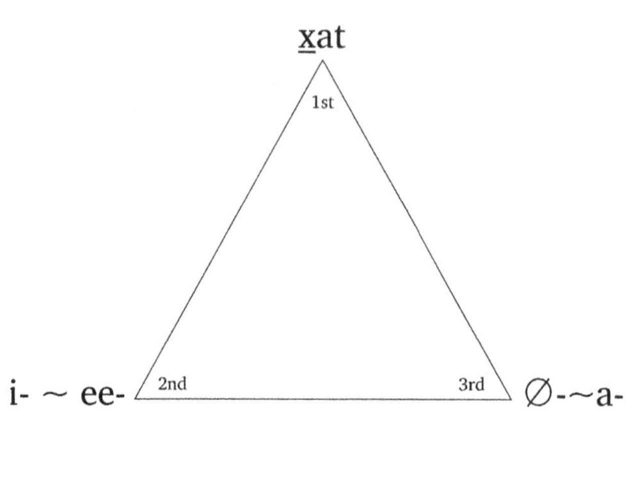

object

x̲a-
1st
i-
2nd
3rd
∅-

subject

x̱át	me independent pronoun: first person singular
wa.é	you independent pronoun: second person singular
hú	them independent pronoun: third person singular
ax̱	my possessive pronoun: first person singular
i~ee	your possessive pronoun: second person singular
du	their possessive pronoun: third person singular
x̱at	me object pronoun: first person singular
i- ~ ee-	you object pronoun: second person singular
∅~a- *	them / it object pronoun: third person singular

* a third person object *and* subject will shift the pronoung from ∅- to a-

x̱a-	i subject pronoun: first person singular
i-	you subject pronoun: second person singular
∅-	they / it subject pronoun: third person singular

What do you have and what do you see?

Question and Answer Drills	
ḵa	and
daa sá i jeewú?	what do you have? daa =sá i jee-wú what =name your.(2s.P) possession-is.at
__ ax̱ jeewú	i have ___. __ ax̱ jee-wú __ my.(1s.P) possession-is.at

daa sá ax̱ jeewú?	what do i have? daa =sá ax̱ jee-wú what =name my.(1s.P) possession-is.at
__ i jeewú.	you have ___. __ i jee-wú __ your.(2s.P) possession-is.at
daa sá du jeewú?	what do they have? daa =sá du jee-wú what =name their.(3.P) possession-is.at
__ du jeewú.	they have ___. __ du jee-wú __ their.(3.P) possession-is.at

<table>
<tr><td colspan="2"></td></tr>
<tr><td rowspan="2">__ gé i jeewú?</td><td>do you have ___?</td></tr>
<tr><td>__ gé i jee-wú
__ yes/no? your.(2s.P) possession-is.at</td></tr>
<tr><td colspan="2"></td></tr>
<tr><td rowspan="2">aaa/tléik', __ ax̱ jeewú.

tléik', tlél __ ax̱ jee.</td><td>yes/no, i have ___.

no, i don't have ____.</td></tr>
<tr><td>aaa/tléik' __ ax̱ jee-wú
yes/no __ my.(1s.P) possession-is.at

tléik, tlél __ ax̱ jee
no, not __ my.(1s.P) possession</td></tr>
<tr><td colspan="2"></td></tr>
<tr><td rowspan="2">aadóo sá __ du jeewú?</td><td>who has ___?</td></tr>
<tr><td>aadóo =sá __ du jee-wú
who =name __ their.(3.P) possession-is.at</td></tr>
<tr><td colspan="2"></td></tr>
<tr><td rowspan="2">__ du jeewú __.</td><td>___ has ___.</td></tr>
<tr><td>___ du jee-wú ___
__ thei.(3.P) possession-is.at __
* (noun) du jeewú (name) *</td></tr>
</table>

daa sá iyatéen?	what do you see?	
	daa =sá Ø-i-ÿa-√téen what =name them/it.(3.O)-you.(2s.S)-cl.(Ø,i)-√see	
___ x̱aatéen.	i see ___.	
	Ø-x̱a-ÿa-√téen them/it.(3.O)-i.(1s.S)-cl.(Ø,i)-√see	
___ gé iyatéen?	do you see ___?	
	___ gé Ø-i-ÿa-√téen ___ y/n? them/it.(3.O)-i.(1s.S)-cl.(Ø,i)-√see	
aaa/tléik, ___ x̱aatéen.	yes/no, i see ___.	
	aaa/tléik' Ø-x̱a-ÿa-√téen yes/no them/it.(3.O)-i.(1s.S)-cl.(Ø,i)-√see	

2B

K̲aa X̲'akaneek Kawdu.aag̲ú 2

Translation Exercises 2

Lingít → English

Daa sá i jeewú?	
Daa sá du jeewú?	
Gáaxw x̱aatéen.	
Goosóo dzísk'w?	
Xóots ák.wé?	
x̱át	
ax̱	

English → Lingít

What do they have?	
Do you have money?	
Do you see a boat?	
you	
your	
Is that a seal?	

3A

Wáa sá iduwasáakw?

How are you called?

Haa at.óowu haa ḵusteeyíx̱ sitee.
—Seiginéigéi

Our at.óow are our life.
– Emma Marks, Lukaax̱.ádi

haa=	at=∅-√.óow-u	haa=	ḵu-s-tee-ÿí-x̱	∅-si-√tee
our.(1p.P)=	thing.(4nh.O)=cl.(∅)-√own-relational	haa.(1p.P)=	areal-cl.(d,s)-√be-subordinate-essive	it.(3.O)-cl.(s,i)-√be

Wáa sá iduwasáakw?

Dialogue Practice

Speaker	#	Lingít	Translation	Breakdown	Gloss
A	1	Wáa sá iyatee?	How are you?	wáa =sá i-ÿa-√tee	how =name you.(2s.O)-cl.(∅,i)-√be
B	2	Tlél wáa sá x̲at utí.	I'm okay.	tlél wáa =sá x̲at= u-∅-√tí	not how =name me.(1s.O)= irrealis-cl.(∅)-√be
	3	Wa.é k̲u.aa? / Wa.é déis?	And you? / How about you? *	wa.é k̲u.aa / wa.é déi-sí	you.(2s.i) however / you.(2s.i) now-it.seems
A	4	Ax̲ toowú yak'éi.	I feel good.	ax̲ tú-ÿú ∅-ÿa-√k'éi	my.(1s.P) mind-relational it/them.(3.O)-cl.(∅,i)-√good
	5	Wáa sá iduwasáakw?	How are you called (what is your name)?	wáa =sá i-du-ÿa-√sáakw	how =name you.(1s.O)-people(4h.S)-cl.(∅,i)-√name
B	6	Susie yóo x̲at duwasáakw.	i am called Susie.	Susie yóo= x̲at= du-ÿa-√sáakw	Susie as.precedes= me.(1s.O)= people(4h.S)-cl.(∅,i)-√name
	7	Wa.é k̲u.aa, wáa sá iduwasáakw?	And you, how are you called (what is your name)?	wa.é k̲u.aa wáa =sá i-du-ÿa-√sáakw	you.(2s.i) however how =name you.(2s.O)-people.(4h.S)-cl.(∅,i)-√name
A	8	Jimmy yóo x̲at duwasáakw.	I am called Jimmy.	Jimmy yóo= x̲at= du-ÿa-√sáakw	Jimmy as.precedes= me.(1s.O)= people.(4h1s.S)-cl.(∅,i)-√name

* In all Lingít dialects *wa.é déis* can be translated as 'you next,' but in Interior Lingít *wa.é déis* is used similar to *wa.é k̲u.aa*, which translates to 'how about you?'

Haa Lingítx̱ Sateeyí (Our Lingít Identity)

There are two very important concepts within the Lingít view of the world that this lesson will cover: identity and sense of self in the world. Within what we call *Haa Ḵusteeyí* (Our Way of Life / Our Culture), it is critical to understand who you are, and that is accomplished by knowing your relations—your clan members, same Moiety members, your immediate family, and most importantly your in-laws. Many names within *Haa Ḵusteeyí* are passed down through matrilineal clans, and so it is also important to know *i sáayi*, your namesake, the person who held the name before you, or who also holds it now.

In *Haa Ḵusteeyí* it is socially inappropriate to boast about yourself or your clan in public, so instead you should be addressing your in-laws or a general audience. Because of this fact, you should learn different ways to introduce yourself in case you are called upon to do so. To say __ *áyá x̱at* is to say "I am __." So you want to minimize the amount of times you use this phrase, and instead learn how to say "I am one of the __" or "I am from __." You should acknowledge your father's people, and your connections to the world instead of yourself.

In this chapter, we learn how to introduce ourselves and to talk about where we are from and where we live. Pay attention to the pronouns that are being used and how they are changing for different verbs. Later chapters will focus more on kinship structures, which operate very differently than the ways they may be referenced in American English. Feel free to pass if you are uncomfortable with certain pieces of personal and family information, but understand that these phrases and terms are important in being able to understand how we relate to one another. In Lingít, lineage is linked to identity, so many of the related terms for lineage are introduced in this chapter.

Question and Answer Drill

waa sá iduwasáakw?	how are you called? / what is your name?
	wáa =sá i-du-ÿa-√sáakw how =name you.(2s.O)-someone.(4h.S)-cl.(∅,i)-√name Most speakers would interpret this phrase as "what is your name," and it is translated here as "how are you called" to show the question structure.
(2s.O) – second person singular object pronoun, (4H.S) – independent human subject pronoun, (1s.O) – first person singular object pronoun	
__ yóo x̱at duwasáakw.	i am called ___.
	___ yóo= x̱at= du-ÿa-√sáakw ___ as.precedes= me.(1s.O)= someone.(4H.S)-cl.(∅,i)-√name Note that *yóo* is used when the name is immediately before the verb and *yéi* is used when the name is separated from the verb.

(1s.P) – first person singular possessive pronoun – possessive suffix

__ áyá ax̱ saayí.	my name is ____. / my namesake is ____.
	á-yá / focus-this · ax̱= / my.(1s.P)= · saa-yí / name-relational This is another way to state your name, and does so without using a verb. It can also be used to refer to someone who has or had the same Lingít name.

dleit ḵáa x̱'éinácx̱ __ yóo x̱at duwasáakw.	in English, i am called ____.
	dleit / white/snow · ḵaa / person · x̱'éi-náx̱ / mouth-through · ___ / ___ yóo= / as.precedes= · x̱at= / me.(1s.O)= · du-ÿa-√saakw / someone.(4h.S)-cl.(∅,i)-√name

locative – suffix tying a noun to a specific function of the verb

daaḵw.aa naax̱ sá isitee? daat naax̱ sá isitee?	which clan/tribe are you? / what clan/tribe are you? /
	daaḵw.aa / which.one · naa-x̱ / clan/tribe-essive= · =sá / =name · i-si-√tee / you.(2s.O)-cl.(s,i)-√be daat / what · naa-x̱ / clan/tribe-essive= · =sá / =name · i-si-√tee / you.(2s.O)-cl.(s,i)-√be Speakers might answer this question with clan, Moiety, or crest.

__-x̱ x̱at sitee.	i am ____ (Moiety/tribe/nation).
	___-x̱ / ___-essive · x̱at= / me.(1s.O)= · si-√tee / cl.(s,i)-√be The essive suffix -x̱ denotes the group with this verb.

__ naax̱ x̱at sitee.	i am ____ (Moiety/tribe/nation).
	___ naa-x̱ x̱at= si-√tee ___ clan/tribe-essive me.(1s.O)= cl.(s,i)-√be

Moiety

gooch / g̱ooch

There are two equal sides that clans are grouped into, and these are sometimes called Moieties. A clan identity is inherited through one's mother, and traditional relationships involved marrying into the opposite Moiety. This word can refer to the the wolf Moiety or the animal (Canis lupus columbianus). Inland speakers and some speakers on the coast will refer to the Moiety opposite of Raven clans as G̱ooch. Inland speakers will refer to Yéil clans as Crow people in English and often call the bird raven a crow.

ch'áak'

This word can refer to the the Eagle Moiety or the animal (Haliaeetus leucocephalus). Most coastal speakers will refer to the Moiety opposite of Raven clans as G̱ooch. When speaking to multiple clans, one could say G̱ooch naax̱ siteeyi aa (ones who are a wolf clan), Ch'áak' naax̱ siteeyi aa (ones who are an eagle clan), or Yéil naax̱ siteeyi aa (ones who are a raven clan).

yéil

This word can refer to the the trickster Raven, the Raven Moiety, or the animal (Corvus corax). When telling stories about the trickster Raven, the word is capitalized when writing in Lingít. At times, the trickster Raven will be referred to as *yá Yéil* (this Raven) or *yú Yéil* (that Raven over there), but otherwise the use of the word is identical and determined through context.

__ yádi	child of ____.
	___ yát-i ___ child-relational We honor our father's clan or nation by acknowledging that we are a child of that clan or nation. This can be done in an introduction, after naming your own clan.

__ dachx̱án	grandchild of ____.
	___ dachx̱án ___ grandchild We honor the clans of the parents of our parents by calling ourselves a grandchild of that clan. This can be either the clan of a mother's father or of a father's father.

__ áyá ax̱ daakanóox'u	____ is my outer shell.
	á-yá ax̱= daaka-nóox'-u focus.this my.(1s.P)= surrounding.surface-shell-relational This is a term of high respect, and refers to the mother's mother's father's clan.

___ ax̱ daakanóox'ux̱ sitee.	my outer shell is of the ____.
	ax̱= daaka-nóox'-u-x̱ my.(1s.P)= surrounding.surface-shell-relational-essive ∅-si-√tee them/it.(3.O)-cl.(s,i)-√be

__ yóo duwasáakw haa naakahídi.	our clan house is called __. ___ yóo= ∅-du-ÿa-√saa-kw ___ as.precedes= them/it.(3.O)-someone.(4h.S)-cl.(∅,i)-√name haa= naa-ka-hít-i our.(1p.P)= clan/nation-surface-house-relational
__ áyá haa naakahídi.	___ is our clan house. __ á-yá haa= naa-ka-hít-i ___ focus-this our.(1p.P)= clan/nation-surface-house-relational
__ yóo duwasáakw __ .	__ is called ___. ___ yóo= ∅-du-ÿa-√saa-kw ___ __ as.precedes= them/it.(3.O)-someone.(4h.S)-cl.(∅,i)-√name ___ {name} called {kinship term}. Ex: K̲aaldaakeit yoo duwasáakw ax̲ tláa — my mother is called K̲aaldaakeit.
__ yóo dusáagun __ .	__ used to be called ___. ___ yóo= ∅-du-∅-√saa-kw-un ___. __ as.precedes= them/it.(3.O)-someone.(4h.S)-cl.(∅)-√name-decessive {name} used-to-be-called {kinship term}. The decessive mode means it no longer is the case. Using this verb mode means the person or thing no longer exists or is no longer called by this name.

goot’á k̲wáan sáwé wa.é?

what place is the ancestral home of your people?

goot’á	k̲wáan	sá-wé	wa.é
what.place	ancestral.people.of	name-there	you.(2s.i)

__ k̲wáan áwé uháan.

we are the ancestral people of ___

k̲wáan	á-wé	uháan
ancestral.people.of	focus-there	us.(1p.i)

There are 21 recorded traditional territories of the Lingít, and these are at the heart of the way that Lingít associates the relationship between peoples, clans, and lands. This term is used to refer to non-humans as people by adding a suffix -i the end, as in kóoshdaa k̲wáani (land otter people), x̲áat k̲wáani (salmon people), or aas k̲wáani (tree people).

goox’ sá k̲iydzitee?

where were you born?

goo-x’	=sa	k̲u-<ÿu>-i-dzi-√tee
where-at.(residing)	=name	areal-<perfective>-you.(2s.S)-cl.(d,s,i)-√be

____-x’ k̲ux̲wdzitee.

i was born at ____.

____-x’	k̲u-<ÿu>-x̲a-dzi-√tee
{place}-at.(residing)	areal-<perfective>-i.(1s.S)-cl.(d,s,i)-√be

goox' sá yéi iyatee?	where do you stay? goo-x' =sa yéi= x̲at= ÿa-√tee where-at.(residing) =name thus= me.(1s.O)= cl.(∅,i)-√be The suffix -x' denotes the location with this verb. it can be ∅ in the case of áa (there).
__-x' yéi x̲at yatee.	i am staying at ____. ____-x' yéi= x̲at= ÿa-√tee (place)-at.(residing) thus= me.(1s.O)= cl.(∅,i)-√be
goox' sá k̲eeya.óo?	where do you reside? goo-x' =sa k̲u-i-ÿa-√.oo where-at.(residing) =name areal-you.(2s.S)-cl.(∅,i)-√own The verb here literally means to own property or land at a place.
__-x' k̲ux̲aa.óo.	i reside at ____. ____-x' k̲u-x̲a-ÿa-√.oo (place)-at.(residing) areal-i.(1s.S)-cl.(∅,i)-√own

Lingít Aaní ká saax'ú (Names on Lingít land)

Yaakwdáat / Laax̱aayík / G̱ałyáx̱	Yakutat
	"A lagoon is starting to form already" / "Near the Glacier" (from Eyak «Yuk'uda'd» / «Ła'x̣a'»)
Shg̱agwei	Skagway
	"Heartwooded Place," from Wushig̱agu Yé, referring to the driftwood that was weatherbeaten heartwood
Tlákw.aan / Tlaaguwu.aan	Klukwan
	"Eternal Village"
Deishú	Haines
	"End of the Trail"
Xunaa / Xunniyaa / Gaawt'ak̲.aan	Hoonah
	"Shelter of the North Wind" (from Xóon Niyaa) / "Village Beside the Drum"
Sheet'ká	Sitka
	"On the Outskirts of Sheey" from Sheey a t'iká, which is an unpacking of the name, and Sheey is the island where the airport is in Sitka
Áak'w	Juneau area (north)
	"Little Lake"

T’aak̲ú	Juneau area (South and Douglas)	There are two interpretations of this name: “King Salmon Cove” from t’á-k̲u / “Flooding Geese” from t’aawák̲-g̲alak̲ú
Aangóon	Angoon	“Land Portage”
K̲éex̲’ / Lx̲ex’x̲u.aan	Kake	“Mouth of the Dawn” / “The Village That Never Sleeps”
Séet Ká	Petersburg	“On the Channel”
K̲aachx̲an.áak’w	Wrangell	“Little Lake Near People’s Work” from k̲aa-jixán-áak’w
Kichx̲áan	Ketchikan	“Smell of Dead Fish” / “Near the Wing”
Lawáak	Klawock	Said to be named after «Lawá,» the man who founded Klawock

Tlingit name	English name / meaning
Sháan Séet	Craig
	"? Channel"
Deisleen / Deisl̲een	Teslin
	"Point on a Trail on Which People Hid Themselves" from dei-lu-√seen; or a borrowed name from Dene name for the lake, dèzli, "starts flowing out"
Áatlein	Atlin
	"Big Lake"
Naataasehéen(i) / Nat'asahéen / Nadashaa Héeni /	Carcross
	Borrowed from a Tagish name of uncertain meaning, or as Ada Haskins said, "Water Flowing from Mountain," or as Ida Calmegane said, "Whitefish River"
T'einyaag̲eey / T'einaag̲eey	Tenakee
	"Bay on the Hindward Side"
K'udeis X̲'é	Pelican
	"Mouth of K'udeis"
G̲unaax̲oo	Dry Bay
	"Among the Dene" from G̲unanaa x̲oo

Áatlein K̲wáan	People of the Atlin Area
Áak'w K̲wáan	People of the Auke Area
Deisl̲een K̲wáan	People of the Teslin Area
G̲alyáx̲ K̲wáan	People of the Kaliakh River Area
G̲unaax̲oo K̲wáan	People of the Dry Bay Area
Henyaa K̲wáan	People of Henyaa (Middle of Prince of Wales Island)
Jilk̲áat K̲wáan	People of the Chilkat Area
Kuyú K̲wáan	People of the Kuiu Island Area
K̲ée̲x' K̲wáan	People of the the Kake Area
Lk̲oot K̲wáan	People of the Chilkoot Area
Saanyaa K̲wáan	People of the Sanyaa / Sanya Area

S'awdáan K̲wáan	People of the Sumdum Area
Sheet'ká K̲wáan	People of the Sitka Area
Shx'at K̲wáan	People of the Shx'at Area
Tak̲jik'.aan K̲wáan	People of the Tuxecan Area (North Prince of Wales Island)
Taagish K̲wáan	People of Carcross and Tagish
Taant'a K̲wáan	People of the Tongass Area
T'aak̲ú K̲wáan	People of the Taku Area
Xudzidaa K̲wáan / Xutsnoowú K̲wáan	People of the Angoon Area
Xunaa K̲áawu	People of the Hoonah and Glacier Bay Areas
Yaakwdáat K̲wáan / Laax̲aayík K̲wáan	People of the Yakutat Area

Introduction template

<table>
<tr><td colspan="3">name</td></tr>
<tr><td rowspan="2">pick one</td><td>__ yóo x̱at duwasáakw.</td><td>i am called ____.</td></tr>
<tr><td>__ áyá ax̱ saayí.</td><td>my name / namesake is ____.</td></tr>
<tr><td colspan="3">name in English</td></tr>
<tr><td colspan="2">dleit ḵáa x̱'éinax̱ __.</td><td>in English ____.</td></tr>
<tr><td colspan="3">clan / tribe / ethnicity</td></tr>
<tr><td colspan="2">__-x̱ x̱at sitee.</td><td>i am ____ (Moiety/tribe/nation).</td></tr>
<tr><td colspan="2">G̱ooch naa / Ch'áak' naa / Yéil naa</td><td>Wolf / Eagle / Raven</td></tr>
<tr><td colspan="3">heritage clans</td></tr>
<tr><td colspan="2">__ yádi</td><td>child of ____.</td></tr>
<tr><td colspan="2">__ dachx̱án</td><td>grandchild of ____.</td></tr>
<tr><td colspan="2">__ áyá ax̱ daakanóox'u</td><td>____ is my outer shell.</td></tr>
<tr><td colspan="3">clan house</td></tr>
<tr><td colspan="2">__ áyá haa naakahídi.</td><td>____ is our clan house.</td></tr>
<tr><td colspan="3">ḵwáan</td></tr>
<tr><td colspan="2">__ ḵwáan áwé uháan.</td><td>we are the people from ____.</td></tr>
<tr><td colspan="3">birthplace</td></tr>
<tr><td colspan="2">____-x' ḵux̱wdzitee.</td><td>i was born at ____.</td></tr>
<tr><td colspan="3">residence</td></tr>
<tr><td rowspan="2">pick one</td><td>__-x' yéi x̱at yatee.</td><td>i am staying at ____.</td></tr>
<tr><td>__-x' ḵux̱aa.óo.</td><td>i reside at ____. / i own land at ___.</td></tr>
</table>

waa sá x̲at duwasáakw?	how am i called? wáa =sá x̲at= du-ÿa-√sáakw how =name me.(1s.O)= someone.(4h.S)-cl.(∅,i)-√name
__ yóo iduwasáakw.	you are called ____. ___ yóo= i-du-ÿa-√saa-kw ___ as.precedes= you.(2s.O)-someone.(4h.S)-cl.(∅,i)-√name
daak̲w.aa naax̲ sá x̲at sitee? / daat naax̲ sá x̲at sitee?	which clan/tribe am i? / what clan/tribe am i? daak̲w.aa naa-x̲ =sá x̲at= si-√tee which.one clan/tribe-essive= =name me.(1s.O)= cl.(s,i)-√be daat naa-x̲ =sá x̲at= si-√tee what clan/tribe-essive= =name me.(1s.O)= cl.(s,i)-√be
__-x̲ isitee.	you are ____ (Moiety/tribe/nation). ____-x̲ i-si-√tee ___-essive you.(2s.O)-cl.(s,i)-√be

goox’ sá yéi x̲at yatee?	where am i? goo-x’ =sa yéi= x̲at= ÿa-√tee where-at.(residing) =name thus= me.(1s.O)= cl.(∅,i)-√be
__-x’ yéi iyatee.	you are at ____. ____-x’ yéi= i-ÿa-√tee (place)-at.(residing) thus= you.(2s.O)-cl.(∅,i)-√be
wáa sá duwasáakw?	how are they called; how is it called? wáa =sá ∅-du-ÿa-√sáakw how =name them/it.(3.O)-someone.(4h.S)-cl.(∅,i)-√name
__ yóo duwasáakw.	they are called ____; it is called ____. ____ yóo ∅-du-ÿa-√saa-kw ___ as.precedes them/it.(3.O)-someone.(4h.S)-cl.(∅,i)-√name

daak̲w.aa naax̲ sá sitee? / daat naax̲ sá sitee?	which clan/tribe are they?
	daak̲w.aa naa-x̲ =sá ∅-si-√tee which.one clan/tribe-essive =name them/it.(3.O)-cl.(s,i)-√be daat naa-x̲ =sá ∅-si-√tee what clan/tribe-essive =name them/it.(3.O)-cl.(s,i)-√be

__-x̲ isitee.	they are ____ (Moiety/tribe/nation).
	____-x̲ ∅-si-√tee ___-essive them/it.(3.O)-cl.(s,i)-√be

goox' sá yéi yatee?	where are they?
	goo-x' =sa yéi= ∅-ÿa-√tee where-at.(residing) =name thus= them/it.(3.O)-cl.(∅,i)-√be

__-x' yéi yatee.	they are at ____. / it is at ____.
	____-x' yéi= ∅-ÿa-√tee (place)-at.(residing) thus= them/it.(3.O)-cl.(∅,i)-√be

Lingít plural pronouns

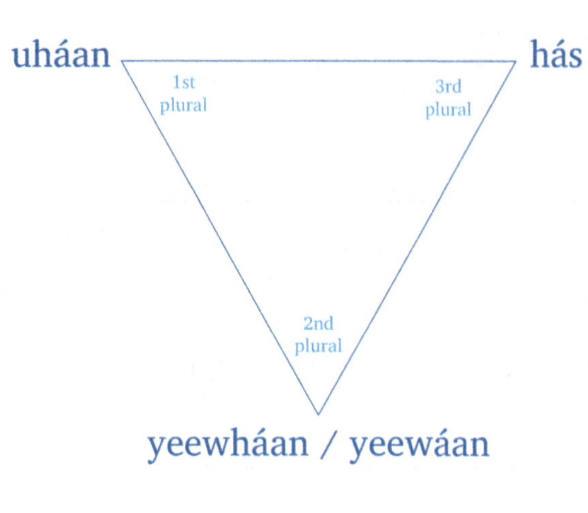

independent

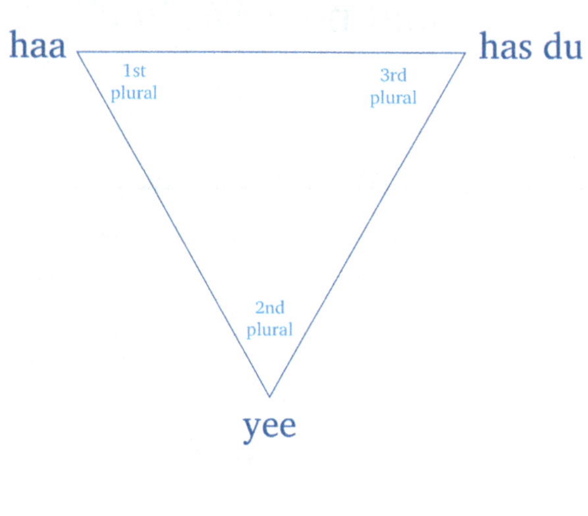

possessive

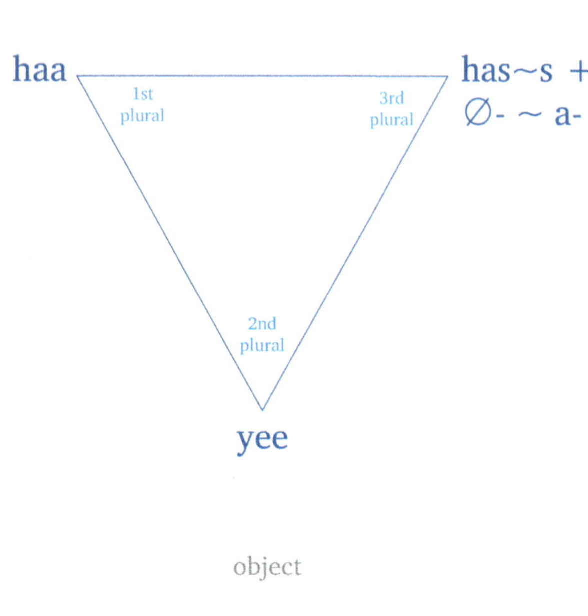

object

tu-

has~s
+ ∅-

1st plural

3rd plural

2nd plural

yi-

subject

uháan	us independent pronoun: first person plural
yeewháan	you all independent pronoun: second person plural
hás	them all independent pronoun: third person plural
haa	our possessive pronoun: first person plural
yee	you all's possessive pronoun: second person plural
has du	them all's possessive pronoun: third person plural
haa	us object pronoun: first person plural
yee	you object pronoun: second person plural
has + ∅~a-	them all object pronoun: third person plural
tu-	we subject pronoun: first person plural
yi-	you all subject pronoun: second person plural
has ∅-	they all subject pronoun: third person plural

Haa Lingítx̱ sateeyí (our Lingít identity)

Lingít clans are divided into two halves, which are often referred to as Moieties (each of two parts). These two sides are *Tléix' Shangukeidí* (Wolf/Eagle) and *Tléix' Laayineidí* (Raven/Crow). Within each Moiety there are many clans, and clan identity is inherited through *haa tláa yinaanáx̱* (on our mother's side/through matrilineal descent). These clans use images and connecting narratives as crests, which are often in the form of an animal, mountain, constellation, or supernatural creature. These images are attached to sacred stories that document why a clan uses particular crests.

Crests, names, stories, houses, objects, and land are all *at.óow*, which literally translates as "an owned thing" but within Lingít culture means "a sacred clan-owned thing." *At.óow* is an important term within *haa ḵusteeyí* (our way of life; our culture). Knowledge of *at.óow* helps solidify understanding of place and belonging, communal ownership and responsibility, and the respect needed to feel the connection between *haa at.óowx'u* (our sacred possessions) and *haa shagóon* (our ancestors; heritage). If something is considered *at.óow* of another clan, remember to not use it or talk publicly about it without that clan's permission.

There are many clans, and many of them are related in groups based on migrations, divisions, and expansions. The following lists are not intended to define which clans came from which, or which ones have the specific ownership of which images. Instead, it is a list of known clans, the meaning of their clan name (if known), and the known primary and secondary crests of the clans. These clans are listed in groups that share a common origin.

This is a growing list, and it is the result of the work of many hands and minds. As we continue to reclaim our knowledge and further our understanding of the complexities of clan relationships, the list will continue to grow and adjust. Understanding these relationships must come at a deeper level than who was first, who is right, who is true. Instead, we must look at the many ways in which we are all related, and how those relationships should define our actions. Be careful how you treat your opposites, and how and why you use a crest or share a clan's stories. Always carry respect in front of you, like a gift that makes the world a better place.

This list is based on an unpublished manuscript by Jeff Leer dated November 1985 and titled "Lingít tribe, clan, and house group names." Leer's basis was Frederica de Laguna's table of "Lingít Tribes and Clans" published in the Northwest Coast volume of the *Handbook of North American Indians*. This was based on a table compiled by George Emmons, as later edited and published in de Laguna's *The Lingít Indians* (an adaptation of Emmons's notes and manuscripts). It has been reorganized and added to with information James Crippen obtained from various elders as well as information from other sources such as Andrew Hope III's "Lingít Map and Tribal List." Additional changes and additions were made by Lance Twitchell and Kanaan Bausler based on the work of Harold Jacobs, consultations with fluent speakers, and Tom Thornton's "Some Lingít Clans Named for Places and Their Distribution" in *Being and Place among the Lingít*.

The last group is Neix̱.ádi, a clan outside of the Wolf/Eagle and Raven/Crow Moieties that could marry into either one. The clan map is partially reproduced with permission from the late Andrew Hope III.

Tléix' Shangukeidí

Kéet Wuligás'i (Killer Whale Migration)

Clan, Meaning, and Origin	Primary Crest(s)	Secondary Crest(s)	Location and Houses
Naanyaa.aayí Group			
Naanya.aayí People of the Upper River	White Bear, Killer Whale	Wolf, Brown Bear, Marmot, Mudshark (Dogfish), Sea Monster, Mountain Goat	Shx'at Ḵwáan X'átgu Hít – Dogfish House X'átgu Naasí Hít – Dogfish Intestines House Ḵóok Hít – Box House Hít Tlein – Big House Tatóok Hít – Cave House Chéx̱'i Hít – Shadow House Aanshuká Hít – End of Town House
S'iknax̱.ádi People of Black Bear Bay; Limestone Inlet on Stephens Passage	Wolf, Killer whale	Brown Bear	Shx'at Ḵwáan X̱'aan Hít – Fire House Ank'u Hít – House of Gentle Courage
Kayaashkiditaan People of the House above the Platform; Lower Stikine	Killer Whale	Wolf	Shx'at Ḵwáan Kayaashkahít – Platform House Kéet Hít – Killerwhale House S'awdáan Ḵwáan Kéet Hít – Killerwhale House
X̱ook'eidí People of Leader Bay; near Wrangell			Shx'at Ḵwáan Shdéen Hít – Steel House Aandaa.óonaa Hít – Cannon House
X̱eil Ḵwáan People of the Foam; Chickamin River, Wrangell			
Daḵl'aweidí Group			
Daḵl'aweidí People of the Inland Sand Bar; Stikine River	Killer Whale, Eagle	Wolf, Dog Spirit, Octopus, Seal, Glacier, Iceberg, Flicker, Shark, Moth	Taant'a Ḵwáan Kéet Hít – Killerwhale House G̱ooch Hít – Wolf House Yasku Hít – Wasgo? House Kóon Hít – Flicker (Woodpecker) House Xutsnoowú Ḵwáan Kéet Hít – Killerwhale House Yaa Ayanasnaḵ Kéet Hít – Killerwhale Chasing After It (Seal) House Kéet Oox̱ú Hít – Killerwhale Tooth House Jilḵáat Ḵwáan Ch'eet Hít – Murrelet House Tleilóo Hít – Butterfly House Kéet Gooshí Hít – Killerwhale Dorsal Fin House Kéet Ḵwáani Hít – Killerwhale People House Kéet L'óot'i Hít – Killerwhale Tongue House Kéet Déx̱'i Hít – Killerwhale Backbone House Áatlein Ḵwáan Deisleen Ḵwáan Taagish Ḵwáan Kéet Hít – Killerwhale House
Tsaagweidí People of the Harbor Seal Ice Floes; Hood Bay (Kake)	Split Killer Whale	Wolf, Seal, Shark	Ḵéex̱' Ḵwáan Aan Yakawlitseix̱i Hít – Stomping the Ground House X̱áay Hít – Yellow-Cedar House

Group	Clan, Meaning, and Origin	Primary Crest(s)	Secondary Crest(s)	Location and Houses
Kéet Wuligás'i	Tagooneidí			Xutsnoowú Ḵwáan
Kéet Wuligás'i	Nees.ádi	Killer Whale		Ḵéex̱' Ḵwáan Kéet Gooshí Hít – Killerwhale Dorsal Fin House
Kéet Wuligás'i	Naasteidí People of the Nass River Rock	Flicker	Wolf, Eagle, Murrelet	Henyaa Ḵwáan Kuyú Ḵwáan Ch'eet Hít – Murrelet House Kóon Hít – Flicker (Woodpecker) House Deikeenoow Hít – Far Out Fort House
Kéet Wuligás'i	S'eet'ḵweidí People of Humpback Cove; Taku	Wolf	Killer Whale, Glacier	S'awdáan Ḵwáan Sít' Hít: Glacier House S'eek Hít: Black Bear House Kéet Hít: Killerwhale House T'aaḵú Ḵwáan Deisleen Ḵwáan
	Teiḵweidí Group			
Teiḵweidí Wuligás'i (People of Rock Carving Migration)	Teiḵweidí People of Payne Island; Payne Island off the north shore of Prince of Wales	Brown Bear	Wolf, Murrelet, Golden Eagle, Shark, Thunderbird, Sun, Marmot, Storm Petrel, Mt. Edgecumbe, Eagle	Taant'a Ḵwáan Kaats' Hít – House of Kaats' Shaanáx̱ Hít – Valley House Xóots Hít – Brown Bear House Xeitl Hít – Thunderbird House Wandaa Hít – Around the Edge House Saanyaa Ḵwáan Xóots Hít – Brown Bear House Litkáhít – Ridge House Xóots Ḵoowú Hít – Brown Bear's Den House Kaats' Hít – House of Kaats' G̱ooch Hít – Wolf House Xutsnoowú Ḵwáan Shaanáx̱ Hít – Valley House Xóots Hít – Brown Bear House Sheet'ká Ḵwáan Yaakwdáat Ḵwáan Xeitl Hít – Thunderbird House Gijook Hít – Golden Eagle House Gaaw Hít – Drum House K'atx̱áan Hít – Coward House Tóos' Hít – Shark House Xóots Hít – Brown Bear House Taḵjik'.aan Ḵwáan Saanyaa Hít – Southern Area House
Teiḵweidí Wuligás'i (People of Rock Carving Migration)	Aanshukahíttaan People of the House on the End of Town; Prince of Wales			Henyaa Ḵwáan Aanshukahít – End of Town House
Teiḵweidí Wuligás'i (People of Rock Carving Migration)	Gaawhittaan People of the Drum House; Dry Bay to Ahrnklin River (Aan Tlein) and Yakutat	Golden Eagle		Yaakwdáat Ḵwáan Gaaw Hít – Drum House (same as above Teiḵweidí) Gijook Hít – Golden Eagle House (same as above Teiḵweidí)
Teiḵweidí Wuligás'i (People of Rock Carving Migration)	Was'ineidí People of Sea Lice Creek; Cathedral Falls Creek at head of Hamilton Bay	Rhinoceros Auklet	Wolf, Brown Bear, Eagle	Ḵéex̱' Ḵwáan Tax̱'hít – Tier House

Teikweidí Wuligás'i

Clan, Meaning, and Origin	Primary Crest(s)	Secondary Crest(s)	Location and Houses
Dagisdinaa Group			
Dagisdinaa Inland Channel Clan; Blake Channel, Wrangell Island	Thunderbird	Wolf, Eagle, Shark, Sun	Jilk̲áat K̲wáan Xeitl Hít – Thunderbird House Shis'g̲i Hít – Sapling House G̲unaax̲oo K̲wáan Yaakwdáat K̲wáan Xeitl Hít – Thunderbird House
Shangukeidí People of Shankw	Thunderbird	Eagle, Brown Bear, G̲unakadeit (Sea Monster)	K̲éex̲' K̲wáan Kóok Hít – Box House Lk̲oot K̲wáan Kawdliyaayi Hít – Lowered (from the Sun) House G̲unaax̲oo K̲wáan
Shankweidí People of Saint Philip Island; Bay of Pines	Thunderbird	Eagle, Brown Bear, G̲unakadeit (Sea Monster)	Henyaa K̲wáan G̲unakadeit Hít – Sea Monster House Xóots Hít – Brown Bear House Tak̲jik'.aan K̲wáan Ch'áak' Hít – Eagle House G̲ooch Hít – Wolf House Tsísk'w Hít – Great Horned Owl House X'átgu Hít – Dogfish House
K̲aax̲'oos.híttaan People of Person's Foot House	Owl	Sockeye, Eagle, Footprint	Henyaa K̲wáan K̲aa X̲'oos Hít – Person's Foot House Tsísk'w Hít – Great Horned Owl House
Lk̲uweidi People of the Flood (?)			Henyaa K̲wáan Yaakwdáat K̲wáan
Kaagwaantaan Group			
Kaagwaantaan People of the Burnt House; Sitka	Wolf or Brown Bear	Eagle, Murrelet, Noble Killer Whale Beaver (Yakutat), Storm Petrel, Halibut, Star	Sheet'ká K̲wáan Aanyádi Hít – Nobleman House Eech Hít – Reef House Ch'áak' Hít – Eagle House Ch'áak' Kúdi Hít – Eagle Nest House Ch'eet Hít – Murrelet House Cháatl Hít – Halibut House Déix̲ X̲'awool Hít – Two Door House G̲ayéis' Hít – Iron House G̲ooch Hít – Wolf House K̲utx̲.ayanaháa Hít – Star House Heenkahít – On The Water House Xóots Hít – Brown Bear House Kaawagaani Hít – Burnt House Koohádaa Hít – Fish-chasing Stick House Jilk̲áat K̲wáan G̲ooch Hít – Wolf House Kéet Hít – Killerwhale House Ligooshi Hít – Dorsal-finned House Lk̲oot K̲wáan Xóots Hít – Brown Bear House Ch'áak' Hít – Eagle House Kaawagaani Hít – Burnt House Gaaw Hít – Drum House Xunaa K̲áawu Xóots Kúdi Hít – Brown Bear Nest House G̲unaax̲oo K̲wáan

Clan, Meaning, and Origin	Primary Crest(s)	Secondary Crest(s)	Location and Houses
K̲ookhittaan People of the Box House; Sitka	Brown Bear	Eagle, Shark, Box	Sheet'ká K̲wáan Tóos' Hít – Shark House K̲óok Hít – Box House K̲utís' Hít – Looking Out House Tl'aadéin Hít – Sideways House
G̲ayes'hittaan People of the Iron House			Sheet'ká K̲wáan G̲ayéis' Hít – Iron House
Chookaneidí Group			
Chookaneidí People of Grass River; Upper Glacier Bay, Berg Bay/Creek	Brown Bear, Porpoise, Spirit Bear	Wolf, Eagle, Murrelet, Glacier, Iceberg, Lady in the Ice, Killer Whale	Xunaa K̲áawu Naanaa Hít / Naanyaa Hít – Upriver House Xáatl Hít – Iceberg House Xóots S'aag̲í Hít – Brown Bear Bones House Yan Wulihashi Hít – Drifted Ashore House Aan Eeg̲ayáak Hít – On the Beach Below Town House Shux'aa X̲áayi Hít – First Yellow-cedar House Sheet'ká K̲wáan Xáatl Hít – Iceberg House Aan Eeg̲ayáak Hít – On the Beach Below Town House
Xinhittaan People of Black Fly House: People of Downriver House (Ixinaa Hít)			? Ixinaa Hít – Downriver House
X̲'ax'aahíttaan People of the Edge House			Sheet'ká K̲wáan X̲'ax'aa Hít – Edge of the Mouth House
Katakw.ádi People of Wilson Cove	Brown Bear	Wolf, Yellow Cedar	Sheet'ká K̲wáan X̲áay Hít – Yellow-cedar House
Xakwnoowkeidí Group			
Xakwnoowkeidí People on the Sandbar Fort; Strawberry Point; Icy Strait, especially upon the peninsula between Lynn Canal and Glacier Bay			
Wooshkeetaan People of the Houses On the Other Side of Each Other	Shark	Wolf, Thunderbird, Bear, Killer Whale, Murrelet, G̲unakadeit (Sea Monster), Eagle	Xunaa K̲áawu Wooshdaa Hít – Around Each Other House Tóos' Déx̲'i Hít – Shark Backbone House Noow Hít – Fort House Xutsnoowú K̲wáan Noow Hít – Fort House Noowshakahít – On the Head of the Fort House Xóots Kúdi Hít – Brown Bear Nest House Sheet'ká K̲wáan Noow Hít – Fort House Áak'w K̲wáan G̲unakadeit Hít – Sea Monster Hít Tlein – Big House Noow Hít – Fort House Tóos' Hít – Shark House Xeitl Hít – Thunderbird House Xóots Hít – Brown Bear House K̲óok Hít – Box House K̲éex̲' K̲wáan Tóos' Hít – Shark House
T'ikanaa			

Teik̲weidí Wuligás'i

	Clan, Meaning, and Origin	Primary Crest(s)	Secondary Crest(s)	Location and Houses
	Yanyeidí Group			
Yanyeidí Wuligás'i (Yanyedí Migration)	Yanyeidí People of the Mainland or People Below the Hemlock; Taku River	Wolf	Killer whale, Brown Bear, Mudshark, Octopus, Hawk, Dorothy Peak Was'as'ei	S'awdáan K̲wáan T'aak̲ú K̲wáan Ch'áal' Hít – Willow House Áatlein K̲wáan Yayuwaa Hít – House Between the Confluence / House on the Face (of the Mountain) Deisl̲een K̲wáan
Yanyeidí Wuligás'i (Yanyedí Migration)	K̲aax̲'us.eetitaan People of the Footprints House	Wolf	Killer whale, Sockeye	T'aak̲ú K̲wáan
Yanyeidí Wuligás'i (Yanyedí Migration)	Tsaat'ineidí People of a Stream Behind a Seal; Young Bay			T'aak̲ú K̲wáan Xóots Hít – Brown Bear House Yayuwaa Hít – House Between the Confluence / House on the Face (of the Mountain)
	Ahtna-Descended Group			
Ahtna/Eyak	G̲alyáx̲ Kaagwaantaan People of the Burnt House at Kaliakh River	Wolf, Beaver		G̲alyáx̲ K̲wáan
Ahtna/Eyak	Jeeshk̲weidí People of Jeeshk̲ú	Wolf, Beaver		G̲alyáx̲ K̲wáan
Ahtna/Eyak	L'ux̲'eidí People of Herring Spawn in Water			Yaakwdáat K̲wáan
Ahtna/Eyak	Laax̲aayík Teik̲weidí			Yaakwdáat K̲wáan

Tléix' Laayineidí

G̱aanax̱.ádi Wuligás'i (People of Sheltered Harbor Migration)

Clan, Meaning, and Origin	Primary Crest(s)	Secondary Crest(s)	Locations and Houses
G̱aanax̱.ádi Group			
G̱aanax̱.ádi People of Sheltered Harbor; Port Stewart in northern Behm Canal	Raven, Starfish	Whale, Golden Eagle, Frog, Musk Ox	Taant'a Ḵwáan Yan Wulihashi Hít – Drifted Ashore House Yéil Hít – Raven House S'áx Hít – Starfish House Yéil S'aag̱í Hít – Raven's Bones House Noow Hít – Fort House Gijook Hít – Golden Eagle House Xaas Hít – Buffalo House Taan Hít – Sea Lion House Ḵutís'hít – Looking Out House Yáay Hít – Whale House X'aagóon Hít – Isthmus Point House Henyaa Ḵwáan Yan Wulihashi Hít – Drifted Ashore House Yaaw Hít – Herring House Yáay Hít – Whale House Deishuhít – End of the Trail House Shís'g̱i Noow Hít – Sapling Fort House Taḵjik'.aan Ḵwáan Yan Wulihashi Hít – Drifted Ashore House Yan Wulihashi Hít 2 – Drifted Ashore House 2 T'aaḵú Ḵwáan Ishkahít – Atop the Fish Hole House Yan Wulihashi Hít – Drifted Ashore House Yéil Hít – Raven House Áak'w Ḵwáan G̱aanax̱aa Hít – G̱aanax̱aa House Yéil Hít – Raven House Galyáx̱ Ḵwáan
Deikée G̱aanax̱.ádi Out to Sea People of Sheltered Harbor; Xaakka.aan (empty clam shell town), Baker Island			Henyaa Ḵwáan
G̱aanax̱teidí People of Sheltered Harbor Rock; Port Stewart in northern Behm Canal	Raven, Frog, Woodworm	Whale, Strong Man and the Sea Lion, Mosquito, Beaver, Land Otter, G̱unakadeit	Jilḵáat Ḵwáan X̱'áakw Hít – Freshwater Marked Sockeye House Yáay Hít – Whale House X̱'aak Hít – Ravine House Ḵutís'hít – Looking Out (to Sea) House Xíxch'i Hít – Frog House Ishkahít – Atop the Fish Hole House Taagish Ḵwáan G̱unaax̱oo Ḵwáan
Taakw.aaneidí People of the Winter Village; Port Chester, Annette Island	Strong Man and the Sea Lion, Woodworm	Whale, Giant Mouse	Henyaa Ḵwáan Yáay Hít – Whale House Taḵjik'.aan Ḵwáan Taan Hít – Sea Lion House
K'ooxineidí People of the Mink/Marten Creek; Port St. Nicholas	Mink/Marten	Raven, Whale, Frog	Henyaa Ḵwáan K'óox Hít – Mink/Marten House

	Clan, Meaning, and Origin	Primary Crest(s)	Secondary Crest(s)	Locations and Houses
Gaanax.ádi Wuligás'i	**Ishkeetaan (Ishkahíttaan)** People of Deep Pool in the River House; East bank of the Chilkat River above Spuhn Point	Frog	Raven, Sea Lion, Sun	**Jilk̲áat K̲wáan** **Ishká Hít** – Atop the Fish Hole House **Áatlein K̲wáan** **Deisl̲een K̲wáan** **Ishkahít** – Atop the Fish Hole House **Taagish K̲wáan** **T'aak̲ú K̲wáan** **Ishkahít** – Atop the Fish Hole House
	Kook̲hittaan People of Cellar House; Migrated from Seenáa (Snettisham) to the interior	Raven (with children)	Musk Ox	**T'aak̲ú K̲wáan** **Áatlein K̲wáan** **Xaas Hít** – Bison/Cattle House **Deisl̲een K̲wáan** **Taagish K̲wáan**
	Took̲a.ádi People of Took̲a			
	K̲ak'w.weidí / K̲ak'weidí People of Basket Bay	Beaver		**Xutsnoowú K̲wáan** **Kaak̲áak'w Hít** – Basket/Arch House
	Deisheetaan Group			
Deisheetaan Wuligás'i (People of the End of the Trail House Migration)	**Deisheetaan** People of the End of the Trail House; End of Beaver Trail street in Angoon or alternatively near Point Craven outside Sitkoh Bay	Beaver, Split Beaver	Raven, Dragonfly, Mosquito, White Frog, Sockeye, Hawk, Bullhead, Needlefish	**Xutsnoowú K̲wáan** **Dáanaa Hít** – Silver House **Deishuhít** – End of the Trail House **Goon Hít** – Spring House **Shdéen Hít** – Steel House **Tuk̲kahít** – Needlefish House **Yéil Hít** – Raven House **Yéil S'aagi Hít** – Raven's Bones House **Kaak̲áak'w Hít** – Basket/Arch House **Áatlein K̲wáan** **Deisl̲een K̲wáan** **Taagish K̲wáan** **Deishuhít** – End of the Trail House **Shx'at K̲wáan** **Deishuhít** – End of the Trail House
	Tuk̲yeidí People of of the Outlet; Outlet of a lake on Xutsnoowú, or Mitchell Bay	Raven, Beaver		**Xutsnoowú K̲wáan**
	Naach'uneidí People of Naach'u Héen; A creek in Whitewater Bay			**Xutsnoowú K̲wáan** **Jilk̲áat K̲wáan**

Taalk̲weidí Wuligás'i (People of the Mountain that Never Flooded Migration)

Clan, Meaning, and Origin	Primary Crest(s)	Secondary Crest(s)	Locations and Houses
Taalk̲weidí Group			
Taalk̲weidí People of Little Flat Basket Bay; Devil's Thumb Mtn, Thomas Bay, east of Cape Fanshaw	Taalk̲unax̲k'ushaa (Devil's Thumb Mountain)	Raven	Shx'at K̲wáan Shaa Hít: Mountain House Kax̲k̲uyandu.aa Hít: Dug Out Foundation House G̲íl' Hít: Cliff House
Kaasx̲'agweidí People of K̲aasx̲'éikw; A small bay between G̲eisa.aan (Kasaan) and Kachx̲ana.áakw (Wrangell), originally Haida		Thunderbird, Frog's Den, Sea Lion	Shx'at K̲wáan Xeitl Hít – Thunderbird House Tl'aadéin Hít – Sideways House Xíxch'i X̲aayí Hít – Frog Lodge House Taan Hít – Sea Lion House
Lukaax̲.ádi People off the Point of It; Duncan Canal	Sockeye	Raven, White Raven, Kingfisher, Mt. Fairweather, Devil's Thumb Mtn., Land Otter, Mt. Ripinsky, Hummingbird	Lk̲oot K̲wáan Yéil Hít – Raven House Yéil Kíji Hít – Raven's Wing House Yéil Kúdi Hít – Raven's Nest House Shaa Hít – Mountain House Kóoshdaa Hít – Land Otter House G̲eisán Hít – Mount Ripinsky House Jilk̲áat K̲wáan Déix̲ X̲'aháadi Hít – Two Door House Xunaa K̲áawu G̲unaax̲oo K̲wáan Shakahít – Prow House
Noowshaka.aayí People on the Head of the Fort			Jilk̲áat K̲wáan
K̲aach.ádi People of Pybus Bay; Pybus Bay, Admiralty Island	Raven, Fresh Water Sockeye	Hummingbird, Frog, Daxana Heen, Land Otter, Halibut, Whale	Shx'at K̲wáan Náalx̲ Hít – Big Halibut House Xíxch'i Hít – Frog House Alk̲áa Hít – Gambling House G̲aach Hít – Mat House Kaawdliyaayi Hít – Lowered House Yáay Hít – Whale House K̲éex̲' K̲wáan X̲'áakw Hít – Freshwater Marked Sockeye House K̲utís' Hít – Looking Out (to Sea) House
Skanax̲.ádi People of the Noisy Beach; Saginaw Bay			K̲éex̲' K̲wáan
Taneidí People of Jumping Fish Creek: Tunehean Creek			K̲éex̲' K̲wáan
X̲'alchaneidí People of the Bad Smelling Mouth; Mudflats on Duncan Canal just west of Wrangell Narrows			Shx'at K̲wáan
K̲uyeik̲'.ádi People of Excursion Inlet			

	Clan, Meaning, and Origin	Primary Crest(s)	Secondary Crest(s)	Locations and Houses
	L'eeneidí Group			
L'eeneidí Wuligás'i	L'eeneidí People of Dog Salmon Creek	Dog Salmon	Raven, Gull, Big Dipper, Mtn. Goat, Lady of the Lake	Áak'w Ḵwáan Ǥaatáa Hít – Trap House Téel' Hít – Dog Salmon House Taḵjik'.aan Ḵwáan Téel' Hít – Dog Salmon House Téel' Yádi Hít – Dog Salmon Child House
L'eeneidí Wuligás'i	Aanx̱'aakhittaan People of the House in the Middle of the Village; Angoon	Dog Salmon	Raven, Eagle, Gull	Xutsnoowú Ḵwáan Aanx̱'aak Hít – Middle of Town House Yanxoon Hít – Logjam House
L'eeneidí Wuligás'i	Teel'hittaan People of the Dog Salmon House; on the point opposite the Barrier Islands	Dog Salmon	Octopus, Raven	Henyaa Ḵwáan
L'eeneidí Wuligás'i	Suḵteeneidí People of the Wide Steam in the Grass; Keku Strait below Hamilton Bay	Dog Salmon	Raven, Snail	Ḵéex̱' Ḵwáan Aanx̱'aak Hít – Middle of Town House Shaa Hít – Mountain House Táax̱' Hít – Snail House Wandaa Hít – Armor House Yéik Hít – Spirit House
L'eeneidí Wuligás'i	Yax̱teitaan People of the Big Dipper House; Auke Bay			Áak'w Ḵwáan Yax̱té Hít – Big Dipper House
	Kiks.ádi Group			
Kiks.ádi Wuligás'i (people of Helm Bay Migration)	Kiks.ádi People of Helm Bay; Helm Bay in western Behm Canal	Frog	Raven, Sun, Herring, Herring Rock, Owl, Sea Lion, Woodworm, Bullhead, Snail	Saanyaa Ḵwáan Wéix̱' Hít – Bullhead House Yéil Hít – Raven House Xíxch'i Hít – Frog House Shx'at Ḵwáan Ǥagaan Hít – Sun House Tax̱'hít – Snail House Xíxch'i Hít – Frog House Sheet'ká Ḵwáan At Uwaxiji Hít – Strong House Ǥagaan Hít – Sun House Kax̱átjaa Hít – Jumping Herring House Noowtuhít – Inside the Fort House Noow Dagaanyaa Hít – Outside the Fort House S'é Hít – Clay House Shdéen Hít – Steel House Tináa Hít – Copper Shield House X'aakahít – On the Point House
Kiks.ádi Wuligás'i (people of Helm Bay Migration)	Teeyhittaan People of the Yellow Cedar Bark House	Frog	Raven	Shx'at Ḵwáan Teey Hít – Yellow Cedar Bark House

	Clan, Meaning, and Origin	Primary Crest(s)	Secondary Crest(s)	Locations and Houses
Kiks.ádi Wuligás'i	Teeyeeneidí People of the Yellow Cedar Bark Stream	Dog Salmon	Raven, Frog, Octopus, Land Otter, Starfish	Henyaa Ḵwáan Yéil Hít – Raven House Yan Wulihashi Hít – Drifted Ashore House Teey Hít – Yellow Cedar Bark House Taḵjik'.aan Ḵwáan Gaxkahít – Gaaxká House Héenkahít – On the Water House S'áx Hít – Starfish House Yéil Hít – Raven House Yéil Yádi Hít – Little Raven House Ḵéex' Ḵwáan Kóoshdaa Hít – Land Otter House Teey Hít – Yellow Cedar Bark House
	L'uknax̱.ádi Group			
L'uknax̱.ádi Wuligás'i (People of L'uknax̱ Migration)	L'uknax̱.ádi People of Deep Bay; A salmon stream North of Klukwan or Deep Bay?	Coho	Raven, Frog, Octopus, Sea Lion, Whale	Sheet'ká Ḵwáan Daginaa Hít / Diginaa Hít – Out in the Ocean Salmon Box H. Ḵutá Hít – Sleep House L'ook Hít Tlein – Big Coho House L'ook Hít Yádi – Little Coho House Shgaadaayí Hít – Yakutat Creek House Taan Hít – Sea Lion House Ixinaa Hít – House at Lower End of Town Ixinaa Hít 2 – House at Lower End of Town 2 Xíxch'i Hít – Frog House Yáay Hít – Whale House Áak'w Ḵwáan L'ook Hít – Coho House G̱unaax̱oo Ḵwáan Dleit Xíxch'i Hít – White Frog House Yaakwdáat Ḵwáan Shaa Hít – Mountain House (Mount Fairweather) Daginaa Hít / Diginaa Hít – Out in the Ocean Salmon Box H. Eech Hít – Reef House Eech Hít 2 – Reef House 2
	X'at'ka.aayí People on the Island; Island in Lituya Bay	Coho	Raven, Water Ouzel	Sheet'ká Ḵwáan Kayaashkahít – Platform House L'ook Hít – Coho House G̱unaax̱oo Ḵwáan Xunaa Ḵáawu
	Kayaashkiditaan People of the Platform House	Coho		Sheet'ká Ḵwáan Kayaashkahít – Platform House
	T'aḵdeintaan People of the House toward the Side; Island on the outer coast beyond Cape Spencer, or inside Lituya Bay	Black Legged Kittiwake	Frog, Whale, Mt. Fairweather, Freshwater Coho, Sockeye, Bullhead, Snail, Venus	Sheet'ká Ḵwáan G̱unax̱oo Hít – House Among the Dene Xunaa Ḵáawu T'aḵdéin Hít – Toward the Side House X̱'áak'w Hít – Freshwater Marked Sockeye House X̱'áak'w Yádi Hít – Little Freshwater Marked Coho House Yéil Hít – Raven House Yéil Kúdi Hít – Raven's Nest House K'óox Dísi Hít – Marten Moon House Teet Hít – Wave House Ḵaa Shaayí Hít – Man's Head House G̱aanax̱áa Hít – G̱aanax̱áa House

Clan, Meaning, and Origin	Primary Crest(s)	Secondary Crest(s)	Locations and Houses
L'uknax̱.ádi Group — L'uknax̱.ádi Wulig̱ás'i (People of L'uknáx̱ Migration)			
Tax̱'hittaan People of the Snail House; Xunaa Káawu (Hoonah)	Black Legged Kittiwake	Snail	Xunaa Ḵáawu Tax̱'hít – Snail House
Xaas.hittaan People of the Ox House			Taant'a Ḵwáan T'aaḵú Ḵwáan Xunaa Ḵáawu Sheet'ká Ḵwáan Yaakwdáat Ḵwáan
Ḵoosk'eidí People of Shg̱aadaayihéen (stream north of Mount Fairweather)	Raven	Coho, Musk Ox, Mouse	Sheet'ká Ḵwáan Xaas Hít – Bison/Cattle House Xunaa Ḵáawu Xaas Hít – Bison/Cattle House G̱unaax̱oo Ḵwáan Xaas Hít – Bison/Cattle House
Shg̱aadaayihin.aayí People of Shg̱aadaayi Héen; a stream that drains Great Plateau Glacier, north of Mount Fairweather on the Gulf Coast	Raven	Coho, Musk Ox, Mouse	
Ahtna-Descended Group — Ahtna/Eyak Wulig̱ás'i			
Kwáashk'i Ḵwáan Humpy Creek People (from Eyak) K'inéix̱ Ḵwáan Copper River People (from Ahtna); Copper River	Mt. St. Elias, Moon, North Star, Humpy	Owl, Raven	Yaakwdáat Ḵwáan Aanyuwaa Hít – In Front of Town House Tsísk'w Hít / Tsísk'u Hít – Owl House Dís Hít – Moon House Yéil S'aag̱í Hít – Raven's Bones House Noow Hít – Fort House Shaa Hít – Mountain House (Yas'éitashaa / Was'éitashaa - Mount Saint Elias)
Stax̱.ádi People of Stax̱			
Unknown			
Kuyuweidí People of Kooyú	Star, Puffin		Kuyú Ḵwáan X̱ík Hít – Puffin House Ḵutx̱.ayanaháa Hít – Star House
Watineidí People of Watin (?); Wattahéen Creek in Hoonah Sound (?)			

Neix̲.ádi

Clan, Meaning, and Origin	Primary Crest	Secondary Crest	Location and Houses
Neix̲.ádi People of Neix̲	Eagle, Beaver, Halibut, King Crab, Giant Clam		Saanyaa K̲wáan Ch'áak' Hít – Eagle House Ch'áak' X̲'oosí Hít – Eagle Foot House S'igeidí X̲aayí Hít – Beaver Lodge House Ch'áak' Kúdi Hít – Eagle Nest House Ch'áak' Koowú Hít – Eagle Fan-Tail House Cháatl Hít – Halibut House X̲'eet' Hít – Giant Clam House X'éix̲ Hít – King Crab House K̲éedu Hít – Beaver Dam House

The map on the following page, which is also in the preface of this workbook, is inspired by the *Traditional Tlingit Country* map that was created by Tlingit Readers, Inc. Andrew Hope III had asked that the map be included in language teaching materials. Previous versions of this workbook contains the map, but it has been replaced with this one to match the spellings included in the list of clans in this chapter. Much work has gone into capturing the clan names, houses, locations, and crests. This list will be updated as corrections and suggestions arrive. The *Traditional Tlingit Country* map was created by Andy Hope, designed by Sue Kraft with artwork provided courtesy of Mike Jackson, and produced by Peter Metcalfe, who coordinates distribution and sales through Tlingit Readers, Inc.

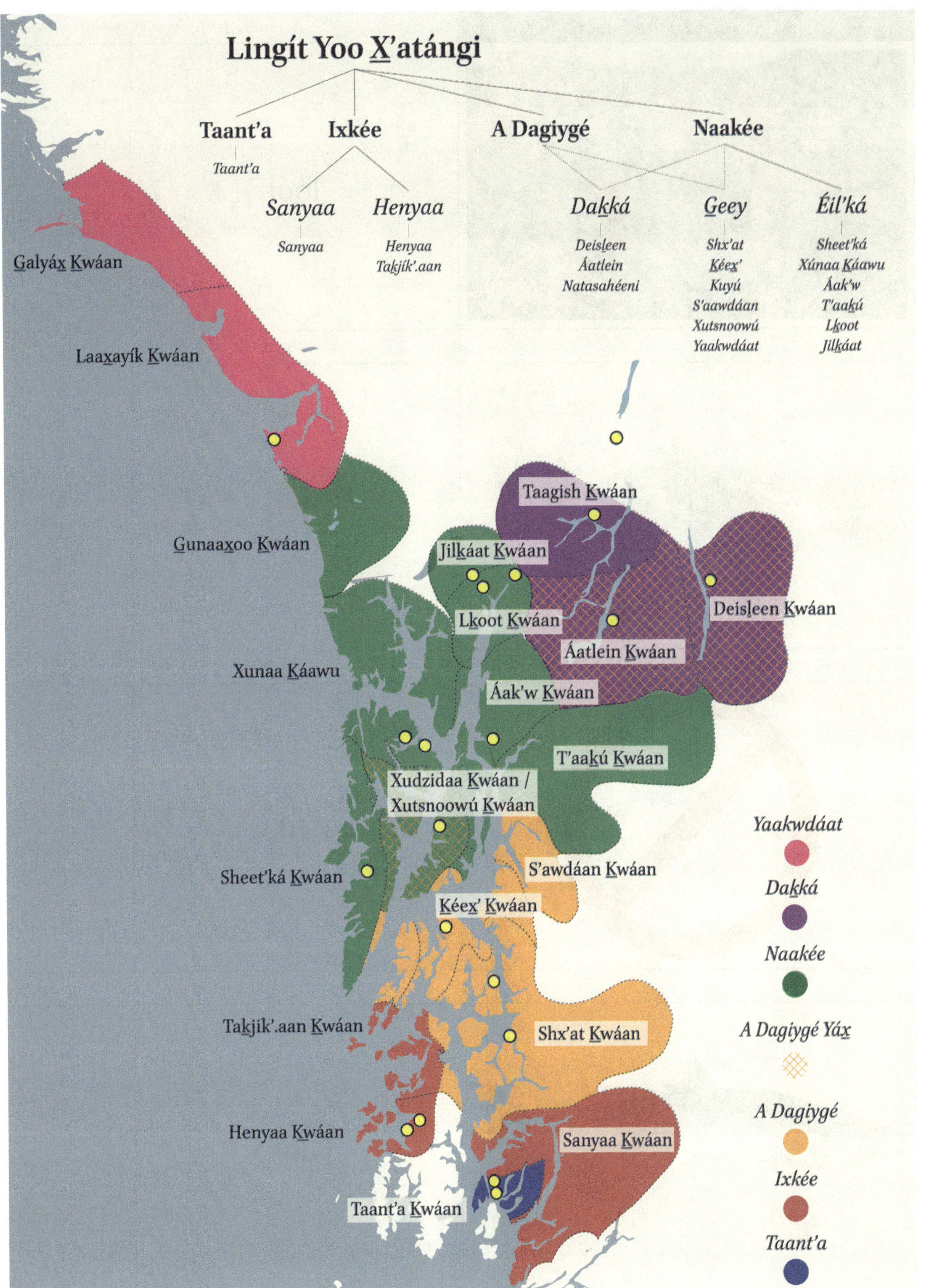
Lingít Yoo X̲'atángi
Taant'a
Ixkée
A Dagiygé
Naakée
Taant'a
Sanyaa
Henyaa
Dak̲ká
G̲eey
Éil'ká
Sanyaa
Henyaa
Tak̲jík'.aan
Deisl̲een
Áatlein
Natasahéeni
Shx'at
K̲éex̲'
Kuyú
S'aawdáan
Xutsnoowú
Yaakwdáat
Sheet'ká
Xúnaa K̲áawu
Áak'w
T'aak̲ú
L̲koot
Jilk̲áat
Galyáx̲ K̲wáan
Laax̲ayík K̲wáan
Gunaax̲oo K̲wáan
Taagish K̲wáan
Jilk̲áat K̲wáan
Deisl̲een K̲wáan
L̲koot K̲wáan
Áatlein K̲wáan
Xunaa K̲áawu
Áak'w K̲wáan
T'aak̲ú K̲wáan
Xudzidaa K̲wáan /
Xutsnoowú K̲wáan
Sheet'ká K̲wáan
S'awdáan K̲wáan
K̲éex̲' K̲wáan
Tak̲jik'.aan K̲wáan
Shx'at K̲wáan
Henyaa K̲wáan
Sanyaa K̲wáan
Taant'a K̲wáan
Yaakwdáat
Dak̲ká
Naakée
A Dagiygé Yáx̲
A Dagiygé
Ixkée
Taant'a

<table>
<tr><th>Vocabulary</th><th colspan="2">l</th></tr>
<tr><td></td><td>lóol</td><td>fireweed;
pink (color)</td></tr>
<tr><td colspan="3">dl</td></tr>
<tr><td></td><td>dleit</td><td>snow;
white (color)</td></tr>
<tr><td colspan="3">tl</td></tr>
<tr><td></td><td>tléik’</td><td>no</td></tr>
<tr><td colspan="3">l’</td></tr>
<tr><td></td><td>l’ook</td><td>coho,
silver salmon</td></tr>
</table>

tl’		
	tl’eex	garbage, trash, rubbish, mess
x’		
	x’áax’	apple
x’w-		
	x’wán	boot(s)
-x’w		
	dzéex’w	small clams

k̲		
	k̲ákw	basket
k̲w-		
	–k̲wáan	people of (a place)
-k̲w		
	náak̲w	octopus
k̲'		
	k̲'ateil	pitcher

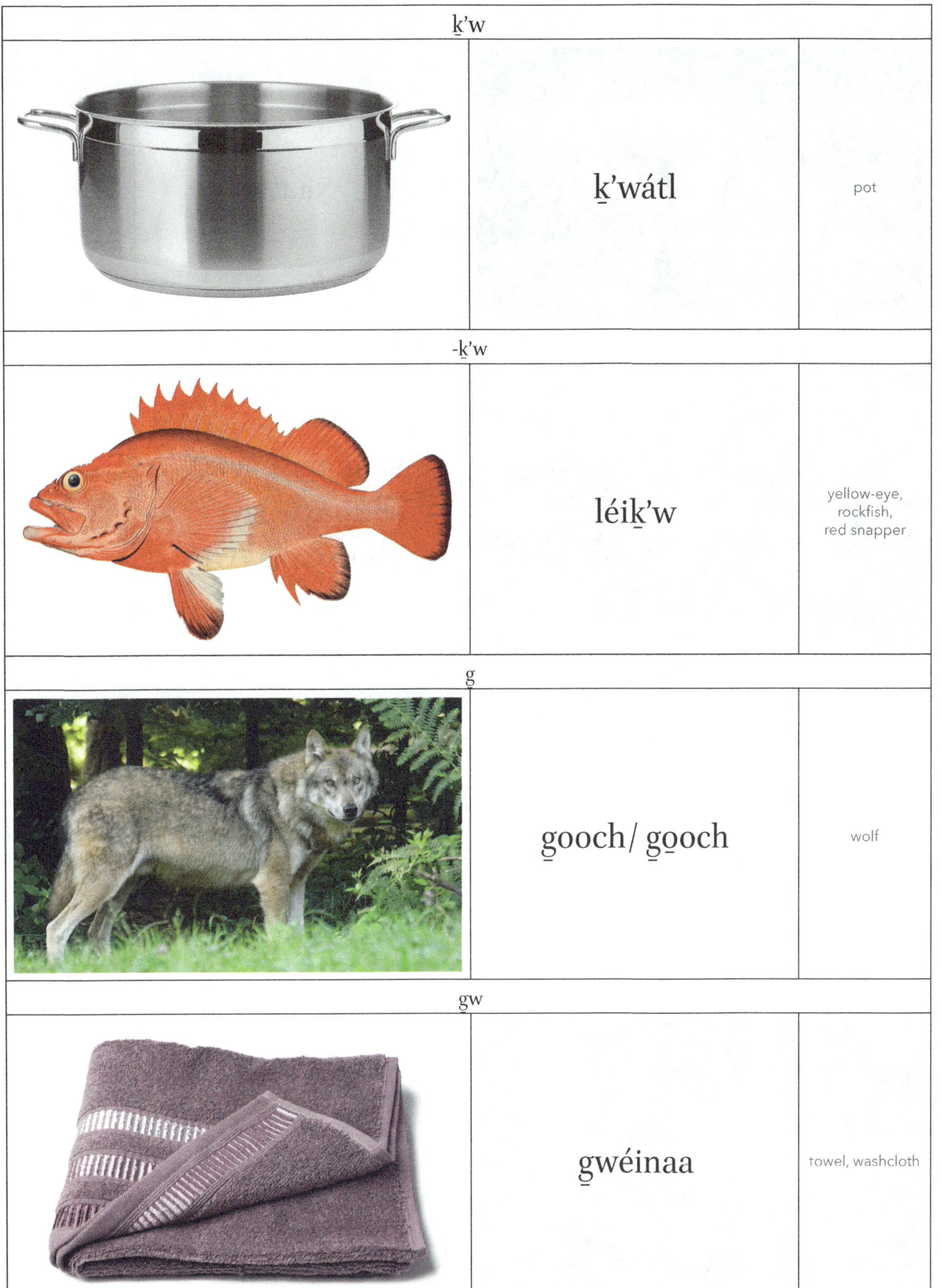

k̲'w		
	k̲'wátl	pot
-k̲'w		
	léik̲'w	yellow-eye, rockfish, red snapper
g		
	g̲ooch/ g̲o̲och	wolf
gw		
	g̲wéinaa	towel, washcloth

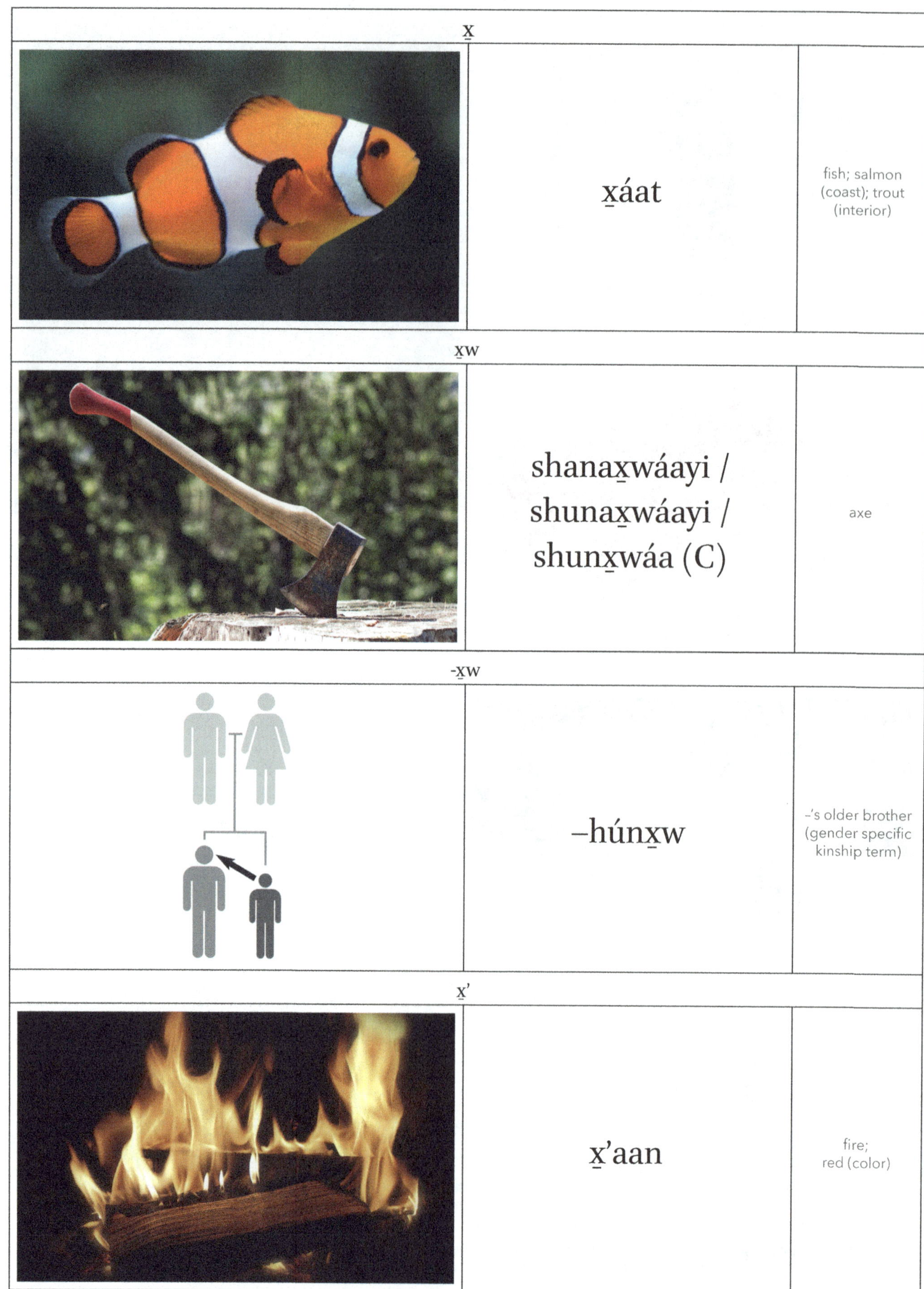

x̱		
	x̱áat	fish; salmon (coast); trout (interior)
x̱w		
	shanax̱wáayi / shunax̱wáayi / shunx̱wáa (C)	axe
-x̱w		
	–húnx̱w	-'s older brother (gender specific kinship term)
x̱'		
	x̱'aan	fire; red (color)

x̱'w		
	x̱'wáat'	Dolly Varden trout
-x̱'w		
	néx̱'w	cloudberry
	tl'átk	earth; dirt; soil
	k'oodás' / goodás' (Y)	shirt; tunic

	tléiḵw	berries
	du tl'eiḵ / du tl'eeḵ	their-(s) finger
Lingít Counting		
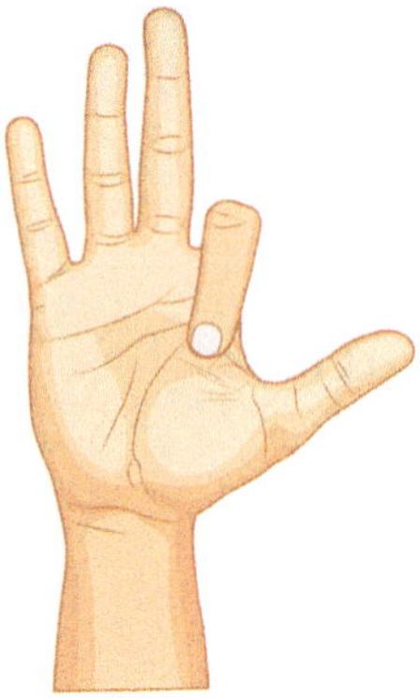	tléix'	one
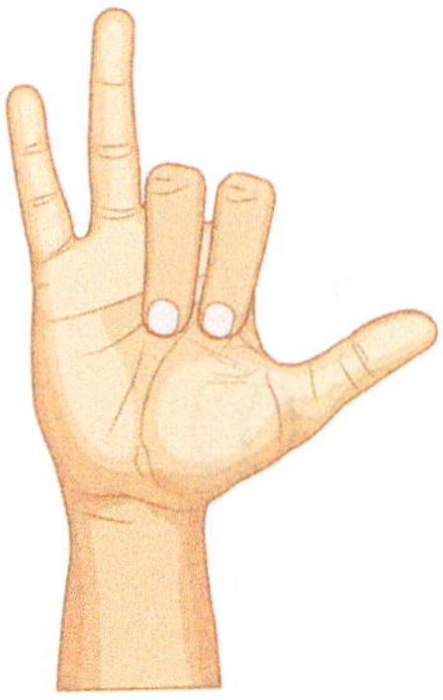	déix̱ / déex̱	two

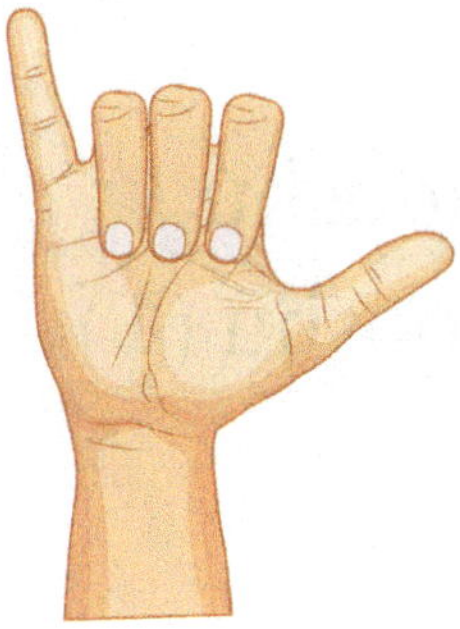	nás'k	three
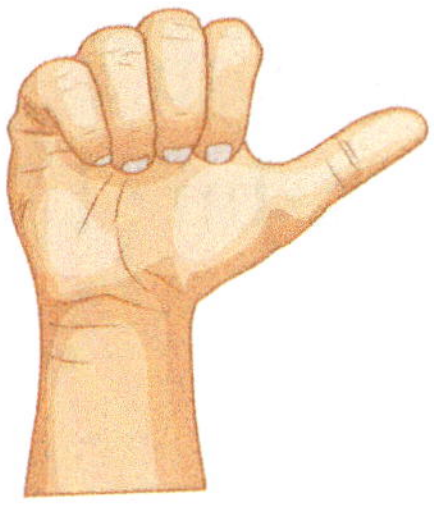	daax'oon	four
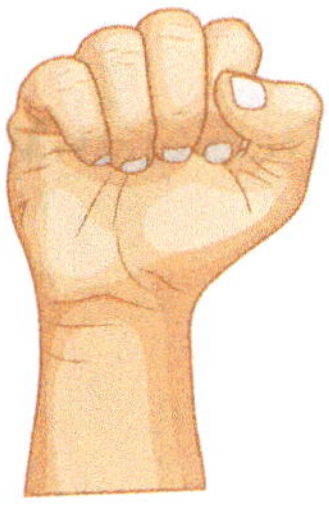	keijín	five
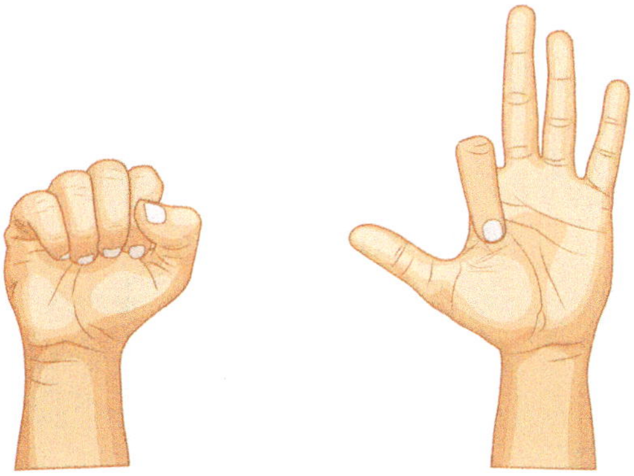	tleidooshú / tleitwooshú (T)	six

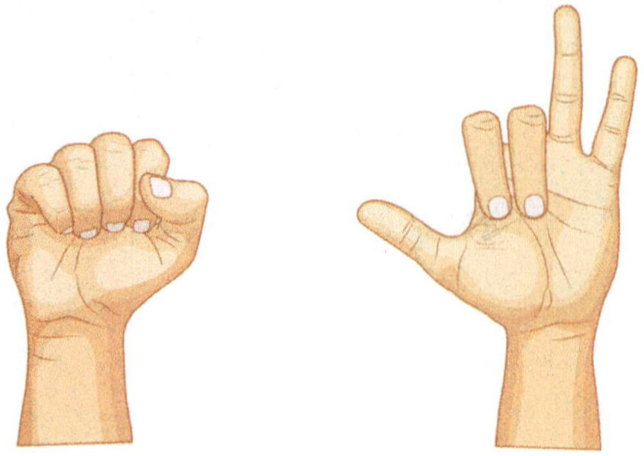	dax̱adooshú / dax̱atwooshú (T)	seven
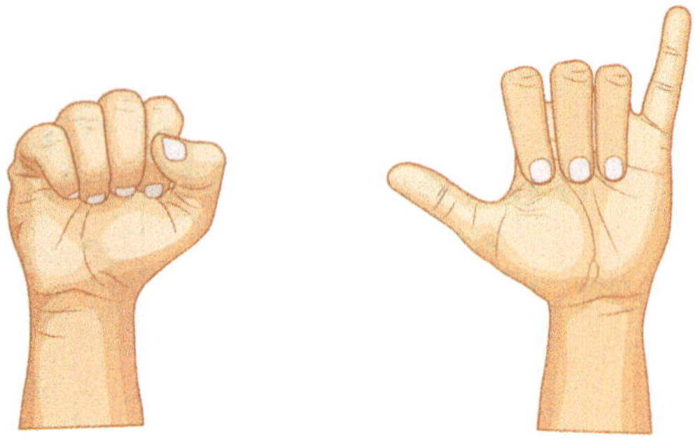	nas'gadooshú / nas'gatwooshú (T)	eight
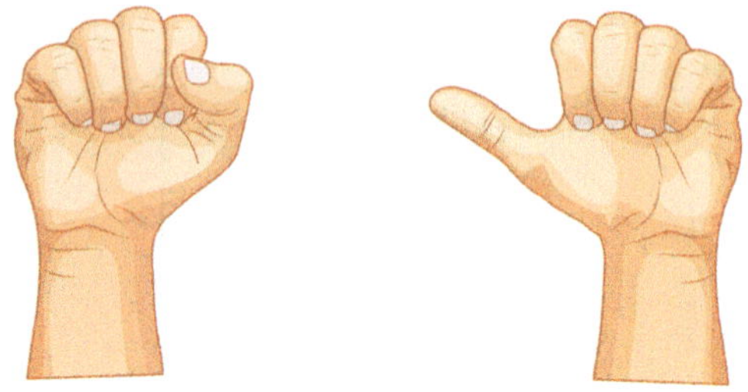	gooshúḵ / goosháḵw	nine
	jinkaat	ten

3B

K̲aa X̲'akaneek Kawdu.aag̲ú 3

Translation Exercises 3

Lingít → English

Wáa sá iduwasáakw?	
Wáa sá duwasáakw?	
Kaagwaantaanx̲ sitee.	
Yéil naax̲ x̲at sitee.	
Uháan áyá.	
Seattle-x' yéi x̲at yatee.	
Xáatl Hít áyá haa naakahídi.	

English → Lingít

They are called Susie in English	
Child of Lukaax̲.ádi	
I am at Angoon	
Which clan are you?	
Where do you reside (own land)?	
We are Áatlein K̲wáan.	

4A

Wáa sá k̲uwatee?

How is the Weather?

Yá Lingít'aaní g̱eix' woosh jín toolshát yeisú
— Katyé

In this world, we're still holding each other's hands
– David Kadashan

(Dauenhaeuer, Haa Tuwunáagu Yís 236-237)

yá	lingít'aaní	g̱ei-x'	woosh	jín	tu-l-√shát	yeisú
right.here	world	within.confines-at.(residing)	reciprocal	hand	we.(1p.S)-cl.(d,l)-√hold	still

Wáa sá k̲uwatee?

Dialogue Practice

A	1	Gáande kk̲wagóot.	I'm going to go outside. gáan-de <ga-u-g̲a>-x̲a-∅-√góot outside-towards <future>-i.(1s.S)-cl.(∅)-√walk/go In classic Lingít, this could mean "going outside" or "going to the bathroom." Today, most speakers use «gáande» for outside and «gánde» for going to the bathroom.
B	2	Gáande aneelg̲ein!	Look outside! gáan-de a-<na>-i-l-√g̲ein outside-towards a.theme-<command>-you.(2s.S)-cl.(d,l)-√look-at
	3	Wáa sá k̲uwatee?	How is the weather? wáa =sá k̲u-ÿa-√tee how =name areal-cl.(∅,i)-√be
A	4	K̲uligóos',	It's cloudy, k̲u-li-√góos' areal-cl.(l,i)-√cloud
	5	k̲a séew daak wusitán.	and it's raining. k̲a séew daak <ÿu>-si-√tán and rain out.to.open <perfective>-cl.(s,i)-√long.object.moves
B	6	I kinaak.ádi yéi na.oo!	Put your jacket on! i= kinaak-át-i yéi= na-∅-√oo your.(2s.P)= over.thing.(4n.i)-relational thus= <command>-cl.(∅)-√use/wear
	7	X̲'oosx̲ idayék̲ i s'él' x'wáni!	Put on your rubber boots! x̲'oos-x̲ i-da-√yék̲ i s'él' x'wán-i foot-contact.with you.(2s.S)-cl.(d,∅)-√pull your.(2s.P) rubber boot(s)-relational
A	8	Aaa, yéi kg̲watée.	Yes, it will be. aaa yéi= ∅-<ga-u-g̲a>-∅-√tée yes thus= them/it.(3.O)-<future>-cl.(∅)-√be

Lingít verbs

Previous lessons focused on repetition of phrases and substitution drills where we learn a pattern and then fill in the blanks with a noun to use the sentence to express ourselves. In this lesson, we will continue doing so, and will be learning a series of verbs that allow us to describe the weather in many possible conditions. This is talking about how the weather is now, which is often a verb mode that is called *im<perfective>-* Verb mode in Lingít refers to the way the verb is talking about a state, action, or motion. Sometimes it functions similar to tense in English, such as past (rained), present (is raining), and future (will rain).

In later lessons we will look at how we can talk about the way the weather was using a verb mode called *perfective*, the way it will be using a verb mode called *future*, and also the way it is becoming right now using a verb mode called *progressive im<perfective>-*

When thinking about how the Lingít language works, it is important to remember that Lingít is more concerned with the whether or not the verb happened instead of when the verb occurs. In English, we often refer to things as *past tense*, *present tense*, and *future tense*. In Lingít, we will be using the terms *perfective*, *imperfective*, and *future*. The reason for this is that Lingít is an event-driven language, which means that when the verb occurred is less important that whether or not it has happened. Because of this, sometimes we have verbs in Lingít that do not change when talking about present tense or past tense, but that is certainly not the case every time. For now, focus on the phrases and try to use them in your day to day communication.

The parts that make up the verb are shown below the phrases, and later lessons will describe how these parts are written (segmented) and labeled (glossed).

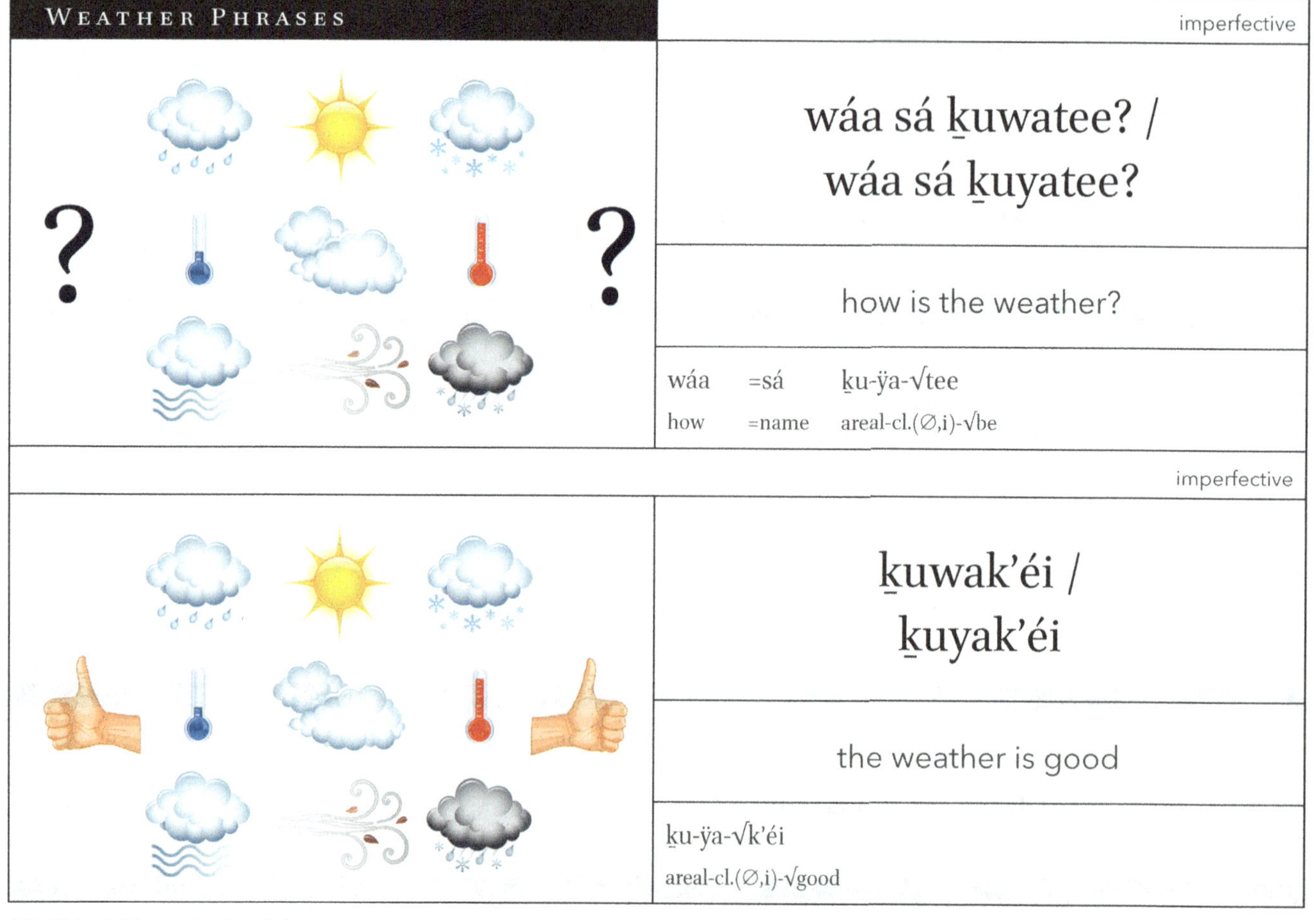

Weather Phrases	imperfective
	wáa sá ḵuwatee? / wáa sá ḵuyatee?
	how is the weather?
	wáa =sá ḵu-ÿa-√tee how =name areal-cl.(∅,i)-√be
	imperfective
	ḵuwak'éi / ḵuyak'éi
	the weather is good
	ḵu-ÿa-√k'éi areal-cl.(∅,i)-√good

perfective

awdigaan / oodigaan (Y)

it is sunny; it was sunny

a-<ÿu>-di-√gaan

a.theme-<perfective>-cl.(d,∅,i)-√burn/light

imperfective

ḵuligóos'

it is cloudy

ḵu-li-√góos'

areal-cl.(l,i)-√cloud

imperfective

ḵuwat'áa / ḵuyat'áa

the weather is hot

ḵu-ÿa-√t'áa

areal-cl.(∅,i)-√warm/hot

imperfective

ḵusi.áat'

the weather is cold

ḵu-si-√.áat'

areal-cl.(s,i)-√cold

___ ágé?	is it ___?
	___ á-gé ___ focus.yes/no? *use one of the weather verbs*

aaa/tléik'. ___.	yes/no. it's ___.
	Answer yes or no, and then with the appropriate weather verb.

Adverbs

	adverb
k̲únáx̲	really
	k̲ú-náx̲ areal-through/via This is an adverb, which usually appear before the verb it modifies, but this one can occur after the verb.

	adverb
k̲údáx̲ ~ k̲útx̲	too much
	k̲ú-dáx̲ areal-from This is an adverb, and appears before the verb it modifies.

perfective

dleit daak wusitán

it is snowing; it was snowing

dleit	daak	<ÿu>-si-√tán
snow	out.to.open	<perfective>-cl.(s,i)-√long.object.moves

perfective

séew daak wusitán

it is raining; it was raining

séew	daak	<ÿu>-si-√tán
rain	out.to.open	<perfective>-cl.(s,i)-√long.object.moves

kadás'

hail

kaklahéen

wet snow; sleet

	kaséix̱jaa	fine rain

imperfective

	ḵuwdigwás'
	it is foggy; it was foggy
	ḵu-<ÿu>-di-√gwás' areal-<perfective>-cl.(d,∅,i)-√fog

perfective

	ayawditee / ayamditee (T,C)
	it is windy; it was windy
	a-ÿa-<ÿu>-di-√tee a.theme-face-<perfective>-cl.(d,∅,i)-√windy/stormy

perfective

	ayakaawadán
	it is snowing heavily; it was snowing heavily (leaving snowdrifts)
	a-ÿa-ka-<ÿu>-ÿa-√dán a.theme-face-surface-<perfective>-cl.(∅,i)-√snow-accumulate

imperfective (-)

tlél ḵooshk'é

the weather is bad

tlél	ḵu-u-sh-√k'é
not	areal-irrealis-cl.(sh)-√good

perfective

x̱at yaawasík

i'm weathered in

x̱at	ÿa-<ÿu>-ÿa-√sík
me.(1s.O)	face-<perfective>-cl.(∅,i)-√weathered.in

This verb has previously been interpreted as "i am delayed," but that would usually be: x̱at yawdi.aa

perfective

x̱at wuditl'ák'

i'm wet

x̱at=	<ÿu>-di-√tl'ák'
me.(1s.O)=	<perfective>-cl.(d,∅,i)-√become.wet

eesháan!

poor thing!

This word is a Lingít interjection, so its meaning can change depending on context. It is used to describe something poor, someone suffering, or to tease.

Vocabulary		
	ḵáa	man; person
	ḵóok / ḵó̲ok	box
	kóoḵ / kó̲oḵ	cellar; pit
	éiḵ / éeḵ	beach

	shaaḵ	driftwood (log or wood that has been in the water for a long time and has gotten waterlogged)
	táḵl	hammer
	láḵt	bentwood box
	k’óox	marten

	g̱áach	mat; doormat; rug
	guwakaan / ḵuwakaan	deer; peacemaker
	g̱áx̱	rabbit
	lug̱wéinaa	tissue; handkerchief (lit. nose wiper)

	s'áaw	dungeness crab
	s'éex'át	shrimp
	s'íx'	bowl; dish
	ús'aa	soap

	óos'i	laundry
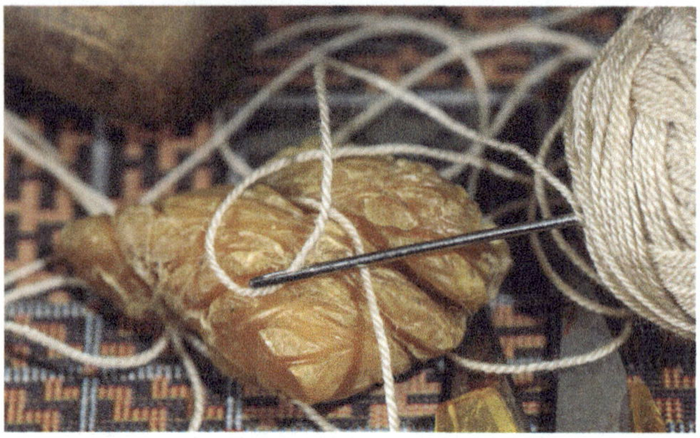	tás daaneis'í	wax for sewing
	cháas'	humpy, pink salmon
	tóos'	shark

	néesʼ	sea urchin
	sʼísaa	cloth; sail (on ship)
	tʼáa ká	floor
	kanatʼá	blueberry; blue huckleberry (Vaccinium ovalifolium)

xít'aa
broom
x̠út'aa
adze
sít'
glacier
dleey
meat; muscle

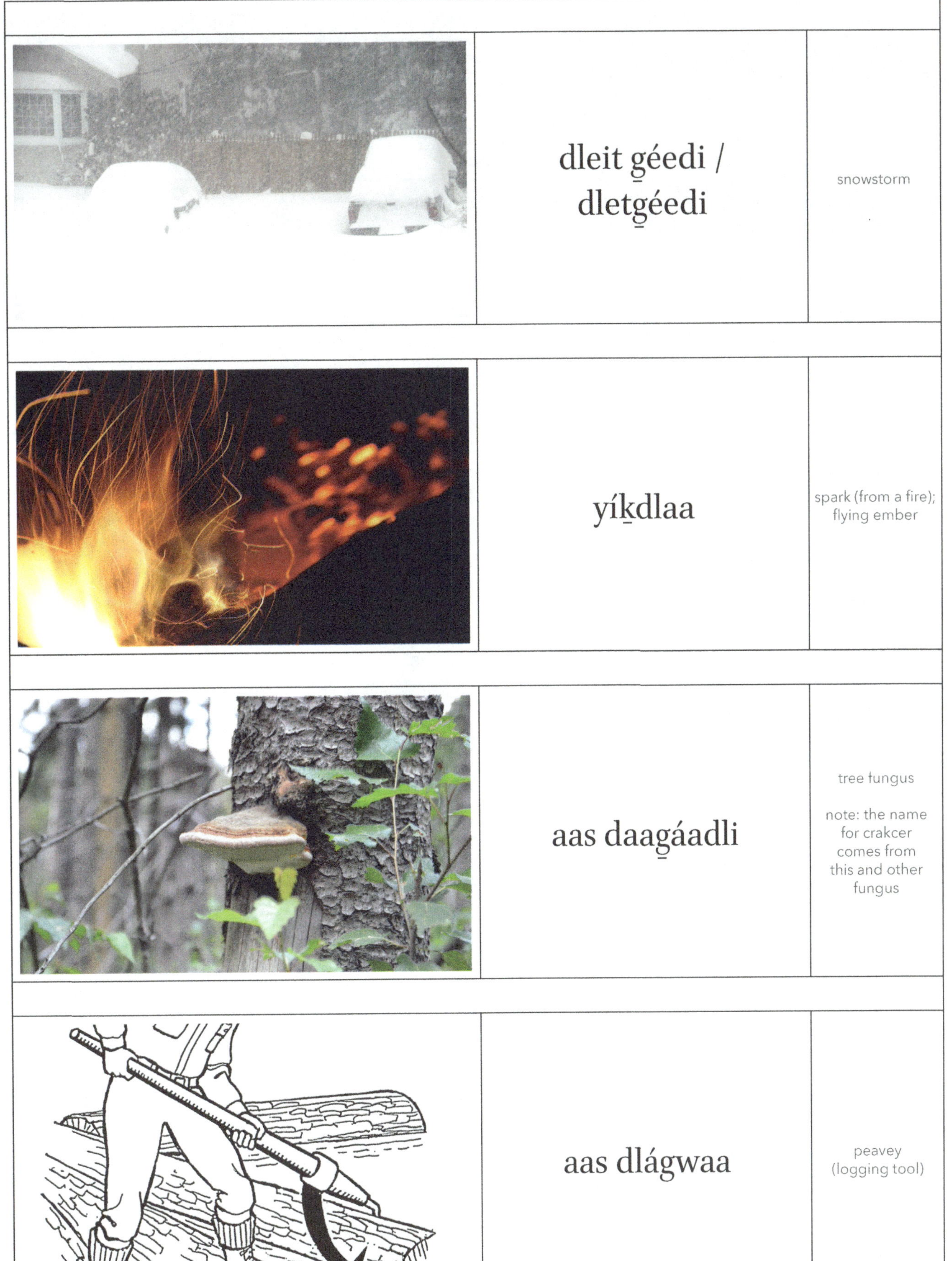

	dleit g̱éedi / dletg̱éedi	snowstorm
	yíḵdlaa	spark (from a fire); flying ember
	aas daag̱áadli	tree fungus note: the name for crakcer comes from this and other fungus
	aas dlágwaa	peavey (logging tool)

4B

K̲aa X̲'akaneek Kawdu.aag̲ú 4

Translation Exercises 4

Lingít → English

Wáa sá ḵuwatee?	
Ḵusi.áat' ágé?	
Ḵúnáx̱ ḵuwat'áa.	
Ḵuwdigwás'.	
Ayakaawadán.	
X̱at yaawasík.	
Ḵuwak'éi.	

English → Lingít

Is the weather warm?	
It is raining.	
Do you see a boat?	
It's cloudy.	
I'm wet.	
It's bad weather.	

5A

Wáa sá sh teedinook?

How do you feel?

Has du yeeg̲áa kanḵadlákwch.
Ch'a yeisú has du yeeg̲áa kax̲adlaakw
yáx̲ yatee
has du yoo x̲'atángi átx̲ x̲alayeix̲i.

— Keihéenák'w

I'm always reaching out to them.
I'm still in that mode, reaching out to them for help,
it's like that
when I use their language.

– John Martin, T'aḵdeintaan

has du=	yee-g̲áa	ka-<na-ÿu>-x̲a-∅-√dlákw-<ch>
all.them's.(3p.P)=	waiting.for-going.after	surface-<<perfective>-habitual>-i.(1s.S)-cl.(∅)-√scratch-<habitual>

ch'a	yeisú	has du=	yee-g̲áa	ka-x̲a-∅-√dlaakw	yáx̲	∅-ÿa-√tee
just	still	all.them's.(3p.P)=	waiting.for-going.after	surface-i.(1s.S)-cl.(∅)-√scratch	like	them/it.(3.O)-cl.(∅,i)√be

has du=	yoo=	x̲'atánk-i	át-x̲	∅-x̲a-la-√yeix̲-i
all.them's.(3p.P)=	to/fro=	language.relational	thing.(4n.i)-essive	it.(3.O)-i.(1s.S)-cl.(l)√make.subordinate

Wáa sá sh teedinook?

The following dialogue practice helps us begin thinking about communicating feelings and various states of being. When practicing this dialogue, start by saying each phrase and focusing on tone, vowel length, and sounding like the speakers you can listen to on the recordings from *Beginning Lingít*. After you have mastered these phrases individually, then shift your focus to the grammatical breakdown listed next to the phrases. The top line is a translation of the phrase, or what we might call the "English equivalent." Beneath that are two lines. The top one is segmenting the phrase to show all the components that are in there, including components that are not heard or seen when written, but reveal how the language is functioning. This section is best practiced with a partner. The most important things here are: 1) having a good flow to your words and honoring the vowel length tone, and 2) expressing emotion and trying to avoid sounding like a robot repeating sentences. Have fun!

Dialogue Practice			
A	1	Wáa sá sh teedinook?	How are you feeling? wáa =sá sh= tu-i-di-√nook how =name self.(rfx.O)= inside-you.(2s.S)-cl.(d,∅,i)-√feel
B	2	Tlél wáa sá sh toox̱danook.	I feel okay. tlél wáa =sá sh= tu-x̱a-di-√nook not how =name self.(rfx.O)= inside-i.(1s.S)-cl.(d,∅,i)-√feel
	3	Wáa sá iyatee?	How are you? wáa =sá i-ÿa-√tee? how =name you.(2s.O)-cl.(∅,i)-√be
A	4	Tlél tlax̱ x̱at tooshk'é.	I feel terrible. tlél tlax̱ x̱at= tu-u-sha-√k'é not very me.(1s.O) inside-irrealis-cl.(sh)-√good
	5	Kei x̱at nanéekw shákdéiiyá.	I think i'm getting sick. <kei= x̱at= na>-∅-√néekw shákdéii-yá <up.conj= me.(1s.O)= progressive>-cl.(∅)-√sick suppose-right.here
B	6	Iwdixwétl gwáawéigé?	Could it be that you're tired? i-<ÿu>-di-√xwétl gwáa-wé-gé you.(2s.O)-<perfective>-cl.(d,∅,i)-√tired maybe.there.y/n?

A 7	Tléik'. X̱at yanéekw	No. I'm sick tléik' · x̱at= · ÿa-√néekw no · me.(1s.O) · cl.(∅,i)-√sick
B 2	Aatlein át!	Oh dear! aatlein · át great.amount · thing.(4n.i)
3	Goo sáwé yanéekw?	Where does it hurt? goo · =sá-wé · ∅-ÿa-√néekw where · =name-there · it.(3.O)-cl.(∅,i)-√sick
A 4	Ax̱ leitóox̱ yanéekw.	My throat hurts / I have a sore throat ax̱ · lá-tú-x̱ · ∅-ÿa-√néekw my.(1s.P) · neck-inside-in.contact.with · it-(2s.O)-cl.(∅,i)-√sick
B 6	Át ax̱wdishée iwuneix̱í	I hope you get well á-t · a-<ÿu>-x̱a-di-√shée · i-<ÿu>-∅-√neix̱-i it.(3nh.PPO)-at.(arrived) · a.theme-<perfective>-i.(1s.S)-cl.(d,∅,i)-√hope · you.(2s.O)-<perfective>-cl.(∅)-√become.well-subordinate
7	Gunalchéesh	Thank you [tlél] · <ga-u-na>-l-√chéesh [not] · <?>-cl.(l)-√possible

The dialogue practice above is divided into two speakers (A and B) and there are seven total lines. Take a look at line A4, *ax̱ leitóox̱ yanéekw*. This is a phrase that we can learn and change the body part to talk about aches and pains that may exist throughout the body. This verb, *yanéekw*, can translate to 'illness' or 'pain' and is used in a variety of ways to talk about maladies. To begin using this phrase in more dynamic ways, we are going to take a look at some basic body parts. As we begin to explore body parts, let's first talk about an important language concept in Lingít: alienability.

Body parts

Body parts usually need to belong to something. When speaking English, it would sound strange to say "nose" or "knee" without it belonging to something, such as "your nose" or "bee's knee." This is the same in Lingít, only the rules are a bit more rigid. Body parts are in a category called "inalienable nouns" and are marked with an en dash (–) before the word to show that they must belong to something. This en dash can be replaced by nouns and possessive pronouns. For example, *–lú* can become *i lú* (your nose) or *yéil lú* (raven's beak) but does not usually appear without a possessing noun or possessive pronoun.

ax̲ shá
ax̲ x̲eek
ax̲ jín

ax tl'eik / ax tl'eek
ax wóow
ax x'óol'

ax̲ keey /
ax̲ kiyshá
ax̲ x̲'oos
ax̲ yá

ax̲ shax̲aawú
ax̲ gúk
ax̲ waak̲

ax̱ lú
ax̱ x̱'é
ax̱ oox̱

Now that we've learned some body parts, we will start using some familiar drills with them. Our goals are to locate our own body parts and then to locate the body parts using the images above. One interesting thing to note is that body parts do not usually pluralize. In English, we would say "my head, your head, our heads," whereas Lingít would be «ax̱ shá, i shá, haa shá.» In Intermediate Lingít you will learn about plural nouns, but for now we will learn some phrases to use for talking about body parts.

Question and Answer Drills

ax̱ ____ áyá	this is my ____
	ax̱ ____ á-yá my.(1s.P) {body part} focus-right.here
goosóo i ____?	where is your ____?
	goo-sá-ú i ____? where-name-is.at your.(2s.P) {body part}?

yáadu ax̱ ____	here is my ____
	yáat-u ax̱ ____ this.place-is.at my.(1s.P) {body part}
du ____ áyá	this is her/his ____
	du ____ á-yá their.(3.P) {body part} focus-right.here

imperfective (+)

Simon yéi x̱'ayaḵá ____	Simon says ____
	Simon yéi= x̱'a-ÿa-∅-∅-√ḵá ____ Simon thus= mouth-face-they.(3.S)-cl.(∅)-√say {phrase}

imperfective (-) - irrealis

tlél yéi x̱'awooḵá Simon	Simon isn't saying that
	tlél yéi x̱'a-ÿa-u-∅-∅-√ḵá Simon not thus= mouth-face-irrealis-they.(3.S)-cl.(∅)-√say Simon

Verbs: singular and plural

imperative

i sháat shí!

touch your head!

i	shá-t	<∅>-∅-√shí
your.(2s.P)	head-at.(arrive)	<command>-cl.(∅)-√touch

Notice the suffix (-t) attached to the body parts here. This is a direction suffix which means 'at' and often refers to arriving at a noun. Nouns ending in a short high vowel are regularly lengthened by a suffix.

imperative

i x̱eekt shí!

touch your upper arm!

i	x̱eek-t	<∅>-∅-√shí
your.(2s.P)	upper-arm-at.(arrive)	<command>-cl.(∅)-√touch

imperative

i jínt shí!

touch your hand! /
touch your lower arm!

i	jín-t	<∅>-∅-√shí
your.(2s.P)	hand-at.(arrive)	<command>-cl.(∅)-√touch

imperative

i tl'eiḵt shí! / i tl'eeḵt shí!

touch your finger!

i	tl'eiḵ-t	<∅>-∅-√shí
your.(2s.P)	finger-at.(arrive)	<command>-cl.(∅)-√touch

imperative

i wóowt shí!

touch your chest!

i	wóow-t	<∅>-∅-√shí
your.(2s.P)	chest-at.(arrive)	<command>-cl.(∅)-√touch

imperative

i x̱'óol't shí!

touch your belly!

i	x̱'óol'-t	<∅>-∅-√shí
your.(2s.P)	belly-at.(arrive)	<command>-cl.(∅)-√touch

imperative

i keeyt shí!

touch your knee!

i	keey-t	<∅>-∅-√shí
your.(2s.P)	knee-at.(arrive)	<command>-cl.(∅)-√touch

imperative

i x̱'oost shí!

touch your foot/feet! /
touch your lower leg!

i	x̱'oos-t	<∅>-∅-√shí
your.(2s.P)	foot-at.(arrive)	<command>-cl.(∅)-√touch

imperative

i yát shí!

touch your face!

i	yá-t	<∅>-∅-√shí
your.(2s.P)	face-at.(arrive)	<command>-cl.(∅)-√touch

The body part –yá (face) does not lenghten the vowel when adding a suffix.

imperative

i shaxaawóot shí!

touch your hair!

i	sha-x̱aaw-ú-t	<∅>-∅-√shí
your.(2s.P)	head-hair-relational-at.(arrive)	<command>-cl.(∅)-√touch

imperative

i gúkt shí!

touch your ear!

i	gúk-t	<∅>-∅-√shí
your.(2s.P)	ear-at.(arrive)	<command>-cl.(∅)-√touch

imperative

i waaḵt shí!

touch your eye!

i	waaḵ-t	<∅>-∅-√shí
your.(2s.P)	eye-at.(arrive)	<command>-cl.(∅)-√touch

imperative

i lóot shí!

touch your nose!

i	lú-t	<∅>-∅-√shí
your.(2s.P)	nose-at.(arrive)	<command>-cl.(∅)-√touch

imperative

i x̱'éit shí!

touch your mouth!

i	x̱'é-t	<∅>-∅-√shí
your.(2s.P)	mouth-at.(arrive)	<command>-cl.(∅)-√touch

imperative

i oox̱t shí!

touch your tooth/teeth!

i	oox̱-t	<∅>-∅-√shí
your.(2s.P)	tooth/teeth-at.(arrive)	<command>-cl.(∅)-√touch

imperative

i leitóox̱t shí!

touch your throat

i	lá-tú-x̱-t
your.(2s.P)	neck-inside-in.contact.with-at.(arrived)

<∅>-∅-√shí
<command>-cl.(∅)-√touch

Shaking

imperative

i ____ laxw̱ál!

shake your ____!

i	____	<∅>-la-√x̱wál
your.(2s.P)	{body part}	<command>-cl.(∅)-√tremble/rattle

Plural Form

yee sháat yishí!

you all touch your head!

yee	shá-t	<∅>-yi-∅-√shí
you.all's.(2p.P)	head-at.(arrive)	

<command>-you.all.(2p.S)-cl.(∅)-√touch

Notice the addition of the pronoun here (yi-), which is not needed in singular second person command form unless there is a +D classifier.

imperative

yee x̱eekt yishí!

you all touch your upper arm!

yee	x̱eek-t
you.all's.(2p.P)	upper-arm-at.(arrive)

<∅>-yi-∅-√shí
<command>-you.all.(2p.S)-cl.(∅)-√touch

imperative

yee jínt yishí!

you all touch your hand!

yee	jín-t
you.all's.(2p.P)	hand-at.(arrive)

<∅>-yi-∅-√shí
<command>-you.all.(2p.S)-cl.(∅)-√touch

imperative

yee tl’eik̲t yishí! / yee tl’eek̲t yishí!

you all touch your finger!

yee — you.all’s.(2p.P)
tl’eik̲-t — finger-at.(arrive)

<∅>-yi-∅-√shí
<command>-you.all.(2p.S)-cl.(∅)-√touch

imperative

yee wóowt yishí!

you all touch your chest!

yee — you.all’s.(2p.P)
wóow-t — chest-at.(arrive)

<∅>-yi-∅-√shí
<command>-you.all.(2p.S)-cl.(∅)-√touch

imperative

yee x̱’óol’t yishí!

you all touch your belly!

yee — you.all’s.(2p.P)
x̱’óol’-t — belly-at.(arrive)

<∅>-yi-∅-√shí
<command>-you.all.(2p.S)-cl.(∅)-√touch

imperative

yee keeyt yishí!

you all touch your knee!

yee — you.all’s.(2p.P)
keey-t — knee-at.(arrive)

<∅>-yi-∅-√shí
<command>-you.all.(2p.S)-cl.(∅)-√touch

imperative

yee x̱'oost yishí!

you all touch your foot/feet!

yee — you.all's.(2p.P)
x̱'oos-t — foot/feet-at.(arrive)

<∅>-yi-∅-√shí
<command>-you.all.(2p.S)-cl.(∅)-√touch

yee yát yishí!

you all touch your face!

yee — you.all's.(2p.P)
yá-t — face-at.(arrive)

<∅>-yi-∅-√shí
<command>-you.all.(2p.S)-cl.(∅)-√touch

imperative

yee shax̱aawóot yishí!

you all touch your hair!

yee — you.all's.(2p.P)
sha-x̱aawú-t — head-hair-at.(arrive)

<∅>-yi-∅-√shí
<command>-you.all.(2p.S)-cl.(∅)-√touch

imperative

yee gúkt yishí!

you all touch your ear!

yee — you.all's.(2p.P)
gúk-t — ear-at.(arrive)

<∅>-yi-∅-√shí
<command>-you.all.(2p.S)-cl.(∅)-√touch

imperative

yee waak̲t yishí!

you all touch your eye!

yee — you.all's.(2p.P)
waak̲-tí — eye-at.(arrive)

<Ø>-yi-Ø-√shí
<command>-you.all.(2p.S)-cl.(Ø)-√touch

---

yee lóot yishí!

you all touch your nose!

yee — you.all's.(2p.P)
lú-t — nose-at.(arrive)

<Ø>-yi-Ø-√shí
<command>-you.all.(2p.S)-cl.(Ø)-√touch

---

imperative

yee x̲'éit yishí!

you all touch your mouth!

yee — you.all's.(2p.P)
x̲'é-t — mouth-at.(arrive)

<Ø>-yi-Ø-√shí
<command>-you.all.(2p.S)-cl.(Ø)-√touch

---

imperative

yee oox̲t yishí!

you all touch your tooth/teeth!

yee — you.all's.(2p.P)
oox̲-t — tooth/teeth-at.(arrive)

<Ø>-yi-Ø-√shí
<command>-you.all.(2p.S)-cl.(Ø)-√touch

imperative

yee leitóox̱t yishí!

you all touch your throat

yee — you.all's.(2p.P)
lá-tú-x̱-t — neck-inside-in.contact.with-at.(arrived)
<∅>-yi-∅-√shí — <command>-you.all.(2p.S)-cl.(∅)-√touch

Shaking

imperative

yee ____ yilax̱wál!

you all shake your ____!

yee — you.all's.(2p.P)
___ — {body part}
<∅>-yi-la-√x̱wál — <command>-cl.(∅)-√tremble/rattle

Pointing

imperative

i sháat ch'éx̱' / ch'íx̱'!

point at your head!

i — your.(2s.P)
shá-t — head-at.(arrive)
<∅>-∅-√ch'éx̱' — <command>-cl.(∅)-√poke/point

It is common to hear this with the suffx -de instead of -t (i sháade) and also sometimes with a different conjugation prefix (i sháade nach'éix̱').

imperative

i x̱eekt ch'éx̱' / ch'íx̱'!

point at your upper arm!

i — your.(2s.P)
x̱eek-t — upper.arm-at.(arrive)
<∅>-∅-√ch'éx̱' — <command>-cl.(∅)-√poke/point

imperative

i jínt ch’éx̱’ / ch’íx̱’!

point at your hand!

i	jín-t	<∅>-∅-√ch’éx̱’
your.(2s.P)	hand-at.(arrive)	<command>-cl.(∅)-√poke/point

imperative

**i tl’eiḵt ch’éx̱’ /
i tl’eeḵt ch’íx̱’!**

point at your finger!

i	tl’eiḵ-t	<∅>-∅-√ch’éx̱’
your.(2s.P)	finger-at.(arrive)	<command>-cl.(∅)-√poke/point

imperative

i wóowt ch’éx̱’ / ch’íx̱’!

point at your chest!

i	wóow-t	<∅>-∅-√ch’éx̱’
your.(2s.P)	chest-at.(arrive)	<command>-cl.(∅)-√poke/point

imperative

i x̱’óol’t ch’éx̱’ / ch’íx̱’!

point at your belly!

i	x̱’óol’-t	<∅>-∅-√ch’éx̱’
your.(2s.P)	belly-at.(arrive)	<command>-cl.(∅)-√poke/point

imperative

i keeyt ch’éx̲’ / ch’íx̲’!

point at your knee!

i	keey-t	<∅>-∅-√ch’éx̲’
your.(2s.P)	knee-at.(arrive)	<command>-cl.(∅)-√poke/point

imperative

i x̲’oost ch’éx̲’ / ch’íx̲’!

point at your foot/feet!

i	x̲’oos-t	<∅>-∅-√ch’éx̲’
your.(2s.P)	foot/feet-at.(arrive)	<command>-cl.(∅)-√poke/point

imperative

i yát ch’éx̲’ / ch’íx̲’!

point at your face!

i	yá-t	<∅>-∅-√ch’éx̲’
your.(2s.P)	face-at.(arrive)	<command>-cl.(∅)-√poke/point

imperative

i shax̲aawóot ch’éx̲’ / ch’íx̲’!

point at your hair!

i	sha-x̲aawú-t	<∅>-∅-√ch’éx̲’
your.(2s.P)	hair-at.(arrive)	<command>-cl.(∅)-√poke/point

imperative

i gúkt ch’éx̱’ / ch’íx̱’!

point at your ear!

i	gúk-t	<Ø>-Ø-√ch’éx̱’
your.(2s.P)	ear-at.(arrive)	<command>-cl.(Ø)-√poke/point

imperative

i waaḵt ch’éx̱’ / ch’íx̱’!

point at your eye!

i	waaḵ-t	<Ø>-Ø-√ch’éx̱’
your.(2s.P)	eye-at.(arrive)	<command>-cl.(Ø)-√poke/point

imperative

i lóot ch’éx̱’ / ch’íx̱’!

point at your nose!

i	lú-t	<Ø>-Ø-√ch’éx̱’
your.(2s.P)	nose-at.(arrive)	<command>-cl.(Ø)-√poke/point

imperative

i x̱’éit ch’éx̱’ / ch’íx̱’!

point at your mouth!

i	x̱’é-t	<Ø>-Ø-√ch’éx̱’
your.(2s.P)	mouth-at.(arrive)	<command>-cl.(Ø)-√poke/point

imperative

i ooxt ch'éx̱' / ch'íx̱'!

point at your tooth/teeth!

i	oox̱-t	<∅>-∅-√ch'éx̱'
your.(2s.P)	tooth/teeth-at.(arrive)	<command>-cl.(∅)-√poke/point

imperative

i leitóox̱t ch'éx̱' / ch'íx̱'!

point at your throat

i	lá-tú-x̱-t	<∅>-∅-√ch'éx̱'
your.(2s.P)	neck-inside-in.contact.with-at.(arrived)	<command>-cl.(∅)-√poke/point

Plural Form

imperative

yee sháat yeech'éx̱' / yeech'íx̱'!

you all point at your head!

yee	shá-t	<∅>-yi-∅-√ch'éx̱'
you.all's.(2p.P)	head-at.(arrive)	<command>-cl.(∅)-√poke/point

imperative

yee x̱eekt yeech'éx̱' / yeech'íx̱'!

you all point at your upper arm!

yee	x̱eek-t	<∅>-yi-∅-√ch'éx̱'
you.all's.(2p.P)	upper-arm-at.(arrive)	<command>-cl.(∅)-√poke/point

imperative

yee jínt yeech'éx̱' / yeech'íx̱'!

you all point at your hand!

yee	jín-t	<∅>-yi-∅-√ch'éx̱'
you.all's.(2p.P)	hand-at.(arrive)	<command>-cl.(∅)-√poke/point

imperative

yee tl'eiḵt yeech'éx̱' / yee tl'eeḵt yeech'íx̱'!

you all point at your finger!

yee	tl'eiḵ-t	<∅>-yi-∅-√ch'éx̱'
you.all's.(2p.P)	finger-at.(arrive)	<command>-cl.(∅)-√poke/point

imperative

yee wóowt yeech'éx̱' / yeech'íx̱'!

you all point at your chest!

yee	wóow-t	<∅>-yi-∅-√ch'éx̱'
you.all's.(2p.P)	chest-at.(arrive)	<command>-cl.(∅)-√poke/point

imperative

yee x̱'óol't yeech'éx̱' / yeech'íx̱'!

you all point at your belly!

yee	x̱'óol'-t	<∅>-yi-∅-√ch'éx̱'
you.all's.(2p.P)	belly-at.(arrive)	<command>-cl.(∅)-√poke/point

imperative

yee keeyt yeech’éx̱’ / yeech’íx̱’!

you all point at your knee!

yee	keey-t	<∅>-yi-∅-√ch’éx̱’
your.(2s.P)	knee-at.(arrive)	<command>-cl.(∅)-√poke/point

imperative

yee x̱’oost yeech’éx̱’ / yeech’íx̱’!

you all point at your foot/feet!

yee	x̱’oos-t	<∅>-yi-∅-√ch’éx̱’
your.(2s.P)	foot/feet-at.(arrive)	<command>-cl.(∅)-√poke/point

imperative

yee yát yeech’éx̱’ / yeech’íx̱’!

you all point at your face!

yee	yá-t	<∅>-yi-∅-√ch’éx̱’
your.(2s.P)	face-at.(arrive)	<command>-cl.(∅)-√poke/point

imperative

yee shax̱aawóot yeech’éx̱’ / yeech’íx̱’!

you all point at your hair!

yee	sha-x̱aaw-ú-t
your.(2s.P)	head-hair-relational-at.(arrive)

<∅>-yi-∅-√ch’éx̱’
<command>-cl.(∅)-√poke/point

imperative

yee gúkt yeech’éx̱’ / yeech’íx̱’!

you all point at your ear!

yee	gúk-t	<∅>-yi-∅-√ch’éx̱’
you.all’s.(2p.P)	ear-at.(arrive)	<command>-cl.(∅)-√poke/point

imperative

yee waaḵt yeech’éx̱’ / yeech’íx̱’!

you all point at your eye!

yee	waaḵ-t	<∅>-yi-∅-√ch’éx̱’
you.all’s.(2p.P)	eye-at.(arrive)	<command>-cl.(∅)-√poke/point

imperative

yee lóot yeech’éx̱’ / yeech’íx̱’!

you all point at your nose!

yee	lú-t	<∅>-yi-∅-√ch’éx̱’
you.all’s.(2p.P)	nose-at.(arrive)	<command>-cl.(∅)-√poke/point

imperative

yee x̱’éit yeech’éx̱’ / yeech’íx̱’!

you all point at your mouth!

yee	x̱’é-t	<∅>-yi-∅-√ch’éx̱’
you.all’s.(2p.P)	mouth-at.(arrive)	<command>-cl.(∅)-√poke/point

yee oox̱t yeech’éx̱’ / yeech’íx̱’!	imperative you all point at your tooth/teeth! yee — you.all’s.(2p.P) oox̱-t — tooth/teeth-at.(arrive) <∅>-yi-∅-√ch’éx̱’ — <command>-cl.(∅)-√poke/point
yee leitóox̱t yeech’éx̱’ / yeech’íx̱’!	imperative you all point at your throat yee — you.all’s.(2p.P) lá-tú-x̱-t — neck-inside-in.contact.with-at.(arrived) <∅>-yi-∅-√ch’éx̱’ — <command>-cl.(∅)-√poke/point

Verbs: states of being

goosóo wé yanéekw? / goosóo wé néekw? / goo sáwé yanéekw	question where is the hurt/sick? goo-sá-ú — where-say-is.at wé — there ÿa-√néekw — cl.(∅,i)-√sick/hurt
ax̱ ____ yanéekw	imperfective my ____ hurts / my ____ is sick ax̱ — my.(1s.P) ____ — {body part} ÿa-√néekw — cl.(∅,i)-√sick/hurt

du ____ yanéekw	her/his ____ hurts; her/his ____ is sick
	du ___ ÿa-√néekw their.(3.P) ___ cl.(∅,i)-√sick/hurt

question

i ____ gé yanéekw?	does your ___ hurt / is your ___ sick?
	i ___ gé ÿa-√néekw your.(2s.P) ___ yes/no? cl.(∅,i)-√sick/hurt

perfective

ax̱ éet yaan.uwaháa	i'm hungry
	ax̱ ée-t my.(1s.P) empty.base-at.(arrived) yaan-<ÿu>-ÿa-√háa hunger-<perfective>-cl.(∅,i)-√move.imperceptibly

perfective

ax̱ éet yataawaháa	i'm sleepy
	ax̱ ée-t my.(1s.P) empty.base-at.(arrived) ÿa-tá-<ÿu>-ÿa-√háa face-cl.(∅,i)-sleep-<perfective>-cl.(∅,i)-√move.imperceptibly

perfective

x̱at wudixwétl

i'm tired

x̱at=	<ÿu>-di-√xwétl
me.(1s.O)=	<perfective>-cl.(d,∅,i)-√become.tired

perfective

x̱at shaawakúx

i'm thirsty

x̱at	sha-<ÿu>-ÿa-√kúx
me.(1s.O)	head-<perfective>-cl.(d,∅,i)-√dry.out

perfective

i éet gé yaan.uwaháa?

are you hungry?

i	ée-t	gé
your.(2s.P)	empty.base-at.(arrived)	yes/no?

yaan-<ÿu>-ÿa-√háa
hunger-<perfective>-cl.(∅,i)-√move.imperceptibly

question

i éet gé yataawaháa?

are you sleepy?

i	ée-t	gé
your.(2s.P)	empty.base-at.(arrived)	yes/no?

ÿa-tá-<ÿu>-ÿa-√háa
face-cl.(∅,i)-sleep-<perfective>-cl.(∅,i)-√move.imperceptibly

question

iwdixwétl gé?

are you tired

i-<ÿu>-di-√xwétl	gé
you.(2s.O)-<perfective>-cl.(d,∅,i)-√tired	yes/no?

question

ishaawakúx gé?

are you thirsty?

i-sha-<ÿu>-ÿa-√kúx	gé
you.(2s.O)-head-<perfective>-cl.(d,∅,i)-√dry.out	yes/no?

question

daa sá i éet uwaháa?

what are you hungry for?
/ what are you wanting?

daa	sá	i	ée-t
what	name	your.(2s.P)	empty.base-at.(arrived)

<ÿu>-ÿa-√háa
<perfective>-cl.(∅,i)-√move.imperceptibly

perfective

____ ax̱ éet uwaháa

i'm hungry for ____; i want ____

____	ax̱	ée-t
	my.(1s.P)	empty.base-at.(arrived)

<ÿu>-ÿa-√háa
<perfective>-cl.(∅,i)-√move.imperceptibly

Vocabulary

	útlx̱i	boiled fish
	at x̱'éeshi	dry fish
	náayadi	half-dry fish
	x̱áat x̱'úx̱u	fish flesh

	tax̱héeni	soup; broth
	at kahéeni	juice
	tléiḵw	berries
	tsaa eix̱í / tsaa eex̱í	seal oil

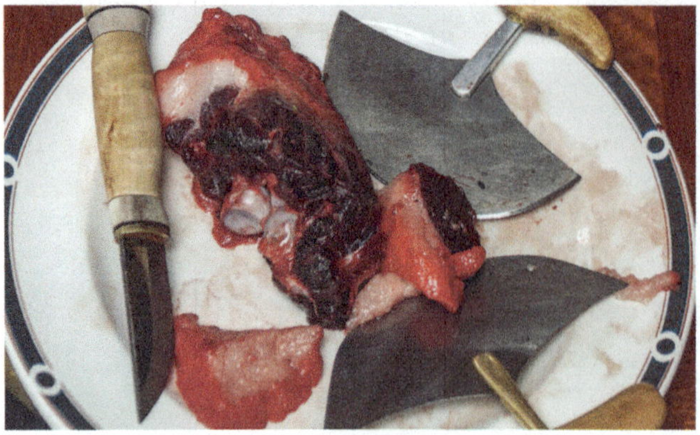	tsaa dleeyí	seal meat
	g̱uwakaan dleeyí / ḵuwakaan dleeyí	deer meat
	g̱áatl	pilot bread
	k'únts' / k'wúnts'	potatoes

	shaaw	gumboots, chiton
	s'áaw	Dungeness crab
	gáal'	clams
	kaháakw	salmon eggs

	s'ikshaldéen	Hudson Bay tea, Labrador tea
	laak̲'ásk	black seaweed (common)
	k̲'áach'	red seaweed (ribbon)

Pronouns in verbs

Now that we have learned some phrases about states of being, we can start examining how pronouns are working in these phrases. When using verbs in Lingít, you will be using three sets of pronouns. Thinking back on our pronoun triangles, we can learn to spot which type of pronoun is being used and then switch it to change the person between 1st (me), 2nd (you), and 3rd (they). Notice how they change in the following verbs.

	Object	Subject	Relational
1st	x̲at	x̲a-	ax̲
2nd	i- ~ ee-	i-	i ~ ee
3rd	∅- ~ a-	∅-	du

N + tuwáa(-x') + S-s-√góo[×] (*ga state verb – subject intransitive*)

for N to want, like, desire S; for S to be pleasing to N	N {noun} · tú-ÿá(-x') inside-face-at.(residing) · S-s-√góo subject-cl.(s)-√enjoy/happy
	question
daa sá i tuwáa sigóo?	what do you want? / what do you like?
	daa =sá i= tú-ÿá si-√góo what =name your.(2s.P)= inside-face cl.(s,i)-√enjoy/happy Note the pronoun use in this verb, which will change the possessive pronoun before –tuwáa to show who is wanting or liking. The use of the subject pronoun here is rare, and may seem like it would be an object pronoun. For example: ax̱ tuwáax' isigóo (i want you) and i tuwáa x̱asigóo (you want me). The -x' suffix will appear when the next word starts with a vowel. Many speakers will have the suffix almost every time, but it may
	imperfective (+)
____ ax̱ tuwáa sigóo	i want ____ / i like ___
	___ ax̱= tú-ÿá si-√góo ___ my.(1s.P)= inside-face cl.(s,i)-√enjoy/happy
	question
daa sá du tuwáa sigóo?	what do they want?
	daa =sá du= tú-ÿá si-√góo what =name their.(3.P)= inside-face cl.(s,i)-√enjoy/happy

	imperfective (+)
____ du tuwáa sigóo	they want ____
	____ du= tú-ÿá si-√góo ____ their.(3.P)= inside-face cl.(s,i)-√enjoy/happy
	question
____ gé i tuwáa sigóo?	do you want ____?
	____ gé i= tú-ÿá si-√góo ____ yes/no? your.(2s.P)= inside-face cl.(s,i)-√enjoy/happy
	imperfective (+)
aaa. ____ ax̱ tuwáa sigóo	yes. i want ____
	aaa ____ ax̱= tú-ÿá si-√góo yes ____ my.(1s.P)= inside-face cl.(s,i)-√enjoy/happy

The phrases we learned so far have verbs in simple modes, and we are going to learn some more complicated ways to use Lingít. We can learn how verbs work by using a theme that shows the skeleton of the verb, revealing the parts within a verb that we can change to communicate. This verb theme was developed by Jeff Leer and Keri Eggleston. A capital letter 'N' is a noun, 'O' is an object pronoun, and 'S' is a subject pronoun.

When a Lingít verb is negative, there are predictable changes that happen. The word *tléil* (not) will appear before the verb. This word can also appear as *tlél*, *hél*, *tíl*, and sometimes fully contracted to *l*. A verb in Lingít has several things in the prefix, which is the part that appears before the stem. The stem contains the root of the verb, which has meaning, and the prefix tells us information about the verb.

The Verb Theme

wanting / liking

tlél + N + tuwáa(-x') + u-S-sh-√gú ˣ (*ga state verb – subject intransitive*)

preverb — prefix — stem

This marker notes that the vowel in the stem will not change. Vowel change in the root is called stem variation, which notes the vowel length and tone.

for N to not want, not like, not desire S; for S to be unpleasant to N	tlél N tú-ÿa(-x') not {noun} inside-face-at.(residing) u-S-sh-√gú irrealis.subject-cl.(sh)-√enjoy/happy

Some of the terms that are used for the parts of the verb are 'preverb', which are words that are separate from the verb but are necessary parts of the verb phrase. These affect the meaning, and include words like *tlél* (not), *ḵúnáx̱* (really), and sets of words like *sh tóot* (inside the self) and *i een* (with you). The verb itself is made up of a 'prefix' and a 'stem', and learning to use verbs in ways beyond memorization involves making prefixes and stems through sound combinations.

The prefix may contain information about who might be doing the verb, to whom it is happening, whether or not it has happened, and some other information. You will notice that verbs make most of the changes in the prefix and that parts will combine with each other in complicated yet predictable ways. There are important differences between 'I want' (*ax̱ tuwáa sigóo*) and 'I don't want' (*tlél ax̱ tuwáa ushgú*) and you need to learn these differences and use them to speak accurately.

progressive imperfective

tlél ax̱ tuwáa ushgú ____ / tlél ax̱ tóo ushgú ____	i don't want ____ / i don't like tléik' tlél ax̱ tú-ÿá(-x') no not my.(1s.P) inside-face-at.(residing) u-S-sh-√gú irrealis.subject-cl.(sh)-√enjoy/happy

needing

N + eetí-náx̱ + O-∅-√tee ʰ ¹ (*na state verb – object intransitive*)

preverb — prefix — stem

The ʰ is also marking stem variation, and this is called a 'fading stem.' The ¹ is marking that there are other √tee verb roots that are homonyms, but have different meaning.

for O to need N; for O to lack N; for O to require N	N eetí-náx̱ O-∅-√tee ʰ ¹ {noun} stead-through/via object-cl.(∅)-√be

question

daat eetéenáx̱ sá iyatee?	what do you need?
	daat / what · eetí-náx̱ / stead-through · =sá / =name · i-ÿa-√tee / you.(2s.O)-cl.(∅,i)-√be

imperfective (+)

____ eetéenáx̱ x̱at yatee	i need ____
	____ / ____ · eetí-náx̱ / stead-through · x̱at= / me.(1s.O)= · ÿa-√tee / cl.(∅,i)-√be

imperfective (-)

tlél + N + eetí-náx̱ + O-u-∅-√tí (*na state verb – object intransitive*)

preverb · prefix · stem

for O to not need N; for O to not lack N; for O to not require N	tlél / not √be · N / {noun} · eetí-náx̱ / stead-through/via · O-u-∅-√tí / object.irrealis-cl.(∅)-

imperfective (-)

tlél ____ eetéenáx̱ x̱at utí	i don't need ____
	tlél / not · ____ / ____ · eetí-náx̱ / stead-through · x̱at= / me.(1s.O)= · u-∅-√tí / irrealis-cl.(∅,i)-√be

	x̱'aan	fire; red (color)
	x̱'oon	fur seal
	x̱'éen	wall crest; wall screen
	x̱'uskeit	leggings (lit. thing over the legs)

	shadakóox̱’	woven hat with rings
	s’áax̱’	gray cod
	keitl	dog
	cháatl	halibut

	xeitl	thunderbird; thunder
	tláak̲	sharp arrow (for killing)
	tleikatánk	red huckleberries
	tlóox̲ / lóox̲ (C)	bullhead

5B

Ḵaa X̱'akaneek Kawdu.aaguú 5

Translation Exercises 5

Lingít → English

Wáa sá sh teedinook?	
X̲at yanéekw.	
Ax̲ éet yaan.uwaháa.	
I x̲eekt shí!	
I éet gé yataawaháa?	
Daa sá i tuwáa sigóo?	
Náayadi ax̲ tuwáa sigóo.	
Daat eetéenáx̲ sá iyatee?	
Daa sá du tuwáa sigóo?	

English → Lingít

How are you?	
My throat hurts.	
I'm tired.	
I'm thirsty.	
I want salmon eggs.	
I don't want pilot bread. / I don't like pilot bread.	
I need dry fish.	
I don't need potatoes.	

6A

Aadóo sáwé?

Who is that?

Shóogonáx̱,
aadéi yáat kawdiyayi yé,
yá Lingít,
shayadiheni aa yéi sh kalneek
yá ixkéenáx̱ áyá,
haat haa wsidáḵ,
Yáa ixkée.

— Shaadaax'

For the things that happened
to the Lingíts,
in the beginning,
many say we migrated here
through the south,
the south.

– Robert Zuboff, Ḵak'weidí

(*Haa Shuká*, Dauenhauer and Dauenhauer)

shóogu-náx̱	aa-dé	yá-t	∅-ka-<ÿu>-di-√ya-yi	yé
first-through/via	that-way	here-at.(arrived)	it.(3.O)-surface-<perfective>-cl.(d,∅,i)-√occur.relational	way

yá	Lingít	sha-ya-di-√háa-<n>-i	aa
right.here	human/Lingít	head-face-cl.(d,∅,i)√become.many.<imperfective>.relational	one(s).(part.i)

yéi=	sh=	ka-∅-l-√neek	yá	ixkée-náx̱	á-yá
thus=	self.(rfx.O)=	surface-they.(3.S)-cl.(d,l)-√tell	right-here	downstream/south-through/via	focus-right.here

haa-t	haa	<ÿu>-si-√dáḵ
here-at.(arrived)	us.(1p.O)	<perfective>-cl.(s,i)-√move.permanently

yá	ixkée
right.here	downstream/south

Aadóo sáwé?

Start this lesson off with the following dialogue exercise. Take turns being A and B, paying close attention to the relationship between an elder and her/his grandchild.

Try to use emotion when speaking, and also focus on having a flow to your language that makes it sound like a native speaker.

Dialogue Practice			
A	1	[kawdigwál: k'úx, k'úx, k'úx]	[knocks: knock, knock, knock] ka-<ÿu>-Ø-di-√gwál surface-<perfective>-they.(3.S)-cl.(d,Ø,i)-√beat/hit/knock/stab
B	2	Neil gú!	Come in! neil <Ø>-Ø-√gú into.building <command>-cl.(Ø)-√walk/go.(singular)
	3	Aadóo sáwé? / Áa sáwé?	who's that? aadóo =sá-wé? who =name-there
A	4	X̱át áyá.	It's me. x̱át á-yá me.(1s.i) focus-right.here
B	5	Aaa. Ax̱ dachx̱ánk'.	Yes. My grandchild. aaa ax̱ dachx̱án-k' yes my.(1s.P) grandchild.little
B	6	Tlél iyax̱wateen.	I didn't recognize you. tlél i-ya-<u-ÿu>-x̱a-Ø-√teen not you.(2s.O)-face-<negative perfective>-i.(1s.S)-cl.(Ø)-√see
	7	Yak'éi haat yigoodí.	It's good that you've come. Ø-ya-k'éi haa-t they/it.(3.O)-cl.(Ø,i)-√good hither-at.(arriving) <ÿu>-i-Ø-√gút-i <perfective>-you.(2s.S)-cl.(Ø)-√walk/go.(singular)-subordinate

B	8	Wáa sáwé?	What's up? wáa =sá how =name
A	9	Ax̲ tláa jeetx̲ utlx̲í áyá haat x̲wasi.ín.	I've brought some boiled fish from my mother ax̲= tláa jee-dáx̲ my.(1s.P)= mother possession.-rom utlx̲í á-yá haa-t boiled.fish focus-right.here hither-at.(arrived) Ø-<ÿu>-x̲a-si-√ín them/it.(3.O)-<perfective>-i.(1s.S)-cl.(Ø,i)-√carry.in.container
B	10	Ax̲ adée!	Oh, my precious! ax̲= adée my.(1s.P)= dear.thing
	11	Goodáx̲ át sáwé?	Where is it from? goo-dáx̲ át sá-wé where.from thing.(4n.i) name-that
A	12	Ast'eix̲ wook̲oox̲ ax̲ éesh dziyaak ts'ootaat.	my father went fishing just this morning. ast'eix̲ <ÿu>-Ø-ÿa-√k̲oox̲ fishing <perfective>-they.(3.S)-cl.(Ø,i)-√go.by.boat/car ax̲= éesh dziyaak ts'ootaat my.(1s.P)= father little.while.ago morning
B	13	Gunalchéesh, hó hó.	Thank you very much. gunalchéesh ho-ho thank.you emphasis
A	14	I jiyís yéi at nak̲asaneiyí.	Let me do something for you. i jee-yís your.(2s.P)= possession-for.benefit yéi= at= <na-g̲a>-x̲a-sa-√nei-<yí> thus= thing.(4n.O)= <hortative>-i.(1s.S)-cl.(s)-√do-<hortative>
B	15	Héen eetéenáx̲ x̲at yatee.	I need water. héen eetí-náx̲ x̲at= ÿa-√tee water stead-through/via me.(1s.O)= cl.(Ø,i)-√be

A	16	Héix' haat x̲wasi.ín.	I've brought it here.	hé-x' / here-at.(residing) · haa-t / hither-at.(arriving) <ÿu>-x̲a-si√.ín / <perfective>-i.(1s.S)-cl.(s,i)-√carry.in.container
B	17	Gunalchéeshík' / Gunalchéeshk'.	Thanks, dear	gunalchéesh-i-k' / thank.you-peg.vowel-little
	18	Goosóo i tláa?	Where is your mother?	goo-sá-ú / where-name-is.at · i= / your.(2s.P)= · tláa / mother
A	19	Neilú hú.	She's home	neil-ú / home-is.at · hú / them.(3.i)
B	20	Goosóo i kéek'?	Where's your little sister/brother?	goo-sá-ú / where-name-is.at · i / your.(2s.P) · kéek' / younger.sibling.(same gender)
A	21	Sgóonu hú.	They are at school	sgóon-ú / school-is.at · hú / them.(3.i)
	22	Kk̲wagóot de.	I'm going to go now	<ga-u-ga>-x̲a-∅-√góot / <future>-i.(1s.S)-cl.(∅)-√walk/go.(singular) · de / now
	23	Tsu i x̲ándei kk̲wagóot seig̲ánin.	I'll come see you again tomorrow.	tsu / again · i / your.(2s.P) · x̲án-de / beside-towards <ga-u-ga>-x̲a-∅-√góot / <future>-i.(1s.S)-cl.(∅)-√walk/go-(sg) · seigánin / tomorrow

B	24	Yak'éi ix̱wsateení.	It's good to see you. ∅-ÿa-√k'éi them/it.(3.O)-cl.(∅,i)-√good i-<ÿu>-x̱a-sa-√teen-í you.(2s.O)-<perfective>-i.(1s.S)-cl.(s)-√see-subordinate
	25	Aaa, tsu haagú x'wán / Aaa, tsu haakw x'wán. [1]	Yes, come back again aaa tsu haa-∅-√gú x'wán yes again hither-cl.(∅)-√walk/go.(singular) be-sure-to/may-you
A	26	Gunalchéesh.	Thank you. gunalchéesh thank.you

1. It is common for verb modes ending in -√gú to contract to -√kw when followed by an enclitic, such as: haakw dé (come here now), haakw s'é (come here for a moment), naakw dé (go now), etc.

Kinship terms

Lingít kinship terms are rooted in matrilineal clan law, so it is important to understand the Lingít way of looking at family, friends, and in-laws. Often we see the word 'friends' translated in Lingít as *ax̱ x̱oonx'i yán* (my clan relatives, friends). This term would not necessarily include those from the opposite clan, who generally are *ax̱ kaani yán* (my in-laws) and can also have specific relationships which are dictated by clan genealogy.

These terms are fluid and are not determined by lineage alone. If two people grow closer to one another through friendship or marriage, they may choose to use a kinship term for one another instead of calling each other by name. A kinship term is a form of greeting and is often used in public and in ceremony to show a closeness to a clan or individual. In Lingít culture, the clan is the primary form of identity, and an individual should always be conscious of the clans of others, especially clan opposites. When speaking in public at a Lingít event the speaker should always address clan opposites, and should be careful not to boast about the self or one's own clan. An insult to the opposite clan in public could result in a debt that the clan of the speaker is responsible for paying.

The terms for siblings are not limited to biological siblings, as in English, but instead they refer to all members of the same clan who are of the same gender and generation. Because of this, there is no equivalent for English kinship terms such as "cousin." In addition, close clan ties can determine the appropriate kinship term regardless of age or biological relationship.

The father's clan is shown the most respect and love in public. Paternal refers to *ḵaa éesh yinaanáx̱* (a person's father's lineage) and maternal is *ḵaa tláa yinaanáx̱* (a person's mother's lineage). A Lingít person is the same clan as their mother, and one must always protect the relationships between clans by putting clan law before the individual. Speak carefully, and try not to insult a clan by using their at.óow without permission (including their histories, songs, names, and crests).

Lingít kinship terms are listed in the same manner as body parts: with the en dash placeholder – as in – *tláa* (–'s mother). This placeholder must be replaced by another pronoun or noun. For example: *ax̱ tláa* (my mother), *i tláa* (your mother), *G̱ooch Tláa* (wolf mother), and *naa tláa* (clan mother).

du ___ áwé.	that is her/his ___/ du= ___ á-wé their.(3.P)= {kinship term} focus-there
–tláa	mother
–éesh	father
–káak	maternal uncle
–tláak'w	maternal aunt
–sáni	paternal uncle
–aat	paternal aunt
–léelk'w	grandparent

i ___ ák.wé?	is that your ___?
	i / ___ / á-gé-wé your.(2s.P) / {kinship term} / focus-yes/no?-there
♀	female specific kinship terms
–shátx̱	(female's) older sister
–kéek'	(female's) younger sister
–éek'	(female's) brother
♂	male specific kinship terms
–húnx̱w	(male's) older brother
–kéek'	(male's) younger brother
–dlaak'	(male's) sister

–yádi	child
–yátx'i	children
–sée / –séek'	daughter
–yéet	son
–dachx̲án	grandchild
–kéilk'	maternal niece/nephew
–káalk'w	paternal niece/nephew
–x̲úx̲	husband
–shát	wife
–x̲án.aa	spouse; partner
–chaan	mother-in-law
–wóo	father-in-law

x̱át áyá	this is me
	x̱át á-yá me.(1s.i) focus-right.here
ax̱ léelk'w áyá yáadu	this is my grandparent right here
	ax̱= léelk'w á-yá yáat-u my.(1s.P)= grandparent focus-right.here this.place-is.at
du dachx̱án áyá x̱át	i am her/his grandchild
	du= dachx̱án á-yá x̱át their.(3.P)= grandchild focus-right.here me.(1s.i)
ax̱ léelk'w dachx̱án áyá x̱át	i am my grandparent's grandchild
	ax̱ léelk'w dachx̱án á-yá x̱át my.(1s.P) grandparent grandchild focus-right.here me.(1s.i)

ax̱ éesh áyá	this is my father
	ax̱= éesh á-yá my.(1s.P)= father focus-right.here
ax̱ léelk'w yéet áwé, ax̱ éesh	my father is my grandparents' son
	ax̱= léelk'w yéet á-wé ax̱= éesh my.(1s.P)= grandparent son focus-there my.(1s.P)= father
ax̱ éesh yéet áyá x̱át	i am my father's son
	ax̱= éesh yéet á-yá x̱át my.(1s.P)= father son focus-right.here me.(1s.i)
ax̱ éesh sée áyá x̱át / ax̱ éesh séek' áyá x̱át	i am my father's daughter
	ax̱ éesh sée á-yá x̱át my.(1s.P) father daughter focus-right.here me.(1s.i) In some communities *–sée* is 'daughter' and *sée* is 'doll,' where the difference is that doll does not require a relating noun before it. In other communities, both *–sée* and *sée* are 'doll' and *–séek'* is 'daughter'

goosóo i éesh?	where is your father?
	goo-sá-ú / where-name-is.at · i= / your.(2s.P)= · éesh / father

wéidu ax̱ éesh.	there is my father.
	wéit-u / that.place-is.at · ax̱= / my.(1s.P)= · éesh / father

imperfective (+)

aadóo sá iyatéen?	who do you see?
	aadóo / who · =sá / =name · ∅-i-ÿa-√téen / them/it.(3.O)-you.(2s.S)-cl.(∅,i)-√see

imperfective (+)

ax̱ éesh x̱aatéen.	i see my father.
	ax̱= / my.(1s.P)= · éesh / father · ∅-x̱a-ÿa-√téen / them/it.(3.O)-i.(1s.S)-cl.(∅,i)-√see

i sáni ák.wé?	is that your paternal uncle? i= / your.(2s.P)= · sáni / paternal.uncle · á-gé-wé / focus-yes/no-there
aaa, ax̱ sáni áwé.	yes, that is my paternal uncle. aaa / yes · ax̱= / my.(1s.P)= · sáni / paternal-uncle · á-wé / focus-there

imperfective (+)

wáa sá yatee i tláa?	how is your mother? wáa / how · =sá / =name · ∅-ÿa-√tee / them/it.(3.O)-cl.(∅,i)-√be · i= / your.(2s.P)= · tláa / mother

imperfective (+)

ax̱ tláa yak'éi.	my mother is good/fine. ax̱ / my.(1s.P) · tláa / mother · ∅-ÿa-√k'éi / them/it.(3.O)-cl.(∅,i)-√good

imperfective (+)

wáa sá duwasáakw i aat?	how is your paternal aunt called?

wáa =sá ∅-du-ÿa-√sáakw
how =name them/it.(3.O)-someone.(4h.S)-cl.(∅,i)-√name

i= aat
your.(2s.P)= paternal-aunt

imperfective (+)

Susie yóo duwasáakw ax̱ aat.	my paternal aunt is called Susie.

Susie yóo ∅-du-ÿa-√sáakw
Susie as.preceeds them/it.(3.O)-someone.(4h.S)-cl.(∅,i)-√name

ax̱= aat
my.(1s.P)= paternal.aunt

daak̲w.aa naa sáwé i éesh?	which clan is your father?

daak̲w-aa naa =sá-wé i= éesh
which.one(s)-(part.i) clan/tribe =name-that your.(2s.P)= father

imperfective (+)

Yéil naax̱ sitee ax̱ éesh.	my father is Raven Moiety/Tribe.

yéil naa-x̱ ∅-si-√tee ax̱= éesh
raven clan/tribe.essive them/it.(3.O)-cl.(s,i)-√be my.(1s.P)= father

goot'á ḵwáan sáwé i éesh?	what is the ancestral place of your father's people?
	goot'á / what.place — ḵwáan / ancestral.people.of — sá-wé / name.there — i= / your.(2s.P)= — éesh / father

Áak'w Ḵwáan áwé.	it is Áak'w Ḵwáan.
	áa-k'w / lake.little — ḵwáan / ancestral.people.of — á-wé / focus-there

imperfective (+)

goox' sá yéi yatee i tláa?	where is your mother staying?
	goo-x' / where-at.(residing) — =sá / =name — yéi= / thus= — ∅-ÿa-√tee / them/it.(3.O)-cl.(∅,i)-√be — i= / your.(2s.P) — tláa / mother

imperfective (+)

Aangóonx' yéi yatee aḵ tláa.	my mother stays at Aangóon.
	aan-góon-x' / land-portage-.at.(residing) — yéi= / thus= — ∅-ÿa-√tee / them/it.(3.O)-cl.(∅,i)-√be — aḵ= / my.(1s.P) — tláa / mother

	imperfective (+)
____-x' yéi yatee ax̱ ____.	my ____ stays at ____.
	____-x' {place}-at.(residing) yéi= thus= ∅-ÿa-√tee them/it.(3.O)-cl.(∅,i)-√be my.(1s.P) ax̱= my.(1s.P) ____ {kinship term}

	imperfective (+)
daat eetéenáx̱ sá yatee i éesh?	what does your father need?
	daat what eetí-náx̱ stead.through/via =sá =name ∅-ÿa-√tee them/it.(3.O)-cl.(∅,i)-√be i= your.(2s.P) éesh father

	imperfective (+)
óonaa eetéenáx̱ yatee ax̱ éesh.	my father needs a rifle.
	√óon-aa √shoot.one(s).(part.i) eetí-náx̱ remnant.through/via ∅-ÿa-√tee them/it.(3.O)-cl.(∅,i)-√be ax̱= my.(1s.P) éesh father

	imperfective (+)
____ eetéenáx̱ yatee ax̱ ____.	my ____ needs ____.
	____ {noun} eetí-náx̱ remnant.through/via ∅-ÿa-√tee them/it.(3.O)-cl.(∅,i)-√be ax̱= my.(1s.P) ____ {kinship term}

imperfective (+)

wáa sá sh tudinook i aat?

how is your paternal aunt feeling?

wáa	=sá	sh	tu-∅-di-√nook
how	=name	self(rflx.O)	inside-they.(3.S)-cl.(d,∅,i)-√feel/touch
i=	aat		
your.(2s.P)	paternal.aunt		

imperfective (+)

ax̱ aat toowú yanéekw.

my paternal aunt is sad.

ax̱	aat	tú-wú	∅-ÿa-√néekw
my.(1s.P)=	paternal.aunt	inside-is.at	them/it.(3.O)-cl.(∅,i)-√sick/hurt

i léelk'w ágé yanéekw?

is your grandparent sick?

i=	léelk'w	á-gé	ÿa-√néekw
your.(2s.P)=	grandparent	focus-yes/no?	cl.(∅,i)-√sick/hurt

imperfective (+)

aaa. ax̱ léelk'w leitóox̱ yanéekw.

yes. my grandparent has a sore throat.

aaa	ax̱=	léelk'w	la-tú-x̱
yes	my.(1s.P)=	grandparent	neck.inside-in.contact.with
∅-ÿa-√néekw			
them/it.(3.O)-cl.(∅,i)-√sick/hurt			

perfective (+)

aadóo éet sá yaan.uwaháa?

who is hungry?

aadóo ée-t =sá
who empty.base-at.(arrived) =name

yaan-<ÿu>-ÿa-√háa
hunger-<perfective>-cl.(∅,i)-√move.imperceptibly

perfective (+)

ax̱ éesh éet yaan.uwaháa.

my father is hungry.

ax̱= éesh ée-t
my= father empty.base-at.(arrived)

yaan-<ÿu>-ÿa-√háa
hunger-<perfective>-cl.(∅,i)-√move.imperceptibly

perfective (+)

aadóo éet sá yataawaháa?

who is sleepy?

aadóo ée-t =sá
who empty.base-at.(arrived) =name

ÿa-ta-<ÿu>-ÿa-√háa
face-sleep-<perfective>-cl.(∅,i)-√move.imperceptibly

perfective (+)

ax̱ sáni éet yataawaháa.

my paternal uncle is sleepy.

ax̱= sáni ée-t
my= paternal.uncle empty.base-at.(arrived)

ÿa-ta-<ÿu>-ÿa-√háa
face-sleep-<perfective>-cl.(∅,i)-√move.imperceptibly

perfective (+)

aadóo sá wudixwétl?

who is tired?

aadóo	=sá	∅-<ÿu>-di-√xwétl
who	=name	them/it.(3.O)-<perfective>-cl.(d,∅,i)-√become.tired

perfective (+)

ax̱ kéilk' wudixwétl.

my maternal niece/nephew is tired.

ax̱=	kéilk'
my.(1P)=	maternal.niece/nephew

∅-<ÿu>-di-√xwétl
them/it.(3.O)-<perfective>-cl.(d,∅,i)-√tire/exhaust

perfective (+)

aadóo sá shaawakúx?

who is thirsty?

aadóo	=sá	∅-sha-<ÿu>-ÿa-√kúx
who	=name	them/it.(3.O)-head-<perfective>-cl.(d,∅,i)-√become.dry

perfective (+)

ax̱ tláa shaawakúx.

my mother is thirsty.

ax̱=	tláa	∅-sha-<ÿu>-ÿa-√kúx
my=	mother	them/it.(3.O)-head-<perfective>-cl.(d,∅,i)-√become.dry

perfective (+)

daa sá i tláak'w éet uwaháa?

what does your maternal aunt want to eat/drink?

daa	sá	i=	tláak'w
what	=name	your.(2s.P)=	maternal.aunt

ée-t	<ÿu>-ÿa-√háa
empty.base-at.(arrived)	<perfective>-cl.(∅,i)-√move.imperceptibly

perfective (+)

x̱áat ax̱ tláak'w éet uwaháa.

my maternal aunt is hungry for fish.

x̱áat	ax̱=	tláak'w
fish	my.(1s.P)=	maternal.aunt

ée-t	<ÿu>-ÿa-√háa
empty.base-at.(arrived)	<perfective>-cl.(∅,i)-√move.imperceptibly

imperfective (+)

daa sá i tláa tuwáa sigóo?

what does your mother want?

daa	=sá	i=	tláa	tú-ÿá	si-√góo
what	=name	your.(2s.P)=	mother	inside-face	cl.(s,i)-√enjoy/happy

imperfective (+)

lítaa ax̱ tláa tuwáa sigóo.

my mother wants a knife.

lítaa	ax̱=	tláa	tú-ÿa	si-√góo
knife	my.(1s.P)=	mother	inside-face	cl.(s,i)-√enjoy/happy

daa sá i éesh jeewú?	what does your father have? daa =sá i= éesh jee-wú what =name your.(2s.P)= father possession-is.at
dáanaa ax̱ éesh jeewú.	my father has money. dáanaa ax̱= éesh jee-wú money my.(1s.P)= father possession-is.at
aadóo jeewú sá wé dáanaa?	who has the money? aadóo jee-wú =sá wé dáanaa who possession-is.at =name there money
ax̱ tláa jeewú wé dáanaa.	my mother has the money. ax̱= tláa jee-wú wé dáanaa my.(1s.P)= mother possession-is.at there money

Kinship terms can be used without a pronoun when directly addressing the relative. This switch is similar to the difference in English between "my mom" when talking to someone else about your mother, and "mom!" when talking directly to your mother. A small number of Lingít kinship terms have special forms when directly addressing a relative. The others stay the same but do not require a pronoun.

sík'	daughter!
yítk'	son!
kélk'	maternal niece/nephew!
kálk'w	paternal niece/nephew!
chx̲ánk'	grandchild!
atléi / atlée	mom!

Vocabulary

	k'wát'	egg
	k'wálx̲	fiddlehead fern sprouts

	dzísk'w / tsísk'w	moose
	tsísk'w / dzísk'w (At, T) / óondách (T) / wesdzí / mesdzí (C)	great horned owl
	at kach'áak'u	carver
	kashóok' gwéil, kashéek'w gwéil	heating pad

shaawát (♀)

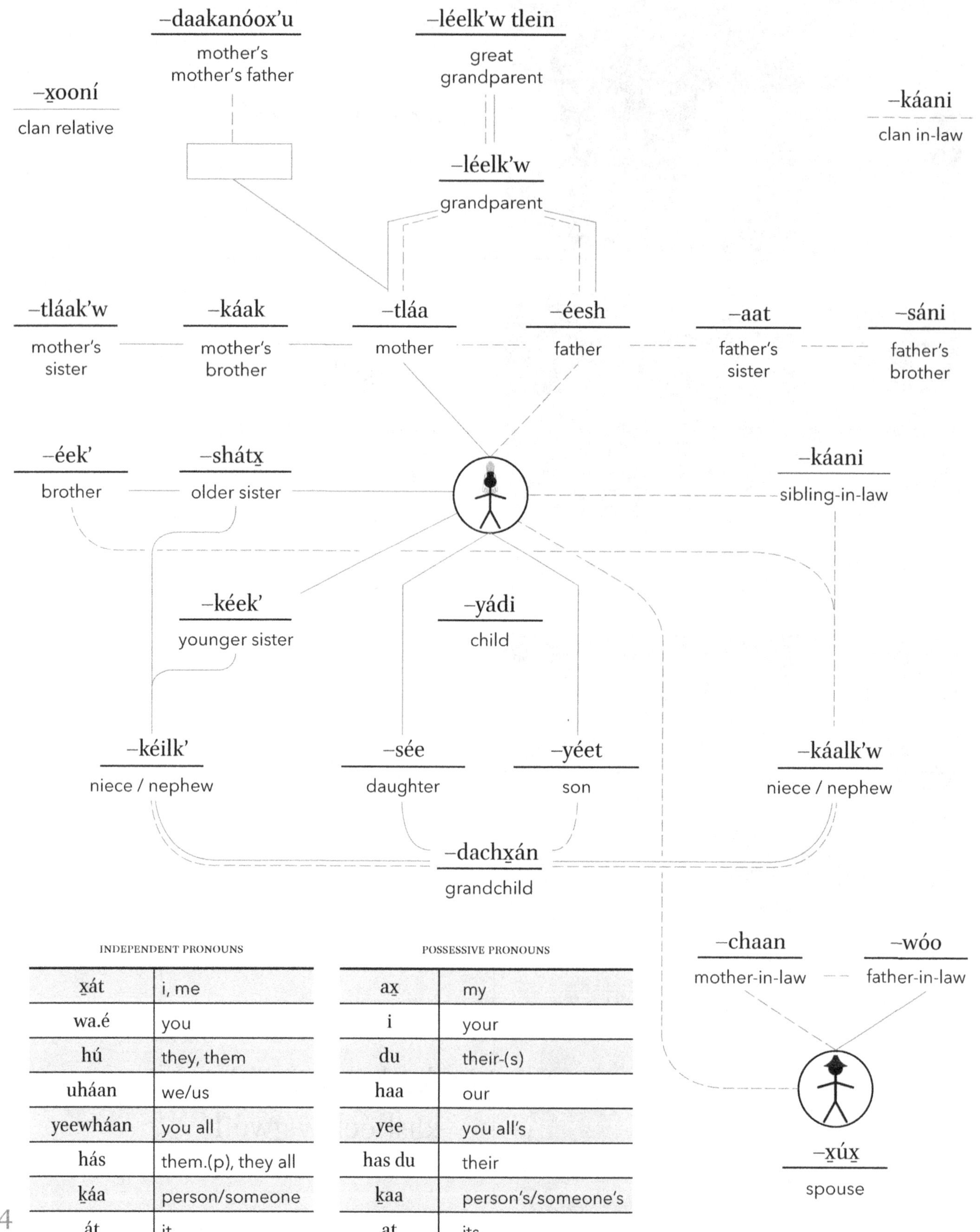

INDEPENDENT PRONOUNS

x̲át	i, me
wa.é	you
hú	they, them
uháan	we/us
yeewháan	you all
hás	them.(p), they all
k̲áa	person/someone
át	it

POSSESSIVE PRONOUNS

ax̲	my
i	your
du	their-(s)
haa	our
yee	you all's
has du	their
k̲aa	person's/someone's
at	its

ḵáa (♂)

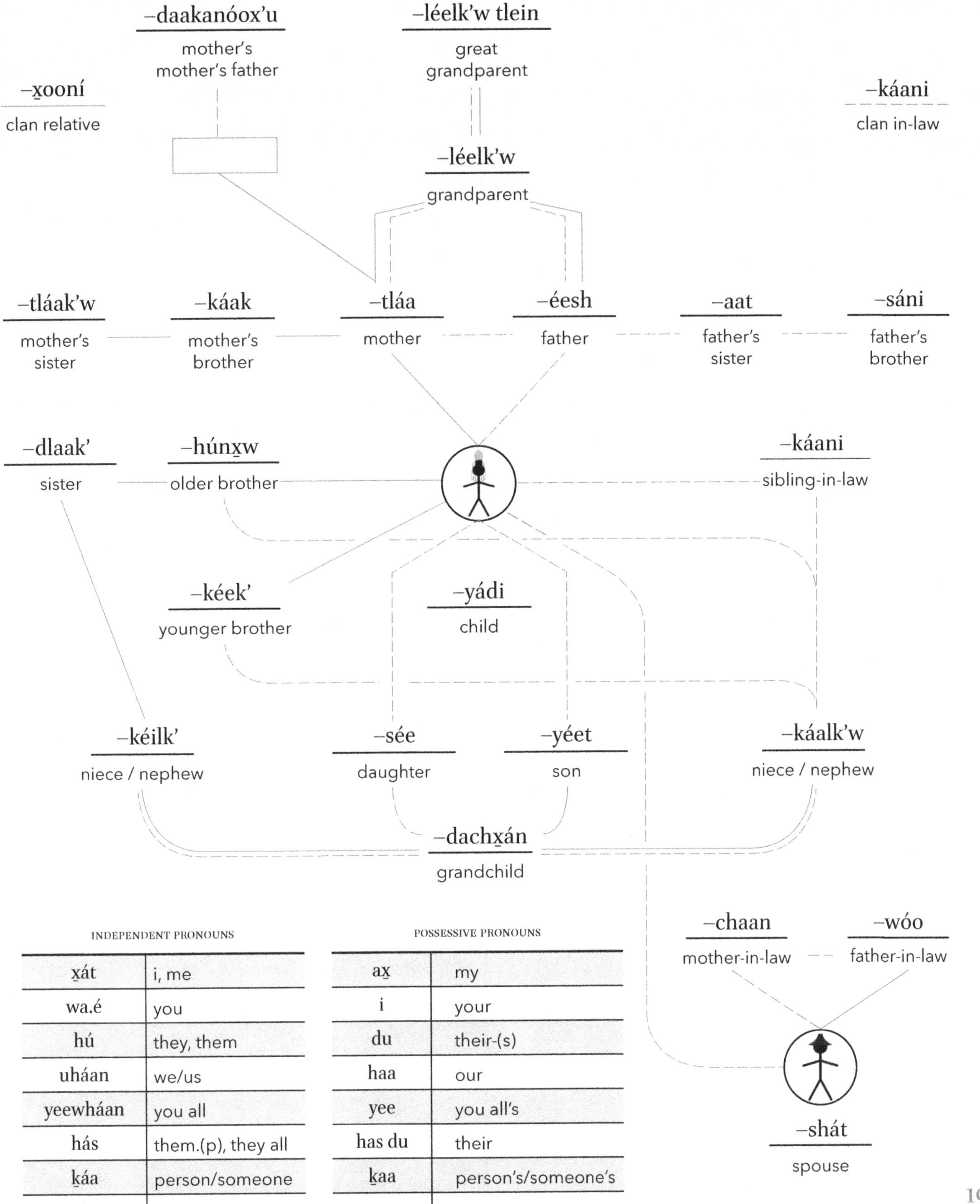

INDEPENDENT PRONOUNS

x̱át	i, me
wa.é	you
hú	they, them
uháan	we/us
yeewháan	you all
hás	them.(p), they all
ḵáa	person/someone
át	it

POSSESSIVE PRONOUNS

ax̱	my
i	your
du	their-(s)
haa	our
yee	you all's
has du	their
ḵaa	person's/someone's
at	its

Tlingit Kinship System

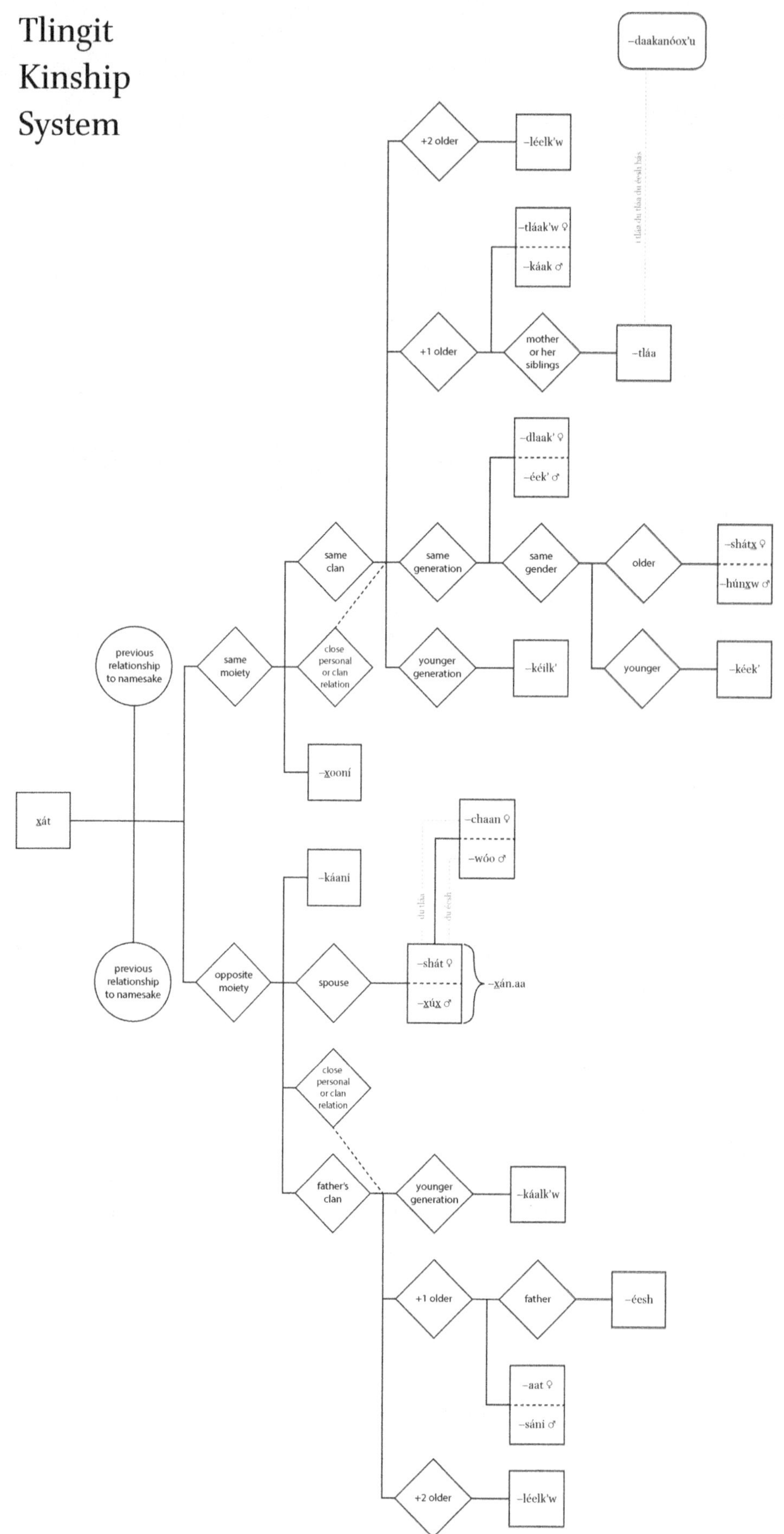

6B

K̲aa X̲'akaneek Kawdu.aag̲ú 6

Translation Exercises 6

Lingít → English

du tláa áwé.	
yak'éi haat yigoodí.	
yak'éi ix̱wsateení.	
i dachx̱án áyá x̱át.	
wáa sá yatee i tláa?	
daaḵw.aa naa sáwé i éesh?	
óonaa eetéenáx̱ yatee ax̱ sáni.	
aadóo éet sá yaan.uwaháa?	
ax̱ kéilk' wudixwétl.	

English → Lingít

is that your father?	
where is your mother?	
who do you see?	
what is your paternal aunt called?	
my grandparent has a sore throat.	
what does your father have?	
what does your mother want?	
who has the money?	

7A

Wáa sá iyatee?

How are you?

Ax̱ éesh yéeyi haa yamsaḵaayín:
a yík wudushk'áatl'i yaakw
tlákw de x'áasde naḵúx̱ch.
— Chukateen

My father used to tell us:
a boat in which people had gone silent
drifts quickly towards the waterfall.
– Jane Smarch, Kooḵhittaan

ax̱= + éesh + =yéeyi + haa= + ÿa-<ÿu>-∅-sa-√ḵaa-yín
my.(1s.P)= + father + =used.to.be + us.(1p.O)= + face-<perfective>-they.(3.S)-cl.(s)-√say-decessive

a= + yík + <ÿu>-du-sh-√ḵ'áatl'-i + yaakw
its.(3n.P)= + in.(shallow.container) + <perfective>-someone.(4h.s)-cl.(d,sh)-√silent.attributive + canoe/boat

tlákw + de + x'áas-de + <na>-∅-∅-√ḵúx̱-<ch>
quickly + now + waterfall-towards + <perfective habitual>-they.(3.s)-cl.(∅)-√go.(by boat/car)-<habitual>

Wáa sá iyatee?

Dialogue Practice				
A	1	wa.é ák.wé?	is that you?	wa.é á-gé-wé you.(2s.i) focus-yes/no?-there
B	2	aaa, x̱át áyá yeisú.	yes, i'm still me.	aaa x̱át á-yá yeisú yes me.(1s.i) focus-right.here still
	3	wáa sá iyatee?	how are you?	wáa =sá i-ÿa-√tee? how =name you.(2s.O)-cl.(∅,i)-√be
A	4	hél wáa sá x̱at utí.	i'm okay	hél wáa =sá x̱at u-∅-√tí not how =voice me.(1s.O) irrealis-cl.(∅)-√be
	5	wa.é déis?	and you?	wa.é de-sé you.(2s.i) now-perhaps
B	6	x̱at wudixwétl.	i'm tired.	x̱at <ÿu>-di-√xwétl me.(1s.O) <perfective>-cl.(d,∅,i)-√become.tired
B	7	hél k'idéin x̱wataa.	i didn't sleep well.	hél √k'é-déin <ÿu>-x̱a-∅-√taa not √good-ly.(adverb) <perfective>-i.(1s.S)-cl.(∅)-√sleep-(singular)
A	8	i gu.aa yáx̱ x'wán!	have strength and courage! / take heart!	i gu.aa yáx̱ x'wán your.(2s.P) best.effort like be-sure-to

The Changing Lingít Verb

As we learn about how verbs work in Lingít, it is important to keep in mind that in English a verb is a word that can be altered with prefixes, suffixes, and other words around it. In Lingít a verb can go through a great deal of change with multiple prefixes, suffixes, and surrounding words. The word that is the verb will begin to change in complicated yet predictable ways.

When you learn to use verbs, you should focus on building a prefix and then attaching the stem. The prefix contains information about to **whom** the verb might be happening (**object**), **who** is doing the verb (**subject**), and information about whether the verb has happened, when it may have happened, and much more. Consider the following examples:

TLINGIT	VERB	ENGLISH	VERB
yéi anasnéin	anasnéin	they are doing it; they are fixing it	doing / fixing
yéi awsinei	awsinei	they did it; they fixed it	did
tlél yéi awusnei	awusnei	they didn't do it; they didn't fix it	do / fix
yéi agux̱sanéi	aguxsanéi	they're going to do it; they're going to fix it	do / fix
tlél yéi agux̱sanei	aguxsanei	they're not going to do it; they're not going to fix it	do / fix
ax̱á	ax̱á	they are eating it; they eat it	eating
tlél oox̱á	oox̱á	they aren't eating it; they don't eat it	eating
aawax̱áa	aawax̱áa	they ate it	ate
tlél awux̱á	awux̱á	they did't eat it	eat
akg̱wax̱áa	akg̱wax̱áa	they are going to eat it	eat
tlél akg̱wax̱aa	akg̱wax̱aa	they aren't going to eat it	eat
yak'éi	yak'éi	they/it is good	good
tlél uk'é	uk'é	they/it aren't good	good
wook'éi	wook'éi	they/it were good	good
tlél wuk'éi	wuk'éi	they/it weren't good	good
kei kg̱wak'éi	kei kg̱wak'éi	they/it will be good	good
tlél kei kg̱wak'éi	kei kg̱wak'éi	they/it won't be good	good
yéi x̱'ayaḵá	x̱'ayaḵá	they/it say that; they are saying that	say
tlél yéi x̱'awuḵá	x̱'awuḵá	they/it isn't saying that; they don't say that	saying
yéi yaawaḵaa	yaawaḵaa	they/it said it	said
tlél yéi yawuḵaa	yawuḵaa	they/it didn't say	say
yéi yakg̱waḵáa	yakg̱waḵáa	they/it will say it	say
tlél yéi yakg̱waḵaa	yakg̱waḵaa	they/it won't say it	say

The Object Pronoun

The **object** usually marks whom the verb happens to, and there is a set of **object pronouns** at the front of the verb. It is one of the first parts spoken and heard. Knowing how to use pronouns opens the door to speaking, and the drills here are intended to help you internalize a list of pronouns.

The use of pronouns differs in Lingít than what you might be used to in English. For example, most state verbs use **object pronouns** in Lingít (me good), whereas English uses **subject pronouns** and a linking verb (i am good). The following examples use both **object** and **subject** pronouns:

	OBJECT	ENGLISH
1S	x̱at	me
2S	i-	you
3	∅-~ a-	them
1P	haa	us
2P	yee	you all
3P	has ∅-~ a-	them all
4H	ḵaa ~ ḵu-	someone
4N	at	something

TLINGIT	OBJECT	ENGLISH	COMPONENTS
x̱at six̱án	x̱at	they love me	x̱at ∅-si-√x̱án
isix̱án	i-	they love you	i-∅-si-√x̱án
asix̱án	a-	they love them	a-∅-si-√x̱án
haa six̱án	haa	they love us	haa ∅-si-√x̱án
yee six̱án	yee	they love you all	yee ∅-si-√x̱án
has asix̱án	has a-	they love them all	has a-∅-si-√x̱án
ḵusix̱án	ḵu	they love people	ḵu-∅-si-√x̱án
at six̱án	at	they love something	at a-∅-si-√x̱án

There are two main types of object pronouns: ones that are written as their own word before the verb and ones that are attached directly to the verb as a prefix. The ones that are attached are marked with a dash (i-). The reasons why some are written as attached and others are disconnected has to do with the ways they combine with other prefixes.

A verb in Lingít has some parts that you should become familiar with, and each of those parts have parts within them. One of the goals of learning Lingít is to understand how to use all of these parts in order to communicate. When you are in the early stages of learning, keep in mind that our goal is communication and not perfection. Errors are a necessary part of learning, and it is okay to use lots of notes and tables when learning the language.

Also, knowing how to understand and speak the language is always the goal. The names of all of these parts will be used to help teach how they work in the Lingít language, but knowing exactly what these things are is less important as speaking and hearing the language.

The Lingít language has a complex set of rules and tends to put things into categories, like types of verbs and nouns and more. One of the goals of Beginning Lingít is to teach these rules in steps so that they continue to build upon each other and reveal the structure of the language as you continue to learn more nouns, phrases, verbs, and other parts of speech.

One of the trickier parts of the Lingít object pronoun involves the third person. The first person is the speaker (me), the second person is the one being spoken to (you), the third person is the one being spoken about to another person (they), and the fourth person in an indefinite thing or person (someone/something). The third person object often is nothing, which we sometimes show with a ∅ symbol. Learners often want to put something there, like *du* 'their,' but there really is nothing there. However, if there is a third person object and a third person subject, then the ∅ will become *a-*, which you will be able to see in future examples when we are changing the object and the subject. For now, focus on the object and how it appears in the verbs we will practice.

Changing the object pronoun in verbs

O-∅-√k'éi (ga state verb – *object intransitive*) for O to be good, fine, pretty	
x̲at yak'éi	i'm good x̲at= ÿa-√k'éi me.(1s.O)= cl.(∅,i)-√good
iyak'éi	you're good i-ÿa-√k'éi you.(2s.O)-cl.(∅,i)-√good
yak'éi	they are good; it is good ∅-ÿa-√k'éi them.(3.O)-cl.(∅,i)-√good
haa yak'éi	we're good haa= ÿa-√k'éi us.(1p.O)= cl.(∅,i)-√good
yee yak'éi	you all are good yee= ÿa-√k'éi you.all.(2p.O)= cl.(∅,i)-√good
has yak'éi	they all are good has= ∅-ÿa-√k'éi 3ph= them.(3.O)-cl.(∅,i)-√good

A Lingít verb is documented using a **verb theme**, which is a skeleton of the verb itself. Don't be scared of this! The capital O means there is an object pronoun there, and you can now select an object pronoun to go into that spot. When working with pronouns in Lingít, keep the following in mind:

- The pronoun occurs in a certain order than cannot be changed (Object-Subject-Verb).
- If a pronoun is in the theme, then it stead there unless the verb goes through major changes.
- If the pronoun is not in the theme, then it cannot be added in.

O-l-√chán ˣ (ga state verb – *object intransitive*) for O to stink, have unpleasant odor, smell bad; for O to smell strongly		
x̲at lichán	i stink; i'm smelly	x̲at= li-√chán me.(1s.O)= cl.(l,i)-√smelly
ilichán	you stink; you're smelly	i-li-√chán you.(2s.O)-cl.(l,i)-√smelly
lichán	they stink; it stinks; they are smelly; it is smelly	∅-li-√chán them.(3.O)-cl.(l,i)-√smelly
haa lichán	we stink; we're smelly	haa= li-√chán us.(1p.O)= cl.(l,i)-√smelly
yee lichán	you all stink; you all are smelly	yee= li-√chán you.all.(2p.O)= cl.(l,i)-√smelly
has lichán	they all stink; they all are smelly	has= ∅-li-√chán 3ph= them.(3.O)-cl.(l,i)-√smelly

3ph is a short form notation for **third person human pluralizer**. While the third person pronoun could be they (human) or it (non-human), the pluralizer *has* is used to pluralize human objects, subjects, or both. There are only **object pronouns** in these verbs, so we know it pluralizes the object. In verbs with both an **object** and a **subject**, it must be understood through context or grammar. Later lessons will examine this with examples and drills, so for know work on seeing where the *has* is placed and how it affects the meaning in these verbs.

O-d+∅-√tl'áak' (∅ event verb – *object intransitive*) for O to be wet (may be thoroughly wet, but not by actual immersion)	
x̱at wuditl'ák'	i'm wet x̱at= <ÿu>-di-√tl'ák' me.(1s.O)= <perfective>-cl.(d,∅,i)-√wet
iwditl'ák' / imditl'ák'	you're wet i-<ÿu>-di-√tl'ák' you.(2s.O)-<perfective>-cl.(d,∅,i)-√wet
wuditl'ák'	they are wet; it is wet ∅-<ÿu>-di-√tl'ák' them.(3.O)-<perfective>-cl.(d,∅,i)-√wet
haa wditl'ák' / haa mditl'ák'	we're wet haa= <ÿu>-di-√tl'ák' us.(1p.O)= <perfective>-cl.(d,∅,i)-√wet
yee wditl'ák' / yee mditl'ák'	you all are wet yee= <ÿu>-di-√tl'ák' you.all.(2p.O)= <perfective>-cl.(d,∅,i)-√wet
has wuditl'ák'	they all are wet has= ∅-<ÿu>-di-√tl'ák' 3ph= them.(3.O)-<perfective>-cl.(d,∅,i)-√wet

O-ya-∅-√seek [1] (∅ event verb – *object intransitive*)

for O to be weathered in

x̱at yaawasík	i'm weathered in	x̱at= ÿa-<ÿu>-∅-√sík me.(1s.O)= face-<perfective>-cl.(∅,i)-√weathered.in
iyaawasík	you're weathered in	i-ÿa-<ÿu>-∅-√sík you.(2s.O)-face-<perfective>-cl.(∅,i)-√weathered.in
yaawasík	they are weathered in; it is weathered in	∅-ÿa-<ÿu>-∅-√sík them.(3.O)-face-<perfective>-cl.(∅,i)-√weathered.in
haa yaawasík	we're weathered in	haa= ÿa-<ÿu>-∅-√sík us.(1p.O)= face-<perfective>-cl.(∅,i)-√weathered.in
yee yaawasík	you all are weathered in	yee ÿa-<ÿu>-∅-√sík you.all.(2p.O)= face-<perfective>-cl.(∅,i)-√weathered.in
has yaawasík	they all are weathered in	has= ∅-ÿa-<ÿu>-∅-√sík 3ph= them.(3.O)-face-<perfective>-cl.(∅,i)-√weathered.in

O-l-√tseen [×] (ga state verb – *object intransitive*)

for O to be strong, powerful

x̱at litseen	i'm strong x̱at= li-√tseen me.(1s.O)= cl.(l,i)-√strong
ilitseen	you're strong i-li-√tseen you.(2s.O)-cl.(l,i)-√strong
litseen	they are strong; it is strong ∅-li-√tseen them.(3.O)-cl.(l,i)-√strong
haa litseen	we're strong haa= li-√tseen us.(1p.O)= cl.(l,i)-√strong
yee litseen	you all are strong yee= li-√tseen you.all.(2p.O)= cl.(l,i)-√strong
has litseen	they all are strong has= ∅-li-√tseen 3ph them.(3.O)-cl.(l,i)-√strong

O-∅-√néekw [1] × (ga state verb – *object intransitive*)

for O to be sick; for O to hurt, be in pain

x̲at yanéekw	i'm sick x̲at= ÿa-√néekw me.(1s.O)= cl.(∅,i)-√sick/hurt
iyanéekw	you're sick i-ÿa-√néekw you.(2s.O)-cl.(∅,i)-√sick/hurt
yanéekw	they are sick; it is sick ∅-ÿa-√néekw them.(3.O)-cl.(∅,i)-√sick/hurt
haa yanéekw	we're sick haa= ÿa-√néekw us.(1p.O)= cl.(∅,i)-√sick/hurt
yee yanéekw	you all are sick yee= ÿa-√néekw you.all.(2p.O)= cl.(∅,i)-√sick/hurt
has yanéekw	they all are sick has= ∅-ÿa-√néekw 3ph= them.(3.O)-cl.(∅,i)-√sick/hurt

O-l-√ch’éix̱’w [1] (∅ event verb – *object intransitive*)

for O to be dirty

x̱at wulich’éx̱’w	i’m dirty	x̱at= <ÿu>-li-√ch’éx̱’w me.(1s.O)= <perfective>-cl.(l,i)-√dirty
iwlich’éx̱’w / imlich’éx̱’w	you’re dirty	i-<ÿu>-li-√ch’éx̱’w you.(2s.O)-<perfective>-cl.(l,i)-√dirty
wulich’éx̱’w	they are dirty; it is dirty	∅-<ÿu>-li-√ch’éx̱’w them.(3.O)-<perfective>-cl.(l,i)-√dirty
haa wlich’éx̱’w / haa mlich’éx̱’w	we’re dirty	haa= <ÿu>-li-√ch’éx̱’w us.(1p.O)= <perfective>-cl.(l,i)-√dirty
yee wlich’éx̱’w / yee mlich’éx̱’w	you all are dirty	yee= <ÿu>-li-√ch’éx̱’w you.all.(2p.O)= <perfective>-cl.(l,i)-√dirty
has wulich’éx̱’w	they all are dirty	has= ∅-<ÿu>-li-√ch’éx̱’w 3ph= them.(3.O)-<perfective>-cl.(l,i)-√dirty

O-tu-l-√.aan [2] × (ga state verb – *object intransitive*) for O to be kind; for O to be gentle		
x̱at tuli.aan	i'm kind	
	x̱at= me.(1s.O)=	tu-li-√.aan inside-cl.(l,i)-√kind/gentle/pleasant
ituli.aan	you're kind	
	i-tu-li-√.aan you.(2s.O)-inside-cl.(l,i)-√kind/gentle/pleasant	
tuli.aan	they are kind; it is kind	
	∅-tu-li-√.aan them.(3.O)-inside-cl.(l,i)-√kind/gentle/pleasant	
haa tuli.aan	we're kind	
	haa= us.(1p.O)=	tu-li-√.aan inside-cl.(l,i)-√kind/gentle/pleasant
yee tuli.aan	you all are kind	
	yee= you.all.(2p.O)=	tu-li-√.aan inside-cl.(l,i)-√kind/gentle/pleasant
has tuli.aan	they all are kind	
	has= 3ph=	∅-tu-li-√.aan them.(3.O)-inside-cl.(l,i)-√kind/gentle/pleasant

O-sa-∅-√.áat' (∅ event verb – *object intransitive*)

for O (person) to feel cold

x̱at seiwa.át'	i'm cold	x̱at= sa-<ÿu>-ÿa-√.át' me.(1s.O)= voice-<perfective>-cl.(∅,i)-√cold
iseiwa.át'	you're cold	i-sa-<ÿu>-ÿa-√.át' you.(2s.O)-voice-<perfective>-cl.(∅,i)-√cold
seiwa.át'	they are cold; it is cold	∅-sa-<ÿu>-ÿa-√.át' them.(3.O)-voice-<perfective>-cl.(∅,i)-√cold
haa seiwa.át'	we're cold	haa= sa-<ÿu>-ÿa-√.át' us.(1p.O)= voice-<perfective>-cl.(∅,i)-√cold
yee seiwa.át'	you all are cold	yee= sa-<ÿu>-ÿa-√.át' you.all.(2p.O)= voice-<perfective>-cl.(∅,i)-√cold
has seiwa.át'	they all are cold	has= ∅-sa-<ÿu>-ÿa-√.át' 3ph= them.(3.O)-voice-<perfective>-cl.(∅,i)-√cold

O-l-√ch'éeyáḵw ˣ (ga state verb – *object intransitive*) for O to be slow		
x̱at lich'éeyáḵw	i'm slow x̱at= li-√ch'éeyáḵw me.(1s.O)= cl.(l,i)-√slow	
ilich'éeyáḵw	you're slow i-li-√ch'éeyáḵw you.(2s.O)-cl.(l,i)-√slow	
lich'éeyáḵw	they are slow; it is slow ∅-li-√ch'éeyáḵw them.(3.O)-cl.(l,i)-√slow	
haa lich'éeyáḵw	we're slow haa= li-√ch'éeyáḵw us.(1p.O)= cl.(l,i)-√slow	
yee lich'éeyáḵw	you all are slow yee= li-√ch'éeyáḵw you.all.(2p.O)= cl.(l,i)-√slow	
has lich'éeyáḵw	they all are slow has= ∅-li-√ch'éeyáḵw 3ph= them.(3.O)-cl.(l,i)-√slow	

O-ka-∅-√déix' ˣ (ga state verb – *object intransitive*) for O to be ashamed; for O to be feel shame	
x̱at kaadéix' / x̱at kayadéix'	i'm ashamed x̱at= ka-ÿa-√déix' me.(1s.O)= horizontal-cl.(∅,i)-√shame
ikaadéix' / ikayadéix'	you're ashamed i-ka-ÿa-√déix' you.(2s.O)-horizontal-cl.(∅,i)-√shame
kaadéix' / kayadéix'	they are ashamed; it is ashamed ∅-ka-ÿa-√déix' them.(3.O)-horizontal-cl.(∅,i)-√shame
haa kaadéix' / haa kayadéix'	we're ashamed haa= ka-ÿa-√déix' us.(1p.O)= horizontal-cl.(∅,i)-√shame
yee kaadéix' / yee kayadéix'	you all are ashamed yee= ka-ÿa-√déix' you.all.(2p.O)= horizontal-cl.(∅,i)-√shame
has kaadéix' / has kayadéix'	they all are ashamed has= ∅-ka-ÿa-√déix' 3ph= them.(3.O)-horizontal-cl.(∅,i)-√shame

O-sh-√g̱eiḵ ˣ / O-sh-√g̱eeḵ ˣ (ga state verb – *object intransitive*)

for O to be stingy, unwilling to give or share much

x̱at shig̱eiḵ	i'm stingy	x̱at= shi-√g̱eiḵ me.(1s.O)= cl.(sh,i)-√stingy
ishig̱eiḵ	you're stingy	i-shi-√g̱eiḵ you.(2s.O)-cl.(sh,i)-√stingy
shig̱eiḵ	they are stingy; it is stingy	∅-shi-√g̱eiḵ them.(3.O)-cl.(sh,i)-√stingy
haa shig̱eiḵ	we're stingy	haa= shi-√g̱eiḵ us.(1p.O)= cl.(sh,i)-√stingy
yee shig̱eiḵ	you all are stingy	yee= shi-√g̱eiḵ you.all.(2p.O)= cl.(sh,i)-√stingy
has shig̱eiḵ	they all are stingy	has= ∅-shi-√g̱eiḵ 3ph= them.(3.O)-cl.(sh,i)-√stingy

O-l-√wóotl' × ((ga state verb – *object intransitive*) for O to be mentally strong, persistent	
x̲at liwóotl'	i'm mentally strong x̲at= li-√wóotl' me.(1s.O)= cl.(l,i)-√stubborn
iliwóotl'	you're mentally strong i-li-√wóotl' you.(2s.O)-cl.(l,i)-√stubborn
liwóotl'	they are mentally strong; it is mentally strong ∅-li-√wóotl' them.(3.O)-cl.(l,i)-√stubborn
haa liwóotl'	we're mentally strong haa= li-√wóotl' us.(1p.O)= cl.(l,i)-√stubborn
yee liwóotl'	you all are mentally strong yee= li-√wóotl' you.all.(2p.O)= cl.(l,i)-√stubborn
has liwóotl'	they are all mentally strong has= ∅-li-√wóotl' 3ph= them.(3.O)-cl.(l,i)-√stubborn

(yéi) + O-∅-√tee h 1 (na state verb – *object intransitive*) for O to be (that way)	
yéi x̱at yatee	i'm that way yéi= x̱at= ÿa-√tee thus= me.(1s.O)= cl.(∅,i)-√be
yéi iyatee	you're that way yéi= i-ÿa-√tee thus= you.(2s.O)-cl.(∅,i)-√be
yéi yatee	they are that way; it is that way yéi= ∅-ÿa-√tee thus= them.(3.O)-cl.(∅,i)-√be
yéi haa yatee	we're that way yéi= haa= ÿa-√tee thus= us.(1p.O)= cl.(∅,i)-√be
yéi yee yatee	you all are that way yéi= yee= ÿa-√tee thus= you.all.(2p.O)= cl.(∅,i)-√be
yéi has yatee	they all are that way yéi= has= ∅-ÿa-√tee thus= 3ph= them.(3.O)-cl.(∅,i)-√be

Changing the preverb to make new verbs

N-x' + (yéi) + O-∅-√tee $^{h\,1}$ (na state verb – *object intransitive*) for O to be or stay at N; for O to dwell, live at N; for O to remain at N	
áa yéi x̲at yatee	i stay there á-x' yéi= x̲at= ÿa-√tee there-at.(residing) thus= me.(1s.O)= cl.(∅,i)-√be
áa yéi iyatee	you stay there á-x' yéi= i-ÿa-√tee there-at.(residing) thus= you.(2s.O)-cl.(∅,i)-√be
áa yéi yatee	they stay there; it stays there á-x' yéi= ∅-ÿa-√tee there-at.(residing) thus= them.(3.O)-cl.(∅,i)-√be
áa yéi haa yatee	we stay there á-x' yéi= haa= ÿa-√tee there-at.(residing) thus= us.(1p.O)= cl.(∅,i)-√be
áa yéi yee yatee	you all stay there á-x' yéi= yee= ÿa-√tee there-at.(residing) thus= you.all.(2p.O)= cl.(∅,i)-√be
áa yéi s yatee / áa yéi has yatee	they all stay there á-x' yéi= has= ∅-ÿa-√tee there-at.(residing) thus= 3ph= them.(3.O)-cl.(∅,i)-√be

In these examples, notice how the meaning of the verb changes when specific things are added to the **preverb**. The **preverb** is an area directly before the verb where certain words can change the meaning. As you learn more about Lingít verbs, you will find that learning to change a verb is complicated but predictable.

The O-∅-√tee $^{h\,1}$ (to be) verb has many different meanings once the preverb changes in certain ways. This means that you can learn to change the verb to different modes, and then the verb will be the part that goes through most of the changes. To start thinking about this, see how the verb itself is the same in these examples, but the meaning changes.

N + eetée-náx̱ + O-∅-√tee [h 1] (na state verb – *object intransitive*)

for O to need, lack, require N

<table>
<tr><td rowspan="3">a eetéenáx̱ x̱at yatee</td><td colspan="4">i need it</td></tr>
<tr><td>a=</td><td>eetí-náx̱</td><td>x̱at=</td><td>ÿa-√tee</td></tr>
<tr><td>its.(3n.P)=</td><td>stead-through/via</td><td>me.(1s.O)=</td><td>cl.(∅,i)-√be</td></tr>
<tr><td rowspan="3">a eetéenáx̱ iyatee</td><td colspan="4">you need it</td></tr>
<tr><td>a=</td><td>eetí-náx̱</td><td colspan="2">i-ÿa-√tee</td></tr>
<tr><td>its.(3n.P)=</td><td>stead-through/via</td><td colspan="2">you.(2s.O)-cl.(∅,i)-√be</td></tr>
<tr><td rowspan="3">a eetéenáx̱ yatee</td><td colspan="4">they need it; it needs it</td></tr>
<tr><td>a=</td><td>eetí-náx̱</td><td colspan="2">∅-ÿa-√tee</td></tr>
<tr><td>its.(3n.P)=</td><td>stead-through/via</td><td colspan="2">them.(3.O)-cl.(∅,i)-√be</td></tr>
<tr><td rowspan="3">a eetéenáx̱ haa yatee</td><td colspan="4">we need it</td></tr>
<tr><td>a</td><td>eetí-náx̱</td><td>haa=</td><td>ÿa-√tee</td></tr>
<tr><td>its.(3n.P)</td><td>stead-through/via</td><td>us.(1p.O)=</td><td>cl.(∅,i)-√be</td></tr>
<tr><td rowspan="3">a eetéenáx̱ yee yatee</td><td colspan="4">you all need it</td></tr>
<tr><td>a=</td><td>eetí-náx̱</td><td>yee=</td><td>ÿa-√tee</td></tr>
<tr><td>its.(3n.P)=</td><td>stead-through/via</td><td>you.all.(2p.O)=</td><td>cl.(∅,i)-√be</td></tr>
<tr><td rowspan="3">a eetéenáx̱ has yatee</td><td colspan="4">they all need it</td></tr>
<tr><td>a=</td><td>eetí-náx̱</td><td>has=</td><td>∅-ÿa-√tee</td></tr>
<tr><td>its.(3n.P)=</td><td>stead-through/via</td><td>3ph</td><td>them.(3.O)-cl.(∅,i)-√be</td></tr>
</table>

In this verb and the previous one, the N in the theme stands for **noun**, which often could be a possessive pronoun, such as: du eetéenáx̱ x̱at yatee, "I am in need of them." Any noun can go here, but if it has already been specified then it is common for the possessive pronoun *a* (its) to be here because something needs to be in the N part of the theme.

Most often you will have the noun directly before the rest of the verb phrase, but the word order could change, such as:

káaxwei eetéenáx̱ x̱at yatee (i need coffee)

káaxwei na.oo! a eetéenáx̱ x̱at yatee (buy coffee! i need it)

N + yáx̱ + O-∅-√tee h 1 (na state verb – *object intransitive*) or O to be like N					
a yáx̱ x̱at yatee	i'm like it				
	a=	yáx̱	x̱at=	ÿa-√tee	
	its.(3n.P)=	like	me.(1s.O)=	cl.(∅,i)-√be	
a yáx̱ iyatee	you're like it				
	a=	yáx̱	i-ÿa-√tee		
	its.(3n.P)=	like	you.(2s.O)-cl.(∅,i)-√be		
a yáx̱ yatee	they are like it; it is like it				
	a=	yáx̱	∅-ÿa-√tee		
	its.(3n.P)=	like	them.(3.O)-cl.(∅,i)-√be		
a yáx̱ haa yatee	we're like it				
	a=	yáx̱	haa=	ÿa-√tee	
	its.(3n.P)=	like	us.(1p.O)=	cl.(∅,i)-√be	
a yáx̱ yee yatee	you all are like it				
	a=	yáx̱	yee=	ÿa-√tee	
	its.(3n.P)=	like	you.all.(2p.O)=	cl.(∅,i)-√be	
a yáx̱ has yatee	they all are like it				
	a=	yáx̱	has=	∅-ÿa-√tee	
	its.(3n.P)=	like	3ph=	them.(3.O)-cl.(∅,i)-√be	

This verb has a wide variety of uses. It can be used to say someone is the same clan, as in: *ch'as du yáx̱ yateeyí aa ash x̱ánt uwagút*, 'only the ones like her went by her (often referring to the women of her clan)'. It can also be used to talk about colors with some specific nouns, as in: *x̱'aan yáx̱ yatee*, 'it's red (literally 'it's like fire')'.

This verb is also used for metaphorical concepts, such as: *x'óol' yáx̱ yatee*, which is literally 'it's like a whirlpool' but translates to 'it is chaotic' and can be used to talk about an intense event or something that is out of control. There is also a similar, but slightly different verb: *ayáx̱ yatee*, which is 'it is correct; it is proper'.

tliyéi + yéi + O-∅-√tee [h 1] (na state verb – *object intransitive*)

for O to be still, quiet; for O to stop (car, clock, e.g.); for O to wait

tliyéi yéi x̲at yatee	i am still; i am stopped			
	tliyéi-x'	yéi=	x̲at=	ÿa-√tee
	one.place-at.(residing)	thus=	me.(1s.O)=	cl.(∅,i)-√be
tliyéi yéi iyatee	you are still; you are stopped			
	tliyéi-x'	yéi=	i-ÿa-√tee	
	one.place-at.(residing)	thus=	you.(2s.O)-cl.(∅,i)-√be	
tliyéi yéi yatee	they are still; it is still; they are stopped; it is stopped			
	tliyéi-x'	yéi=	∅-ÿa-√tee	
	one.place-at.(residing)	thus=	them.(3.O)-cl.(∅,i)-√be	
tliyéi yéi haa yatee	we are still; we are stopped			
	tliyéi-x'	yéi=	haa=	ÿa-√tee
	one.place-at.(residing)	thus=	us.(1p.O)=	cl.(∅,i)-√be
tliyéi yéi yee yatee	you all are still; you all are stopped			
	tliyéi-x'	yéi=	yee=	ÿa-√tee
	one.place-at.(residing)	thus=	you.all.(2p.O)=	cl.(∅,i)-√be
tliyéi yéi has yatee	they all are still; they all are stopped			
	tliyéi-x'	yéi=	has=	∅-ÿa-√tee
	one.place-at.(residing)	thus=	3ph=	them.(3.O)-cl.(∅,i)-√be

7B

X̱'akaduneek Yéi Jiné 7

Translation Exercises 7

Lingít → English

x̱at yak'éi	
ilichán	
litseen	
haa yanéekw	
yee wlich'éx̱'w / yee mlich'éx̱'w	
has tuli.aan	
x̱at seiwa.át'	
ilich'éeyáḵw	
haa kaadéix' / haa kayadéix'	

English → Lingít

you all are stingy	
they're mentally strong	
i'm that way	
you stay there	
they/it needs it	
we're like it	
you all are still	
we're cold	

8A

Wáa sá k̲uwanóok?

What are they doing?

“Nineteen twenty-two” ...
dé wtusikóo áwé,
haa jinák̲ yaa nalhásh
haa k̲usteeyí,
haa yoo x̲’atángi.
Yeedát áyá yee a x̲oo aa nx̲alg̲éinin
yées k̲áax’w yá school-x’ yóo ee.
Tsu x̲át áwé kíndaa x̲’éin yaa nax̲aséich.

— K̲aalk̲áawu

In nineteen twenty-two ...
we knew then,
it was drifting out of our hands,
our way of life,
our language.
Now, when I looked at some of you
young people that are going to school.
It makes my head go up with pride.

– Cyril George, K̲ak’weidí

dé	<ÿu>-tu-si-√kóo	á-wé	haa=	jee-nák̲	<ÿaa=	∅-na>-l-√hásh
already	<perfective>-we.(1p.S)-cl.(s,i)-√know	focus-there	our.(1p.P)=	possession-leave.behind	<along=	they/it.(3.O)-progressive>.cl.(l)-√float

haa=	k̲u-s-√tee-yí	haa=	yoo=	x̲’a-∅-√tán-k-i
our.(1p.P)=	area-cl.(d,s)-√be.relational	our.(1p.P)=	to/fro=	mouth-cl.(∅)-√communicate-repeatedly-relational

yeedát	á-yá	yee=	a=	x̲oo	aa
now	focus-right.here	you.all’s.(2p.P)=	its.(3n.P)	among	one(s).(part.i)

a-<na>-x̲a-l-√g̲éin-<in>	yées	k̲áa-x’w	yá	school-x’
a.theme-<contingent>.i(1s.S).cl.(d,l)-√cast.eyes-<contingent/ decessive>	new	person-plural	right.here	school-at.(residing)

yóo	ee	tsu	x̲át	á-wé	kín-daa	x̲’éin	<ÿaa=	na>-x̲a-s-√.áa-ch
to/fro	emtpy.base	again	me	focus-there	upward.around	among	one(s)	<habitual>-i.cl.(d,s)-√inspect-<habitual>

Wáa sá ḵuwanóok?

Dialogue Practice

A	1	Haaw, x̱ooní.	Well, friend.	haaw x̱ooní well friend
B	2	Há'! Yéi yeekoowaat' áwé tlél ix̱wsateenín.	My! For a long time I didn't see you.	há'! yéi= yee-ka-u-ÿa-√wáat' my! thus= time-comparitive-irrealis-cl.(∅,i)-√long á-wé tlél i-<ÿu>-x̱a-sa-√teen-in focus-there not you-<perfective>-i.(1s.S)-cl.(s)-√see-decessive
	3	Wáa sá ḵeeyanóok?	What are you doing?	wáa =sá ḵu-i-ÿa-√nóok how =name areal-you.(2s.S)-cl.(∅,i)-√do/behave
A	4	x̱adaxáash.	i'm cutting	x̱a-da-√xáash i.(1s.S)-cl.(d,∅)-√cut
B	5	daa sá eexáash?	what are you cutting?	daa =sá ∅-i-∅-√xáash what =name it.(3.O)-you.(2s.S)-cl.(∅)-√cut
A	6	x̱áat x̱axáash.	i'm cutting fish.	x̱áat ∅-x̱a-∅-√xáash fish it.(3.O)-i.(1s.S)-cl.(∅)-√cut
A	7	at x̱'éeshi kḵwax'áan	i am going to smoke dryfish.	at x̱'eeshí ∅-<ga-u-ga>-x̱a-∅-√x'áan things.(4n.P) dryfish <future>-i.(1s.S)-cl.(d,∅)-√smoke-(fish)

Conjugating Lingít Verbs

It is now time to begin looking more closely at how verbs function in Lingít. Here are the three ways we need to learn to conjugate verbs in order to use them effectively:

1. **PERSON**

   This is who is doing the verb (subject) and who is affected by the verb (object). As in most things with Lingít, we will learn some basic rules and then see exceptions to those rules, such as using object pronouns for what is actually the subject of the verb and using noun phrases for subjects or objects outside of the verb itself.

2. **MODE**

   In Lingít, verb mode is linked to concepts like whether the verb is completed or not, and if it is happening now or in the future. We will see the complexity of Lingít verb modes over time, but for now you can compare it to past, present, and future in English.

3. **DEPENDENT OR RELATIVE CLAUSES**

   Linking verbs together for cause and effect (it's X that Y) or other ways changes the way the verbs are put together. It is important to learn this so you can begin stringing thoughts together in Lingít. You have already learned phrases that do this, such as *yak'éi i̲xwsateení.*

The following question and answer drill looks at common verbs that work well for a "what are you doing now" type of question. These are conjugated for person using 1st (i), 2nd (you), and third (they) pronouns. The 1st person is used when talking about yourself. The 2nd person is used when talking about the person who are talking to. The 3rd person is used when talking about someone other than who you are talking about.

Keep in mind that the third person subject in pronoun is unmarked. If we did this in English we would say: i did it, you did it, and did it where the third example is the singular they, which we mark here as they.

wáa sá k̲uwanóok?	what are they doing?		
	wáa	=sá	k̲u-∅-ÿa-√nóok
	how	=name	areal-they.(3.S)-cl.(∅,i)-√do/behave
wáa sá k̲eeyanóok?	what are you doing?		
	wáa	=sá	k̲u-i-ÿa-√nóok
	how	=name	areal-you.(2s.S)-cl.(∅,i)-√do/behave
wáa sá k̲ux̲aanóok?	what am i doing?		
	wáa	=sá	k̲u-x̲a-ÿa-√nóok
	how	=name	areal-i.(1s.S)-cl.(∅,i)-√do/behave

(yéi) + k̲u-S-∅-√nook [4] *(na act verb – subject intransitive)*

for S to behave, do, act (in a certain way)

S-∅-√.áa [1] *(positional verb – subject intransitive)* for (singular) S to be seated	
áa	they are sitting ∅-∅-√.áa they.(3.S)-cl.(∅)-√sit/be.situated
ee.áa	you are sitting i-∅-√.áa you.(2s.S)-cl.(∅)-√sit/be.situated
x̱a.áa	i am sitting x̱a-∅-√.áa i.(1s.S)-cl.(∅)-√sit/be.situated

S-∅-√hán [×] *(positional verb – subject intransitive)* for (singular) S to be standing	
hán	they are standing ∅-∅-√hán they.(3.S)-cl.(∅)-√stand/rise
eehán	you are standing i-∅-√hán you.(2s.S)-cl.(∅)-√stand/rise
x̱ahán	i am standing x̱a-∅-√hán i.(1s.S)-cl.(∅)-√stand/rise

at + S-∅-√x̱aa [1] (*∅ act verb – subject intransitive*)

for S to eat

at x̱á	they are eating	at= ∅-∅-√x̱á thing.(4n.O)= they.(3.S)-cl.(∅)-√eat
at eex̱á	you are eating	at= i-∅-√x̱á thing.(4n.O)= you.(2s.S)-cl.(∅)-√eat
at x̱ax̱á	i am eating	at= x̱a-∅-√x̱á thing.(4n.O)= i.(1s.S)-cl.(∅)-√eat

at + S-d+∅-√naa [1] (*∅ act verb – subject intransitive*)

for S to drink

at daná	they are drinking	at= ∅-da-√ná thing.(4n.O)= they.(3.S)-cl.(d,∅)-√drink
at idaná	you are drinking	at= i-da-√ná thing.(4n.O)= you.(2s.S)-cl.(d,∅)-√drink
at x̱adaná	i am drinking	at= x̱a-da-√ná thing.(4n.O)= i.(1s.S)-cl.(d,∅)-√drink

at + S-∅-√look (*∅ act verb – subject intransitive*)

for S to sip (esp. hot liquids)

at lóok	they are sipping	
	at=	∅-∅-√lóok
	thing.(4n.O)=	they.(3.S)-cl.(∅)-√sip.hot.liquid
at eelóok	you are sipping	
	at=	i-∅-√lóok
	thing.(4n.O)=	you.(2s.S)-cl.(∅)-√sip.hot.liquid
at x̲alóok	i am sipping	
	at=	x̲a-∅-√lóok
	thing.(4n.O)=	i.(1s.S)-cl.(∅)-√sip.hot.liquid

at + S-∅-√.een [1] (*∅ act verb – subject intransitive*)

for S to pick (esp. berries) into a container

at een	they are picking (berries)	
	at=	∅-∅-√.een
	thing.(4n.O)=	they.(3.S)-cl.(∅)-√carry.filled.container
at ee.een	you are picking (berries)	
	at=	i-∅-√.een
	thing.(4n.O)=	you.(2s.S)-cl.(∅)-√√carry.filled.container
at x̲a.een	i am picking (berries)	
	at=	x̲a-∅-√.een
	thing.(4n.O)=	i.(1s.S)-cl.(∅)-√carry.filled.container

at + ga-S-d+s-√.ee (∅ *act verb – subject intransitive*) for S to cook for immediate consumption; for S to cook for immediate for self		
at gas.ée	they are cooking (for immediate consumption / for self)	
	at= thing.(4n.O)=	<ga>-∅-s-√.ée <for.self>-they.(3.S)-cl.(d,s)-√cook
at gees.ée	you are cooking (for immediate consumption / for self)	
	at= thing.(4n.O)=	<ga>-i-s-√.ée <for.self>-you.(2s.S)-cl.(d,s)-√cook
at gax̱as.ée	i am cooking (for immediate consumption / for self)	
	at= thing.(4n.O)=	<ga>-x̱a-s-√.ée <for.self>-i.(1s.S)-cl.(d,s)-√cook

at + S-s-√.ee (∅ *act verb – subject intransitive*) for S to cook		
at sa.ée	they are cooking	
	at= thing.(4n.O)=	∅-sa-√.ée they.(3.S)-cl.(s)-√cook
at isa.ée	you are cooking	
	at= thing.(4n.O)=	i-sa-√.ée you.(2s.S)-cl.(s)-√cook
at x̱asa.ée	i am cooking	
	at= thing.(4n.O)=	x̱a-sa-√.ée i.(1s.S)-cl.(s)-√cook

S-d+∅-√xaash (*na act verb – subject intransitive*) for S to cut	
daxáash	they are cutting ∅-da-√xáash they.(3.S)-cl.(d,∅)-√cut/saw
idaxáash	you are cutting i-da-√xáash you.(2s.S)-cl.(d,∅)-√cut/saw
x̱adaxáash	i am cutting x̱a-da-√xáash i.(1s.S)-cl.(d,∅)-√cut/saw

S-d+∅-√xéet' (act) (*g̱a act verb – subject intransitive*) for S to sweep	
daxít'kw	they are sweeping ∅-da-√xít'-kw they.(3.S)-cl.(d,∅)-√sweep/scrape/brush-repeatedly
idaxít'kw	you are sweeping i-da-√xít'-kw you.(2s.S)-cl.(d,∅)-√sweep/scrape/brush-repeatedly
x̱adaxít'kw	i am sweeping x̱a-da-√xít'-kw i.(1s.S)-cl.(d,∅)-√sweep/scrape/brush-repeatedly

S-d+∅-√.óos' (act) (*na act verb – subject intransitive*) for S to wash	
da.ús'kw	they are washing
	∅-da-√.ús'-kw they.(3.S)-cl.(d,∅)-√wash-repeatedly
ida.ús'kw	you are washing
	i-da-√.ús'-kw you.(2s.S)-cl.(d,∅)-√wash-repeatedly
x̱ada.ús'kw	i am washing
	x̱a-da-√.ús'-kw i.(1s.S)-cl.(d,∅)-√wash-repeatedly

S-d+∅-√ḵaa [2] (*∅ act verb – subject intransitive*) for S to sew	
daḵéis'	they are sewing
	∅-da-√ḵáa-s' they.(3.S)-cl.(d,∅)-√sew-in.series
idaḵéis'	you are sewing
	i-da-√ḵáa-s' you.(2s.S)-cl.(d,∅)-√sew-in.series
x̱adaḵéis'	i am sewing
	x̱a-da-√ḵáa-s' i.(1s.S)-cl.(d,∅)-√sew-in.series

ka-S-d+∅-√ch'áak'w (*∅ act verb – subject intransitive*) for S to carve (usually smaller, detailed work) using a knife	
kadach'áak'w	they are carving (smaller, more detailed work)
	ka-∅-da-√ch'áak'w surface-they.(3.S)-cl.(d,∅)-√carve/nick
keedach'áak'w	you are carving (smaller, more detailed work)
	ka-i-da-√ch'áak'w surface-you.(2s.S)-cl.(d,∅)-√carve/nick
kax̱dach'áak'w	i am carving (smaller, more detailed work)
	ka-x̱a-da-√ch'áak'w surface-i.(1s.S)-cl.(d,∅)-√carve/nick

ka-S-s+d-√nei 3 (*∅ act verb – subject intransitive*) for S to knit, weave, or crochet	
kasné	they are knitting, weaving, or crocheting
	ka-∅-s-√né surface-they.(3.S)-cl.(d,s)-√weave.yarns/knit/crochet/make.cloth
keesné	you are knitting, weaving, or crocheting
	ka-i-s-√né surface-you.(2s.S)-cl.(d,s)-√weave.yarns/knit/crochet/make.cloth
kax̱asné	i am knitting, weaving, or crocheting
	ka-x̱a-s-√né surface-i.(1s.S)-cl.(d,s)-√weave.yarns/knit/crochet/make.cloth

a-S-∅-√l'óon × (*na act verb – subject intransitive*) for S to hunt	
al'óon	they are hunting a-∅-∅-√l'oon a.theme-they.(3.S)-cl.(∅)-√hunt
eel'óon	you are hunting a-i-∅-√l'oon a.theme-you.(2s.S)-cl.(∅)-√hunt
ax̱al'óon	i am hunting a-x̱a-∅-√l'oon a.theme-i.(1s.S)-cl.(∅)-√hunt

a-S-s+d-√g̱eiwú × (*na act verb – subject intransitive*) for S to fish with net, seine	
asg̱eiwú	they are seining a-∅-s-√g̱eiwú a.theme-they.(3.S)-cl.(d,s)-√fish.with.net
eesg̱eiwú	you are seining a-i-s-√g̱eiwú a.theme-you.(2s.S)-cl.(d,s)-√fish.with.net
ax̱asg̱eiwú	i am seining a-x̱a-s-√g̱eiwú a.theme-i.(1s.S)-cl.(d,s)-√fish.with.net

a-S-s+d-√t'eix̱ [×] *(na act verb – subject intransitive)* for S to fish with hooks, catch on a hook, troll	
ast'eix̱	they are fishing (with hooks)
	a-∅-s-√t'eix̱ a.theme-they.(3.S)-cl.(d,s)-√fish.with.hook
eest'eix̱	you are fishing (with hooks)
	a-i-s-√t'eix̱ a.theme-you.(2s.S)-cl.(d,s)-√fish.with.hook
ax̱ast'eix̱	i am fishing (with hooks)
	a-x̱a-s-√t'eix̱ a.theme-i.(1s.S)-cl.(d,s)-√fish.with.hook

at S-∅-√.únt [×] *(na act verb – subject intransitive)* for S to shoot (with firearms)		
at únt	they are shooting	
	at= thing.(4n.O)=	∅-∅-√.ún-t they.(3.S)-cl.(∅)-√shoot.firearm
at ee.únt	you are shooting	
	at= thing.(4n.O)=	i-∅-√.ún-t you.(2s.S)-cl.(∅)-√shoot.firearm
at x̱a.únt	i am shooting	
	at= thing.(4n.O)=	x̱a-∅-√.ún-t i.(1s.S)-cl.(∅)-√shoot.firearm

S-d+∅-√tóow [×] (*na act verb – subject intransitive*) for S to read, count	
datóow	they are reading
	∅-da-√tóow they.(3.S)-cl.(d,∅)-√read/count/teach
idatóow	you are reading
	i-da-√tóow you.(2s.S)-cl.(d,∅)-√read/count/teach
x̱adatóow	i am reading
	x̱a-da-√tóow i.(1s.S)-cl.(d,∅)-√read/count/teach

sh tóo at S-l+d-√tóow [×] (*∅ act verb – subject intransitive*) for S to study, teach oneself	
sh tóo at iltóow	they are studying
	sh= tóo at= i-∅-l-√tóow self.(rflx.P)= inside thing.(4n.O)= peg.vowel-they.(3.S)-cl.(d,l)-read/count/teach
sh tóo at eeltóow	you are studying
	sh= tóo at= i-l-√tóow self.(rflx.P)= inside thing.(4n.O)= you.(2s.S)-cl.(d,l)-read/count/teach
sh tóo at x̱altóow	i am studying
	sh= tóo at= x̱a-l-√tóow self.(rflx.P)= inside thing.(4n.O)= i.(1s.S)-cl.(d,l)-read/count/teach

ka-S-sh+d-√xeet (*∅ act verb – subject intransitive*) for S to write, draw, or paint; for S to take a photograph	
kashxeet	they are writing ka-∅-sh-√xeet surface-they.(3.S)-cl.(d,sh,)-√mark/write
keeshxeet	you are writing ka-i-sh-√xeet surface-you.(2s.S)-cl.(d,sh,)-√mark/write
kax̲ashxeet	i am writing ka-x̲a-sh-√xeet surface-i.(1s.S)-cl.(d,sh,)-√mark/write

at S-∅-√shee h 4 (*ga act verb – subject intransitive*) for S to sing	
at shí	they are singing at= ∅-∅-√shí thing.(4n.O)= they.(3.S)-cl.(∅)-√sing
at eeshí	you are singing at= i-∅-√shí thing.(4n.O)= you.(2s.S)-cl.(∅)-√sing
at x̲ashí	i am singing at= x̲a-∅-√shí thing.(4n.O)= i.(1s.S)-cl.(∅)-√sing

a-S-∅-√l'eix̲ [×] (*na act verb – subject intransitive*) for S to dance	
al'eix̲	they are dancing a-∅-∅-√l'eix̲ a.theme-they.(3.S)-cl.(∅)-√dance
eel'eix̲	you are dancing a-i-∅-√l'eix̲ a.theme-you.(2s.S)-cl.(∅)-√dance
ax̲al'eix̲	i am dancing a-x̲a-∅-√l'eix̲ a.theme-i.(1s.S)-cl.(∅)-√dance

S-d+∅-√gwaal (*ga act verb – subject intransitive*) for S to beat (esp. drum), ring (bell); for S to stab	
dagwáal	they are beating (the drum) ∅-da-√gwáal they.(3.S)-cl.(d,∅)-√beat/knock/ring/hit/stab
idagwáal	you are beating (the drum) i-da-√gwáal you.(2s.S)-cl.(d,∅)-√beat/knock/ring/hit/stab
x̲adagwáal	i am beating (the drum) x̲a-da-√gwáal i.(1s.S)-cl.(d,∅)-√beat/knock/ring/hit/stab

S-∅-√gaa<u>x</u> (*ga act verb – subject intransitive*) for (singluar) S to cry, weep; for (singular) S to mourn, lament	
gáa<u>x</u>	they are crying
	∅-∅-√gáa<u>x</u> they.(3.S)-cl.(∅)-√cry
eegáa<u>x</u>	you are crying
	i-∅-√gáa<u>x</u> you.(2s.S)-cl.(∅)-√cry
<u>x</u>agáa<u>x</u>	i am crying
	<u>x</u>a-∅-√gáa<u>x</u> i.(1s.S)-cl.(∅)-√cry

at S-∅-√shoo<u>k</u> (*∅ act verb – subject intransitive*) for S to laugh		
at shoo<u>k</u>	they are laughing	
	at= thing.(4n.O)=	∅-∅-√shoo<u>k</u> they.(3.S)-cl.(∅)-√laugh/smile
at eeshoo<u>k</u>	you are laughing	
	at= thing.(4n.O)=	i-∅-√shoo<u>k</u> you.(2s.S)-cl.(∅)-√laugh/smile
at <u>x</u>ashoo<u>k</u>	i am laughing	
	at= thing.(4n.O)=	<u>x</u>a-∅-√shoo<u>k</u> i.(1s.S)-cl.(∅)-√laugh/smile

yoo tu-S-∅-√taan 5 (*∅ act verb – subject intransitive*)

for (singular) S to think over, consider, make up one's mind

yoo tuwatánk	they are thinking yoo= tu-∅-ÿá-√tán-k to/fro= inside-they.(3.S)-cl.(∅,i)-√communicate-repeatedly
yoo teeyatánk	you are thinking yoo= tu-i-ÿá-√tán-k to/fro= inside-you.(2s.S)-cl.(∅,i)-√communicate-repeatedly
yoo tux̲aatánk	i am thinking yoo= tu-x̲a-ÿá-√tán-k to/fro= inside-i.(1s.S)-cl.(∅)-√communicate-repeatedly

yoo x̲'a-S-∅-√taan 5 (*∅ act verb – subject intransitive*)

for (singular) S to speak, talk

yoo x̲'ayatánk	they are talking yoo= x̲'a-∅-ÿá-√tán-k to/fro= mouth-they.(3.S)-cl.(∅,i)-√communicate-repeatedly
yoo x̲'eeyatánk	you are talking yoo= x̲'a-i-ÿá-√tán-k to/fro= mouth-you.(2s.S)-cl.(∅,i)-√communicate-repeatedly
yoo x̲'ax̲aatánk	i am talking yoo= x̲'a-x̲a-ÿá-√tán-k to/fro= mouth-i.(1s.S)-cl.(∅)-√communicate-repeatedly

sh ka-S-l+d-√neek [×] (*na act verb – subject intransitive*) for S to tell a story		
sh kalneek	they are telling a story	
	sh= self.(rflx.P)=	ka-∅-l-√neek surface-they.(3.S)-cl.(d,l)-√tell/report/interpret
sh keelneek	you are telling a story	
	sh= self.(rflx.P)=	ka-i-l-√neek surface-you.(2s.S)-cl.(d,l)-√tell/report/interpret
sh kax̱alneek	i am telling a story	
	sh= self.(rflx.P)=	ka-x̱a-l-√neek surface-i.(1s.S)-cl.(d,l)-√tell/report/interpret

yéi ji-(na)-S-∅-√nei [h 2] (*na act verb – subject intransitive*) for S to work; for S to do		
yéi jiné	they are working	
	yéi= thus=	ji-∅-∅-√né hand-they.(3.S)-cl.(∅)-√do
yéi jeené	you are working	
	yé=i thus=	ji-i-∅-√né hand-you.(2s.S)-cl.(∅)-√do
yéi jix̱ané	i am working	
	yéi= thus=	ji-x̱a-∅-√né hand-i.(1s.S)-cl.(∅)-√do

ash ka-u-S-l+d-√yát [×] (*na act verb – subject intransitive*)

for S to play (esp. active games)

ash koolyát	they are playing	ash= ka-u-∅-l-√yát itself= surface-irrealis-they.(3.S)-cl.(d,l)-√child
ash keelyát	you are playing	ash= ka-u-i-l-√yát itself= surface-irrealis-you.(2s.S)-cl.(d,l)-√child
ash kux̲alyát	i am playing	ash= ka-u-x̲a-l-√yát itself= surface-irrealis-i.(1s.S)-cl.(d,l)-√child

k̲u-S-s+d-√.ook' [×] (*na act verb – subject intransitive*)

for S to entertain, amuse oneself; for S to play quietly

k̲us.ook'	they are playing quietly, amusing themself	k̲u-∅-s-√.ook' areal-they.(3.S)-cl.(d,s)-√play.quietly/amuse.self
k̲uyis.ook'	you are playing quietly, amusing yourself	k̲u-i-s-√.ook' areal-irrealis-you.(2s.S)-cl.(d,s)-√play.quietly/amuse.self
k̲ux̲as.ook'	I am playing quietly, amusing myself	k̲u-x̲a-s-√.ook' areal-i.(1s.S)-cl.(d,s)-√play.quietly/amuse.self

ch'u this particle appears with other words, as in the following examples: ch'u déix̱ — both ch'u shóogu — the same ch'u tle ~ ch'u tlei — just when; just while ch'u tleix̱ — forever		same; even; still
	ch'eix̱' / ch'eex̱'	thimbleberries
	ch'éen	hair ribbon
	kach'ák'waa	rounded chisel

	éil’	salt; ocean; salt water
	gáal’	clams
	yéil’	elderberries
	téel’	chum, dog salmon

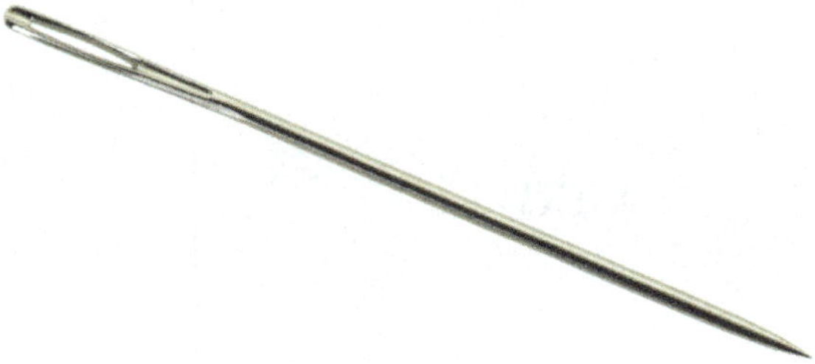	táax'ál'	needle
	l'ook	coho, silver salmon
	l'aak	dress
	l'ax̱keit	mask

 	xákwl'i	soapberries
	kax̱'íl'aa	iron

8B

Ḵaa X̱’akaneek Kawdu.aagú 8

Translation Exercises 8

Lingít → English

Wáa sá k̲uwanóok?	
Sh tóo at x̲altóow.	
Ee.áa.	
Idak̲éis'.	
At x̲ax̲á.	
X̲adatóow.	
Idagwáal.	
Ash koolyát.	
Ax̲asg̲eiwú.	

English → Lingít

You are picking berries.	
I am working.	
What am i doing?	
You are laughing.	
I am standing.	
I am telling a story.	
They are writing.	
I am fishing (with hooks).	

9A

Daa sáwé aX̱á?

What are they eating?

Ch'u tlákwdáx̱
haa dachx̱án
haa kináa kei wtusinúk.
Aaa.
X̱'atulitseen.
Tsu ḵushtuyáx̱ daa sá yaa tushigéiyi át
du jeedéi yatx̱ gatooteeyín
haa dachx̱ánx̱ siteeyi ḵáa.

— Ḵaal.átk'

Even from long ago
we have placed our grandchildren
high above ourselves.
Yes.
We cherish them.
Even those things we treasure
we used to offer up to them,
to those who are our grandchildren.

– Charlie Joseph, Kaagwaantaan

(*Because We Cherish You*, Dauenhauer & Dauenhauer 1981)

ch'u	tlákw-dáx̱	haa	dachx̱án	haa	kináa-x'	kei=	<ÿu>-tu-si-√núk
even	forever-from	our.(1p.P)=	grandchild	our.(1p.P)=	above-at.(residing)	up.conj=	<perfective>-we.(1p.S)-cl.(s,i)-√move.sitting

aaa	∅-x̱'a-tu-li-√tseen	tsu	ḵushtuyáx̱	daa	=sá
yes	them.(3.O)-mouth-we.(1p.S)-cl.(l,i)-√strong	again	doesn't.matter	what	=name

ÿaa=	tu-shi-√géiyi=	át	du	jee-dé	ya(n)-dáx
mentally=	we.(1p.S)-cl.(sh,i)-√treasure.attributive=	thing.(4n.i)	their.(3h.P)=	possession-towards	completion-from

ga-tu-∅-√tee-yín	haa=	dachx̱ánx̱	si-√tee-yi	ḵáa
<hortative>-we.(1pS)-cl.(∅)-√carry.(compact/abstract)-decessive	our.(1p.P)=	grandchild-essive	cl.(s,i)-√be-attributive	person.(4n.i)

Daa sáwé ax̱á?

Dialogue Practice

A	1	wáa sá yaa at nanein i een?	what's happening with you? wáa sá at= <na>-∅-√néi-<n> how =voice thing.(4n.O)= <progressive>-cl.(∅)-√do-<progressive> i= ee-n your.(2s.P)=a empty-base.with
B	2	haaw, ch'a yeedát áwé	well, just right now haaw ch'a yeedát á-wé well just now focus-there
	3	yá x'úx' x̱atóow.	i am reading this book. yá x'úx' ∅-x̱a-∅-√tóow right.here paper/book it.(3.O)-i.(1s.S)-cl.(∅)-√read/count/teach
A	4	daat daat át sáwé?	what it is about? daat daat át =sá-wé what about/around thing.(4n.i) =name-there
	5	aadóoch sá kawshixít?	who wrote it? aadóo-ch =sá ∅-ka-<ÿu>-shi-√xít who.ergative =name it.(3.O) surface <perfective>-cl.(sh,i)-√mark/write
B	6	Lingít sh kalneegí x'úx'u áyá,	it is a book of Lingít stories, Lingít sh ka-l-√neek-í Lingit self.(rflx.O) surface-cl.(d,l)-√tell.relational x'úx'-u á-yá paper/book focus.right-here
	7	Ḵeixwnéi ḵa Xwaayeenáḵ	Nora Dauenhauer and Richard Dauenhauer Ḵeixwnéi ḵa Xwaayeenáḵ Nora Dauenhauer and Richard Dauenhauer
		has akawshixít.	they wrote it. has= a-ka-<ÿu>-∅-shi-√xít 3ph= it.(3.O)-surface-<perfective>-they.(3.S)-cl.(sh,i)-√mark/write
A	8	ax̱ tuwáa sigóo aa x̱wa.oowú.	i want to buy one; i want to buy some. ax̱= tu-ÿáa-x' si-√góo my.(1s.P)= inside-faceat.(residing) cl-(s,i)-√happy aa= <ÿu>-x̱a-ÿa-√.oow-ú one(s).(part.O)= <perfective>-i.(1s.S.)-cl.(∅,i)-√buy.subordinate

The subject in Lingít verbs

The last chapter focused on the **object pronoun** in Lingít verbs, which is usually the one impacted by the verb. The **subject** is usually the one who does the verb. The six **subject pronouns** that we will practice in this chapter are in the table to the right.

1S	x̱a-	i
2S	i-	you
3	∅-	they
1P	tu-	we
2P	yi-	you all
3P	has + ∅-	they all

Keep in mind that the Lingít verb has certain parts that appear in a specific order. The illustration below shows the order of these parts. The object comes first, and then the subject, followed b the classifier and the stem. While practicing the subjects in this chapter, learn these verbs and try and use them.

In this chapter, we will be changing the **subject pronoun** in the verb. Remember that the **object** is usually the one impacted by the verb. In English, these are object pronouns: me, you, her, him, us, you all, and them. The **subject** is the usually the one who does the verb, and in English **subject pronouns** are: i, you, she, he, we, you all, and they.

The pronouns are built into the verb and must appear in a specific order. Note that in most of the third person verbs in this chapter, the **object** becomes a-. This happens when both the **object** and the **subject** are third person singular or plural. In English these would be the **objects** "her, him, it, and them" and the **subjects** "she, he, it, and they."

Changing the subject pronoun in verbs

daa sá ax̱á?	what are they eating? daa =sá a-∅-∅-√x̱á what =name it.(3.O)-they.(3.S)-cl.(∅)-√eat
x̱áat ax̱á.	they are eating fish. x̱áat a-∅-∅-√x̱á fish it.(3.O)-they.(3.S)-cl.(∅)-√eat
____ ax̱á.	they are eating ____. ____ a-∅-∅-√x̱á {food} it.(3.O)-they.(3.S)-cl.(∅)-√eat
ax̱ ____ ____ ax̱á.	my ____ is eating ____. ax̱= ____ ____ a-∅-∅-√x̱á my.(1S.P)= {kinship term} {food} it.(3.O)-they.(3.S)-cl.(∅)-√eat

aadóo sá x̱áat ax̱á?	who is eating fish? aadóo =sá x̱áat a-∅-∅-√x̱á who =name fish it.(3.O)-they.(3.S)-cl.(∅)-√eat
ax̱ éesh x̱áat ax̱á.	my father is eating fish. ax̱= éesh x̱áat a-∅-∅-√x̱á my.(1s.P)= father fish it.(3.O)-they.(3.S)-cl.(∅)-√eat
daa sá eex̱á?	what are you eating? daa =sá ∅-i-∅-√x̱á what =name it.(3.O)-you.(2s.S)-cl.(∅)-√eat
daa sáwé eex̱á?	what is that you are eating? daa =sá-wé ∅-i-∅-√x̱á what =name-there it.(3.O)-you.(2s.S)-cl.(∅)-√eat
x̱áat x̱ax̱á.	i am eating fish. x̱áat ∅-x̱a-∅-√x̱á fish it.(3.O)-i.(1s.S)-cl.(∅)-√eat
tax̱héeni alóok.	they are sipping broth (soup). tax̱héeni a-∅-∅-√lóok soup/broth it.(3.O)-they.(3.S)-cl.(∅)-√sip.hot.liquid
daa sá alóok?	what are they sipping? daa =sá a-∅-∅-√lóok what =name it.(3.O)-they.(3.S)-cl.(∅)-√sip.hot.liquid
____ alóok.	they are sipping ____. ____ a-∅-∅-√lóok {hot liquid} it.(3.O)-they.(3.S)-cl.(∅)-√sip.hot.liquid

tax̱héeni	broth; soup

	cháayu	tea
	káaxwei	coffee

aadóo sá ____ alóok?	who is sipping ____? aadóo =sá ____ a-∅-∅-√lóok who =name {hot liquid} it.(3.O)-they.(3.S)-cl.(∅)-√sip.hot.liquid
aadóo sáwé ____ alóok?	who is that sipping ____? aadóo =sá-wé who =name-there ____ a-∅-∅-√lóok {hot liquid} it.(3.O)-they.(3.S)-cl.(∅)-√sip.hot.liquid
ax̱ ____ ____ alóok.	my ____ is sipping ____. ax= ____ my.(1s.P)= {kinship term} ____ a-∅-∅-√lóok {hot liquid} it.(3.O)-they.(3.S)-cl.(∅)-√sip.hot.liquid
cháayu x̱alóok.	i am sipping tea. cháayu ∅-x̱a-∅-√lóok tea it.(3.O)-i.(1s.S)-cl.(∅)-√sip.hot.liquid

<table>
<tr><td rowspan="2">daa sá eelóok?</td><td>what are you sipping?</td></tr>
<tr><td>daa =sá Ø-i-Ø-√lóok
what =voice it.(3.O)-you.(2s.S)-cl.(Ø)-√sip.hot.liquid</td></tr>
<tr><td rowspan="2">____ x̱alóok.</td><td>i am sipping ____.</td></tr>
<tr><td>____ Ø-x̱a-Ø-√lóok
____ it.(3.O)-i.(1s.S)-cl.(Ø)-√sip.hot.liquid</td></tr>
</table>

<table>
<tr><td rowspan="2">héen adaná.</td><td>they are drinking water.</td></tr>
<tr><td>héen a-Ø-da-√ná
soup/broth it.(3.O)-they.(3.S)-cl.(d,Ø)-√drink</td></tr>
<tr><td rowspan="2">daa sá adaná?</td><td>what are they drinking?</td></tr>
<tr><td>daa =sá a-Ø-dá-√ná
what =voice it.(3.O)-they.(3.S)-cl.(d,Ø)-√drink</td></tr>
<tr><td rowspan="2">____ adaná.</td><td>they are drinking ____.</td></tr>
<tr><td>____ a-Ø-dá-√ná
____ it.(3.O)-they.(3.S)-cl.(Ø)-√drink</td></tr>
</table>

	áanjís kahéeni	orange juice
	wasóos l'aa tux̱áni / wínk	milk

	géewaa	beer
	náaw	liquor

daa sá idaná?	what are you drinking? daa =sá ∅-i-dá-√ná what =name it.(3.O)-you.(2s.S)-cl.(d,∅)-√drink
____ x̱adaná.	i am drinking ____. ___ a-∅-dá-√ná ___ it.(3.O)-they.(3.S)-cl.(∅)-√drink

aadóo sáwé at kahéeni adaná?	who is that drinking juice? aadóo =sá-wé at= ka-héen-i who =name.there thing's.(4n.P)= surface.water.relational a-∅-da-√ná it.(3.O)-they.(3.S)-cl.(d,∅)-√drink
ax̱ sáni at kahéeni adaná.	my paternal uncle is drinking juice. ax̱= sáni_ at= ka-héen-i my.(1s.P)= paternal-uncle thing's.(4n.P) surface.water.relational a-∅-da-√ná it.(3.O)-they.(3.S)-cl.(d,∅)-√drink

daa sá yéi adaané?	what are they doing?
	daa =sá yéi= a-daa-∅-∅-√né what =name thus= it.(3.O)-around/about-they.(3.S)-cl.(∅)-√do
x̱áat ast'eix̱.	they are fishing (with a hook) for fish.
	x̱áat a-∅-s-√t'eix̱. fish it.(3.O)-they.(3.S)-cl.(d,s)-√fish.with.hook

	x̱áat	fish; salmon (coast); trout (interior)
	l'ook	coho, silver salmon
	téel'	chum, dog salmon

	chа́as’	humpy, pink salmon
	g̱aat	sockeye, red salmon
	t’á	chinook, king salmon
	yaaw	herring

	saak	eulachon, hooligan, candlefish
	sháach’	smelt
	took̲	needlefish, sand lance
	cháatl	halibut

	dzánti	flounder
	léiḵ'w	red snapper, yellow eye, rockfish
	chudéi	tom cod
	s'áax̱'	grey cod

	ishk̲een	black cod
	x̲'wáat'	Dolly Varden trout
	x'éitaa	cutthroat trout
	aashát	steelhead

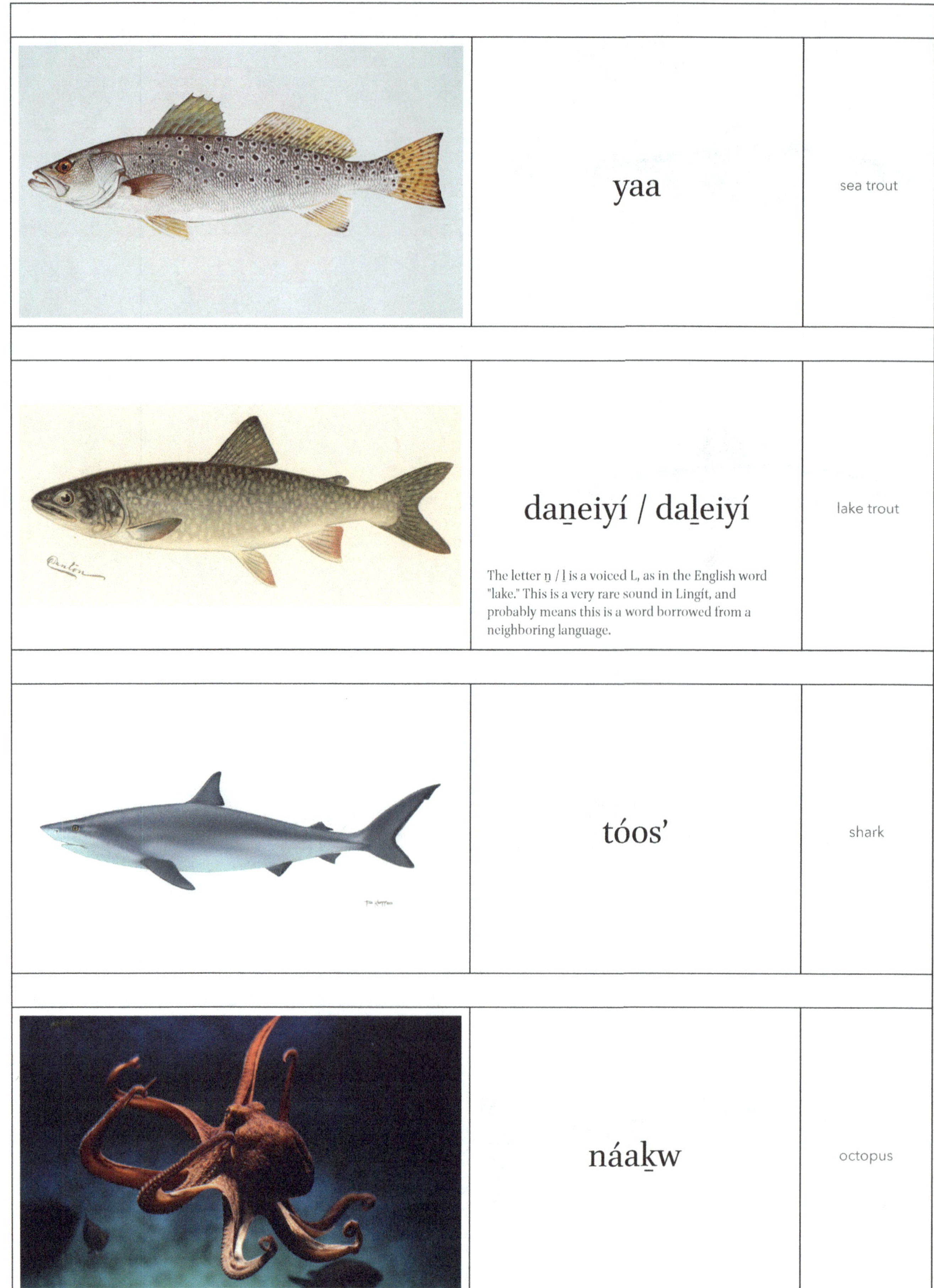

	yaa	sea trout
	daṉeiyí / daḻeiyí The letter ṉ / ḻ is a voiced L, as in the English word "lake." This is a very rare sound in Lingít, and probably means this is a word borrowed from a neighboring language.	lake trout
	tóos'	shark
	náaḵw	octopus

____ axáash.	they are cutting ____.	
	___ a-∅-∅-√xáash ___ them/it.(3.O)-they.(3.S)-cl.(∅)-√cut/saw	
____ asg̱eiwú.	they are fishing ____ (with a net).	
	___ a-∅-s-√g̱eiwú ___ them/it.(3.O)-they.(3.S)-cl.(d,s)-√net	
____ agas.ée.	they are cooking ____ (for self or immediate consumption).	
	___ a-<ga>-∅-s-√.ée ___ them/it.(3.O).<for.self>-they.(3.S)-cl.(d,s)-√cook	
____ ak'éx̱'t	they are gaffing ____.	
	___ a-∅-∅-√k'éx̱'-t ___ it.(3.O)-they.(3.S)-cl.(∅)-√gaff-repeatedly	

Word order & sentence structure

We are going to look into the components of the verb that are changing when conjugating, but first we will look at how sentences are forming as noun phrases interact with verb phrases to make our sentences more dynamic. Lingít has a lot of flexibility in word order, but you will learn that the most important information comes first. The information which comes first in a verb phrase is called theis called the **forephrase**. For example, you can see in the examples above that the noun comes before the verb (l'ook axáash, téel' axáash, etc). When making a statement, the most important information comes first, forming the forephrase, which is easiest to show with answers to questions. Whatever type of information the question is seeking should typically come first in the response. For example:

Daa sá axáash i éesh? → L'ook axáash ax̱ éeshch.

Aadóoch sá axáash wé l'ook? → Ax̱ éeshch áwé xáash wé l'ook.

Daa sá yéi adaané wé l'ook, i éeshch? → Axáash áwé wé l'ook, ax̱ éesh.

These are only samples, and there may be a great deal of variation among speakers in terms of word order. For now, let's take a look at the variety of possibilities within the patterns we have learned in this chapter. You could rearrange the words in the following table to make over a thousand sentences:

POSSESSIVE PRONOUN	KINSHIP TERM	NOUN PHRASE (OBJECT)	VERB
ax̱	éesh	x̱áat	asg̱eiwú
i	tláa	t'á	ast'eix̱
du	léelk'w	cháatl	agas.ée
haa	káak	l'ook	ax̱á
yee	aat	gaat	axáash
has du	sáni	x̱'éitaa	ak'éx̱'t

Another aspect of Lingít grammar for the Lingít student to examine is the placement of the *gé* question particle in Lingít sentences. There is some flexibility in terms of what is being asked, but you should pay close attention to specific sentences that may require the question marker to be placed in specific locations.

I tláa gé t'á axáash? → Aaa. Ax̱ tláa áwé t'á axáash.

T'á gé axáash i tláach? → Aaa. T'á axáash ax̱ tláach.

Axáash gé i tláach wé t'á? → Aaa. Axáash áwé ax̱ tláach wé t'á.

Again, we see how the word order of the question shapes the word order of the answer. Also, the *gé* question marker comes immediately after the item it is specifically questioning. In similar fashion, the type of question determines the appropriate answer. The table on the left below shows how the verb can be inserted and conjugated to the second person singular subject (2s.S = you) and the table on the right shows how to conjugate that verb as an answer with a first person singular subject (1s.S = i). The specifying noun can change, but the verb in the answer should match the verb in the question.

QUESTION PARTICLES	VERB
daa sá	eesg̱eiwú
	eest'eix̱
	gees.ée
	eex̱á
	eexáash
	eek'éx̱'t

NOUN PHRASE (OBJECT)	VERB
x̱áat	x̱asg̱eiwú
t'á	x̱ast'eix̱
cháatl	gax̱as.ée
l'ook	x̱ax̱á
g̱aat	x̱axáash
x̱'éitaa	x̱ak'éx̱'t

To begin untangling how these verbs are working, we should introduce some fundamental concepts in the Lingít verb, and then see how they change when conjugating for person, and then how contraction functions in these changes. To start with, let's take a look at the 1st, 2nd, and 3rd person conjugations of the verbs in the above table.

1S = I	2S = YOU	3 = THEY
x̱asg̱eiwú	eesg̱eiwú	asg̱eiwú
x̱ast'eix̱	eest'eix̱	ast'eix̱
gax̱as.ée	gees.ée	gas.ée
x̱ax̱á	eex̱á	ax̱á
x̱axáash	eexáash	axáash
x̱ak'éx̱'t	eek'éx̱'t	ak'éx̱'t
x̱asa.ée	isa.ée	as.ée

Note that for the verb "to cook" there are two common ways to talk about cooking. For many speakers, *x̱asa.ée* would be interpreted as "i am cooking." With an added suffix ga- (for self), *gax̱as.ée* could be interpreted as "i am cooking for myself." Both examples are shown in these two tables.

At the beginning of this chapter, we looked at a graphic that shows the basic components inside of a verb, and we are going to add one more, and then expand each of these components to see what kinds of options there are within them and then see how it impacts neighboring components. These examples are using transitive verbs, which means there is both an **object** and a **subject** in the verb. Not all verbs have both of these, as **object intransitive** verbs only have an object, **subject intransitive** verbs only have a subject, and **impersonal** verbs have neither object nor subject.

Here is the graphic showing the basic components of a transitive verb:

We are going to add more categories to our verb illustration, explain basically what these components are doing, and then see how they are working in the verbs from this chapter. We have to add to the complexity somewhat in order to see some of the things that are going on in verb conjugation, and this will help us to conjugate verbs for person and for mode. Here is the more complex verb illustration:

We will look at how some of these components are working in the verbs we have learned. Please note that the verb root is often written and documented with a long low vowel (√x̱aa instead of √x̱á), but we are keeping it the same here so you can focus on the **object** and **subject** for now.

Analyzing parts of verbs

PREVERB	OBJECT	THEMATIC	CONJUGATION	SUBJECT	CLASSIFIER	STEM
BASIC DEFINITION & FUNCTION						
determines type of motion, or puts the verb into different modes	impacted by verb (usually)	alters meaning and creates new verb	puts the verb into different modes	does the verb (usually)	denotes completion, middle voice, changes in transitivity, or classification	contains the core meaning of the verb

PREVERB	OBJECT	THEMATIC	CONJUGATION	SUBJECT	CLASSIFIER	STEM	SUFFIX	COMPLETE VERB
—	Ø-	—	—	x̱a-	Ø-	√x̱á	—	x̱ax̱á
—	a-	—	—	Ø-	Ø-	√x̱á	—	ax̱á
—	Ø-	—	—	i-	Ø-	√x̱á	—	eex̱á
—	Ø-	—	—	x̱a-	Ø-	√lóok	—	x̱alóok
—	a-	—	—	Ø-	Ø-	√lóok	—	alóok
—	Ø-	—	—	i-	Ø-	√lóok	—	eelóok
—	Ø-	—	—	x̱a-	da-	√ná [1]	—	x̱adaná
—	a-	—	—	Ø-	da-	√ná [1]	—	adaná
—	Ø-	—	—	i-	da-	√ná [1]	—	idaná
—	Ø-	—	—	x̱a-	s-	√t'eix̱	—	x̱ast'eix̱
—	a-	—	—	Ø-	s-	√t'eix̱	—	ast'eix̱
—	Ø-	—	—	i-	s-	√t'eix̱	—	eest'eix̱
—	Ø-	—	—	x̱a-	Ø-	√xáash	—	x̱axáash
—	a-	—	—	Ø-	Ø-	√xáash	—	axáash
—	Ø-	—	—	i-	Ø-	√xáash	—	eexáash

PREVERB	OBJECT	THEMATIC	CONJUGATION	SUBJECT	CLASSIFIER	STEM	SUFFIX	COMPLETE VERB
—	∅-	—	—	x̱a-	s-	√g̱eiwú	—	x̱asg̱eiwú
—	a-	—	—	∅-	s-	√g̱eiwú	—	asg̱eiwú
—	∅-	—	—	i-	s-	√g̱eiwú	—	eesg̱eiwú
—	∅-	—	—	x̱a-	∅-	√.ée	—	gax̱as.ée
—	a-	—	—	∅-	∅-	√.ée	—	agas.ée
—	∅-	—	—	i-	∅-	√.ée	—	gees.ée
—	∅-	—	na-	x̱a-	∅-	√k'éx̱'	-t	x̱ak'éx̱'t
—	a-	—	na-	∅-	∅-	√k'éx̱'	-t	ak'éx̱'t
—	∅-	—	na-	i-	∅-	√k'éx̱'	-t	eek'éx̱'t

The Lingít verb complex is a lot to digest, but it is at the heart of using the language in dynamic ways. We will continue to use the chart above to show how more components are added to the verb and how it changes the appearance of the verb as well as the meaning. For now, our verbs are going to shift towards the land and sky, so we will start by reviewing some land animals and birds, and add some new ones along the way.

We will also look at other food harvesting nouns and verbs, conjugating them for 1st, 2nd, and 3rd person using the same question and answer formulas as earlier in this chapter. The goal here is to continue to practice changing the subject and seeing how that affects the prefix, and learn new verbs along the way. You should be on your way to making your own sentences now using these verbs and looking up new ones to practice using the verb theme.

VOCABULARY		
	g̱uwakaan / ḵuwakaan	deer; peacemaker
	xóots	brown bear

	s'eek	black bear
	tawéi	mountain sheep
	jánwu / jánu (T) / ján (C) / jínwu (Y)	mountain goat
	dzísk'w / tsísk'w	moose

gáx̱	rabbit
tsaa	seal
taan	sea lion
x̱'óon	fur seal

 kindachooneit	mallard duck
t'aawák̲	Canada goose
g̲úk̲l'	swan
 núkt	blue grouse

Substitution Drills	
____ al'óon.	they are hunting ____. ____ a-∅-∅-√l'óon ____ them/it.(3.O)-they.(3.S)-cl.(∅)-√hunt
aadóo sá ____ al'óon?	who is hunting ____? aadóo =sá ____ a-∅-∅-√l'óon who =voice ____ them/it.(3.O)-they.(3.S)-cl.(∅)-√hunt
ax̱ ____ ____ al'óon.	my ____ is hunting ____. ax̱= ____ ____ a-∅-∅-√l'óon my.(1s.P)= {kinship term} {noun} them/it.(3.O)-they.(3.S)-cl.(∅)-√hunt
daa sáwé i ____ al'óon?	what is your ____ hunting? daa =sá-wé i ____ what =name.there your.(2s.P) {kinship term} a-∅-∅-√l'óon them/it.(3.O)-they.(3.S)-cl.(∅)-√hunt
____ al'óon ax̱ ____.	my ____ is hunting ____. ____ a-∅-∅-√l'óon {noun} them/it.(3.O)-they.(3.S)-cl.(∅)-√hunt ax̱= ____ my.(1s.P)= {kinship term}
daa sá eel'óon?	what are you hunting? daa =sá ∅-i-∅-√l'óon what =name them/it.(3.O)-you.(2s.S)-cl.(∅)-√hunt
____ x̱al'óon.	i am hunting ____. ____ ∅-x̱a-∅-√l'óon ____ them/it.(3.O)-i.(1s.S)-cl.(∅)-√hunt
daa sá a.únt?	what are they shooting at? daa =sá a-∅-∅-√ún-t what =name them/it.(3.O)-they.(3.S)-cl.(∅)-√shoot-repeatedly
____ a.únt.	they are shooting at ____. ____ a-∅-∅-√ún-t ____ them/it.(3.O)-they.(3.S)-cl.(∅)-√shoot-repeatedly

daa sá ee.únt?	what are you shooting at?
	daa =sá ∅-i-∅-√ún-t what =voice them/it.(3.O)-you.(2s.S)-cl.(∅)-√shoot-repeatedly
____ x̱a.únt.	i am shooting at ____.
	___ ∅-x̱a-∅-√ún-t ___ them/it.(3.O)-i.(1s.S)-cl.(∅)-√shoot.-repeatedly

	yalooleit / sáaxw (Y)	cockles
	yaak	mussels
	s'áaw	Dungeness crab

	néesʼ	sea urchin
	yéin	sea cucumber
	sʼéexʼát	shrimp
	gúnx̱aa	abalone

yéi adaané.	they work on it; they are working on it yéi= a-daa-∅-∅-√né thus= them/it.(3.O).around-they.(3.S)-cl.(∅)-√do
daa sá yéi daa.eené?	what are you working on? daa =sá yéi= ∅-daa-i-∅-√né what =voice thus= them/it.(3.O).around-you.(2s.S)-cl.(∅)-√do
____ yéi daax̱ané.	i am working on ____. ____ yéi= ∅-daa-x̱a-∅-√né ____ thus= them/it.(3.O).around-i.(1s.S)-cl.(∅)-√do

PREVERB	OBJECT	THEMATIC	CONJUGATION	SUBJECT	CLASSIFIER	STEM	COMPLETE VERB
—	∅-	—	—	x̱a-	∅-	√l'oon	x̱al'óon
—	a-	—	—	∅-	∅-	√l'oon	al'óon
—	∅-	—	—	i-	∅-	√l'oon	eel'óon
—	∅-	—	—	x̱a-	∅-	√ún	x̱a.únt
—	a-	—	—	∅-	∅-	√ún	a.únt
—	∅-	—	—	i-	∅-	√ún	ee.únt
yéi	∅-	daa-	—	x̱a-	∅	√né	yéi daax̱ané
yéi	a-	daa-	—	∅-	∅-	√né	yéi adaané
yéi	∅-	daa-	—	i-	∅-	√né	yéi daa.eené

kanat'á

blueberries

	was'x'aan tléigu / ch'a.aanáx̱ tléigu / tléik̲w tlénx'	salmonberries
	tléik̲w yádi	raspberries
	shákw / shúk (C)	strawberries
	shaax̱	gray currants

dáxw / dúx / eetl'át (AT)	lowbush cranberries; Lingonberry
kaxwéix̱	high bush cranberries
ch'eix̱' / ch'eex̱'	thimbleberries
yéil'	elderberries

	xákwl'i	soapberries
	tleikatánk	huckleberries
	k̲'eikaxétl'k	bunchberries, Jacob's berries
	k̲'eishkaháagu	bog cranberry

____ a.een.	they are picking ____. ____ a-∅-∅-√.een ____ them/it.(3.O)-they.(3.S)-cl.(∅)-√carry.full.container
aadóo sá ____ a.een?	who is picking ____? aadóo =sá ____ a-∅-∅-√.een who =name {noun} them/it.(3.O)-they.(3.S)-cl.(∅)-√carry.full.container
ax̱ ____ ____ a.een.	my ____ is picking ____. ax̱= ____ ____ my.(1s.P)= {kinship term} {noun} a-∅-∅-√.een them/it.(3.O)-they.(3.S)-cl.(∅)-√carry.full.container
daa sáwé i ____ a.een?	what is your ____ picking? daa =sá-wé i ____ what =name.there your.(2s.P) {kinship term} a-∅-∅-√.een them/it.(3.O)-they.(3.S)-cl.(∅)-√carry.full.container
____ a.een ax̱ ____.	my ____ is picking ____. ____ a-∅-∅-√.een {noun} them/it.(3.O)-they.(3.S)-cl.(∅)-√carry.full.container ax̱= ____ my.(1s.P)= {kinship term}
daa sá ee.een?	what are you picking? daa =sá ∅-i-∅-√.een what =voice them/it.(3.O)-you.(2s.S)-cl.(∅)-√carry.full.container
____ x̱a.een.	i am picking ____. ____ ∅-x̱a-∅-√.een ____ them/it.(3.O)-i.(1s.S)-cl.(∅)-√carry.full.container

	x'úx'	book; paper; letter

	neek x'úx'u	newspaper
	x'úx' daakax'úx'u	envelope
	dus'él' x'úx'u	pull tabs, rippies

____ atóow.	they are reading/counting ____. ____ a-∅-∅-√tóow them/it.(3.O)-they.(3.S)-cl.(∅)-√read/count/teach
____ x̲atóow.	i am reading/counting ____. ____ ∅-x̲a-∅-√tóow them/it.(3.O)-i.(1s.S)-cl.(∅)-√read/count/teach

____ eetóow.	you are reading/counting ____.
	____ {noun} ∅-i-∅-√tóow them/it.(3.O)-you.(2s.S)-cl.(∅)-√read/count/teach
____ sh tóo altóow.	they are studying ____.
	____ {noun} sh= self.(rflx.P)= tóo inside a-∅-l-√tóow them/it.(3.O)-they.(3.S)-cl.(d,l)-√read/count/teach
____ sh tóo x̱altóow.	i am studying ____.
	____ {noun} sh self.(rflx.P)= tóo inside ∅-x̱a-l-√tóow them/it.(3.O)-i.(1s.S)-cl.(d,l)-√read/count/teach
____ sh tóo eeltóow.	you are studying ____.
	____ {noun} sh self.(rflx.P)= tóo inside ∅-i-l-√tóow them/it.(3.O)-you.(2s.S)-cl.(d,l)-√read/count/teach
____ akshaxeet.	they are writing/drawing ____.
	____ {noun} a-ka-∅-sha-√xeet them/it.(3.O)-surface-they.(3.S)-cl.(sh)-√mark/write
____ kax̱shaxeet.	i am writing/drawing ____.
	____ {noun} ∅-ka-x̱a-sha-√xeet them/it.(3.O)-surface-i.(1s.S)-cl.(sh)-√mark/write
____ keeshaxeet.	you are writing/drawing ____.
	____ {noun} a-ka-∅-sha-√xeet them/it.(3.O)-surface-you.(2s.S)-cl.(sh)-√mark/write
akas'él't.	they are tearing/ripping/peeling ____.
	____ ____ a-ka-∅-∅-√s'él'-t them/it.(3.O)-surface-they.(3.S)-cl.(∅)-√tear/peel-repeatedly
kax̱as'él't.	i am tearing/ripping/peeling ____.
	____ ____ ∅-ka-x̱a-∅-√s'él'-t them/it.(3.O)-surface-i.(1s.S)-cl.(∅)-√tear/peel-repeatedly
kees'él't.	you are tearing/ripping/peeling ____.
	____ ____ ∅-ka-i-∅-√s'él'-t them/it.(3.O)-surface-you.(2s.S)-cl.(∅)-√tear/peel-repeatedly

PREVERB	OBJECT	THEMATIC	CONJUGATION	SUBJECT	CLASSIFIER	SUFFIX	STEM	COMPLETE VERB
—	∅-	—	—	x̲a-	∅-	—	√tóow	x̲atóow
—	a-	—	—	∅-	∅-	—	√tóow	atóow
—	∅-	—	—	i-	∅-	—	√tóow	eetóow
—	∅-	—	—	x̲a-	l-	—	√tóow	sh tóo x̲altóow
—	a-	—	—	∅-	l-	—	√tóow	sh tóo altóow
—	∅-	—	—	i-	l-	—	√tóow	sh tóo eeltóow
—	∅-	ka-	—	x̲a-	sha-	—	√xeet	kax̲shaxeet
—	a-	ka-	—	∅-	sha-	—	√xeet	akshaxeet
—	∅-	ka-	—	i-	sha-	—	√xeet	keeshaxeet
—	∅-	ka-	—	x̲a-	∅-	-t	√s'él'	kax̲as'él't
—	a-	ka-	—	∅-	∅-	-t	√s'él'	akas'él't
—	∅-	ka-	—	i-	∅-	-t	√s'él'	kees'él't

daa sá sh tóo eeltóow?	what are you are studying? daa / what; sá / =name; sh / self.(rflx.P); tóo / inside ∅-i-l-√tóow it.(3.O)-you.(2s.S)-cl.(d,l)-√read/count/teach
____ sh tóo x̲altóow.	i am studying ____. ____; sh / self.(rflx.P); tóo / inside ∅-x̲a-l-√tóow them/it.(3.O)-i.(1s.S)-cl.(d,l)-√read/count/teach
al'eix̲	dancing
kashxeet	writing
yéi jiné	work
ast'eix̲	fishing
at shí	singing
dak̲éis'	sewing
kasné	knitting
át wook̲oox̲	driving

al’óon	hunting
datóow	reading
at gas.ee	cooking (for immediate consumption)
at sa.ee	cooking (generally)
daxaash	cutting
da.aak	weaving
dagwaal / gaaw gwaal	drumming
goodé sá yaa neegút?	where are you going? goo-dé =sá where-towards = voice <ÿaa= na>-i-∅-√gút <along= progressive>-you.(2s.S)-cl.(∅)-√walk/go.(singular)
____-de/-dé yaa nx̱agút.	i am going to ____ . ____-de <ÿaa= na>-x̱a-∅-√gút {noun}-towards <along= progressive>-i.(1s.S)-cl.(∅)-√walk/go.(singular)
al’eix̱dé	to dance
yéi jinéide	to work
ash koolyátde	to play
ast’eix̱dé	to fish
al’óonde	to hunt

aya.áx̱ch.	they hear it; they can hear it. a-∅-ÿa-√áx̱ch them/it.(3.O)-they.(3.S)-cl.(∅,i)-√can.hear This verb has an unusualy -ch suffix that has become part of the stem. This suffix usually marks a habitual mode (always does it; always is that way)
x̱aa.áx̱ch.	i hear it; i can hear it. ∅-x̱a-ÿa-√áx̱ch them/it.(3.O)-i.(1s.S)-cl.(∅,i)-√can.hear
iya.áx̱ch.	you hear it; you can hear it. ∅-i-ÿa-√áx̱ch them/it.(3.O)-you.(s2s.s)-cl.(∅,i)-√can.hear
adzinéex'.	they smell it. a-∅-dzi-√néex' them/it.(3.O)-they.(3.S)-cl.(d,s,i)-√smell
x̱adzinéex'.	i smell it. ∅-x̱a-dzi-√néex' them/it.(3.O)-i.(1s.S)-cl.(d,s,i)-√smell
idzinéex'.	you smell it. ∅-i-dzi-√néex' them/it.(3.O)-you.(s2s.s)-cl.(d,s,i)-√smell
jee adinook.	they feel/touch it. jee-x' — possession-at.(residing) a-∅-di-√nook — them/it.(3.O)-they.(3.S)-cl.(d,∅,i)-√feel/touch
jee x̱dinook.	i feel/touch it. jee-x' — possession-at.(residing) ∅-x̱a-di-√nook — them/it.(3.O)-i.(1s.S)-cl.(d,∅,i)-√feel/touch
jee idinook.	you feel/touch it. jee-x' — possession-at.(residing) ∅-i-di-√nook — them/it.(3.O)-you.(2s.S)-cl.(d,∅,i)-√feel/touch

PREVERB	OBJECT	THEMATIC	CONJUGATION	SUBJECT	CLASSIFIER	STEM	SUFFIX	COMPLETE VERB
—	∅-	—	—	x̱a-	∅-	√áx̱ch	—	x̱aa.áx̱ch
—	a-	—	—	∅-	∅-	√áx̱ch	—	aya.áx̱ch
—	∅-	—	—	i-	∅-	√áx̱ch	—	iya.áx̱ch
—	∅-	—	—	x̱a-	dzi-	√néex'	—	x̱adzinéex'
—	a-	—	—	∅-	dzi-	√néex'	—	adzinéex'
—	∅-	—	—	i-	dzi-	√néex'	—	idzinéex'
jee-x'	∅-	—	—	x̱a-	di-	√nook	—	jee x̱dinook
jee-x'	a-	—	—	∅-	di-	√nook	—	jee adinook
jee-x'	∅-	—	—	i-	di-	√nook	—	jee idinook

9B

X̱'akaduneek Yéi Jiné 9

Translation Exercises 9

Lingít → English

Daa sá ax̱á?	
Áanjis kahéeni adaná.	
L'ook ast'eix̱	
Aadóoch sá g̱uwakaan al'óon?	
S'éex'át yéi daax̱ané.	
Kanat'á a.een ax̱ léelk'uch.	
Daa sá sh tóo eeltóow?	
Dus'él' x'úx' akas'él't.	
Jee idinook.	

English → Lingít

I am sipping tea.	
What is your paternal uncle hunting?	
What are you shooting at?	
I am reading a newspaper.	
Where are you going?	
Who is drinking juice?	
I am writing a book.	
I smell it.	

10A

Goodé sá yaa neegút?

Where are you going?

Tle ch'as yeewháan áyá a daa yánde gax̲yináak̲.
Tlél ch'a g̲óot k̲áa.
Yeewháanch áyá a kagéi yís
yee ée wdudlitóow.
Ách áyá a kát tux̲atán.

— K̲eixwnéi

It will just be you all who will stand up for it.
Not another person.
You all, for it,
you were taught.
This is why I hope for it.

– Nora Dauenhauer, Lukaax̲.ádi

tle	ch'as	ÿeewháan	á-yá	a=	daa-x'	ÿán-de
then	just	you.all.(2p.i)	focus-right.here	its.(3n.P)=	around-at.(residing)	shore/completion-toward

<ga-u-ga>-yi-∅-√ náak̲	tlél	ch'a	g̲óot	k̲áa
<future>-you.all.(2p.S)-cl.(∅)-√stand.(plural)	not	just	different	person.(4h.i)

yeewháan-ch	á-yá	a=	kagéi	yís
you.all.(2p.i)-ergative	focus-right.here	its.(3n.P)=	face.to.face	for.(benefit)

yee	ée	∅-<ÿu>-du-dli-√tóow
you.all's.(2p.P)	empty.base	it.(3.O)-<perfective>-someone.(4h.S)-cl.(d,l,i)-√read/count/teach

ách	á-yá	a=	ká-t	tu-<ÿu>-x̲a-ÿa-√tán
because	focus-right.here	its.(3n.P)=	on-at.(arrived)	inside-<perfective>-i.(1s.S)-cl.(∅,i)-√communicate

Goodé sá yaa neegút?

Start this lesson off with the following dialogue exercise that involves travel. Take turns being A and B, paying close attention to the relationship between an elder and her/his grandchild.

Try to use emotion when speaking, and also focus on having a flow to your language that makes it sound like a native Lingít speaker.

Dialogue Practice			
A	1	Goodé sá yaa neegút?	Where are you going to? goo-dé / where-towards =sá / =name <ÿaa= / <along= na>-i-∅-√gút / progressive>-you.(2s.S)-cl.(∅)-√walk/go.(singular)
B	2	Hoon daakahídidéi yaa nx̱agút.	I'm going to the store. hoon / sale daaka-hít-i-dé / surrounding.surface-house-relational-towards <ÿaa= / <along= na>-x̱a-∅-√gút / progressive>-i.(1s.S)-cl.(∅)-√walk/go.(singular)
A	3	Daatg̱áa sáwé?	What for? daat-g̱aa / what-for.(purpose) =sá-wé / =name.there
	4	G̱áatlg̱aa, ax̱ tláa jiyís.	For pilot bread for my mother. g̱áatl-g̱aa / cracker-for.(purpose) ax̱= / my-(1s.P)= tláa / mother jee-yís / possession-for.(benefit)
B	5	Goodé sá yaa neegút, wa.é ḵu.aa?	Where are you going, though? goo-dé / where-towards =sá / =name <ÿaa= / <along= na>-i-∅-√gút / progressive>-you.(2s.S)-cl.(∅)-√walk/go.(singular) wa.é / you.(2s.i) ḵu.aa / on.the.other.hand
			Note the word order for the final sentence. In this case, *wa.é ḵu.aa* functions to call attention to the subject of the sentence. If asked a question, after answering one could say *wa.é ḵu.aa?* on its own to ask the same sentence back.

A	6	Ax̱ aat x̱ánde yaa nx̱agút.	I'm going to my aunt's. ax̱= aat x̱án-de my.(1s.P)= paternal.aunt beside-towards <ÿaa= na>-x̱a-∅-√gút <along= progressive>-i.(1s.S)-cl.(∅)-√walk/go.(singular)
B	7	Daa sá áx' yéi kg̱isanéi?	What are you going to do there? daa =sá á-x' what =name there-at.(residing) yéi= <ga-u-g̱a>-i-sa-√néi thus= <future>-you.(2s.S)-cl.(s)-√do
A	8	Du jiyís at kuḵasa.ée.	I'm going to cook a meal for her. du= jee-yís their.(3p.P)= possession-for.(benefit) at <ga-u-g̱a>-x̱a-s-√.ée thing.(4n.O) <future>-i.(1s.S)-cl.(s)-√cook
B	9	Ḵuwak'éi yáa yakyee.	It's nice weather today. ḵu-ÿa-√k'éi yáa yakyee areal-cl.(∅,i)-√good right.here day
A	10	Aaa. Ḵúnáx̱.	Yes. Really. aaa ḵu-náx̱ yes areal-through/via
	11	Haa káa g̱áa ḵuwatee.	It's good weather for us. haa ká g̱áa ḵu-ÿa-√tee our.(1p.P) on accomodating areal-cl.(∅,i)-√be
B	12	Goodé sá ituwatee?	Where do you want to go? goo-dé =sá i-tu-ÿa-√tee where-towards =name you.(2s.O)-inside-cl.(∅,i)-√be
A	13	Xunaadé x̱at tuwatee.	I want to go to Hoonah. Xóon-nÿaa-dé x̱at= tu-ÿa-√tee north.wind-shield/vicinity-towards me.(1s.O)= inside-cl.(∅,i)-√be
B	14	Góok! Nax̱tooḵoox̱ ch'a yóok' kwshé!	Do it! Let's go soon! góok! <na-g̱a>-tu-∅-√ḵoox̱ go.ahead <hortative>-we-(1p.S)-cl.(∅)-√go.(by boat/car) ch'a yóok' kwshé just immediately i.guess

A	1	Goodáx̱ sáwé yaa ḵineetín?	Where are you traveling from? goo-dáx̱ =sá-wé where-from =name-there <ÿaa= ḵu-na>-i-∅-√tín <along= areal-<progressive>-you.(2s.S)-cl.(∅)-√see
	2	Fairbanks-dáx̱ áyá yaa ḵunx̱atín.	I'm coming from Fairbanks. Fairbanks-dáx̱ á-yá Fairbanks-from focus-right.here <ÿaa= ḵu-na>-x̱a-∅-√tín along= areal.<progressive>-i.(1s.S)-cl.(∅)-√see
B	3	Juneaux’ ḵúx̱de yaa ḵunax̱datín.	I'm returning to Juneau. Juneau-dé ḵux̱-dé Juneau-towards return/revert-towards ÿaa= ḵu-na>-x̱a-da-√tín <along= areal-progressive>-i.(1s.S)-cl.(d,∅)-√see
	4	Wa.é ḵu.aa?	And you? wa.é ḵu.aa you.(2s.i) although
A	5	Sheet’kaadé yaa ḵunx̱atín.	I'm traveling to Sitka. Sheey-t’iká-de Sheey.(Baranof.Island)-outskirts/ocean.side-towards <ÿaa= ḵu-na>-x̱a-∅-√tín along= areal.<progressive>-i.(1s.S)-cl.(∅)-√see
B	6	Ḵux̱ ḵeedatínni ast’eix̱ nax̱tooḵoox̱ kwshé!	When you get back maybe let's go fishing! ḵux̱ ḵu-i-da-√tín-ni return/revert areal-i.(1s.S)-cl.(d,∅)-√see.<conditional> a-s-√t’eix̱ a.theme-cl.(s)-√fish.with.hook na-ga-tu-∅-√ḵoox̱ kwshé <horative>.we-(1p.S)-cl.(∅)-√go-(by.boat/car) i.guess
A	7	Aaa, kei kg̱wak’éi.	Yes, that will be good. aaa <kei= ga-u-ga>-∅-√k’éi yes <up.conj future>-cl.(∅)-√good

Coming and going

imperfective (+)

wáa sá ḵuwanóok?	what are they doing?
	wáa =sá ḵu-∅-ÿa-√nóok how =name areal-they.(3.S)-cl.(∅,i)-√do/behave

progressive imperfective (+)

yaa nagút	them is/are walking along
	<ÿaa= na>-∅-∅-√gút <along= progressive>-they.(3.S)-cl.(∅)-√walk/go.(singular)

imperfective (+)

wáa sá ḵeeyanóok?	what are you doing?
	wáa =sá ḵu-i-ÿa-√nóok how =name areal-you.(2s.S)-cl.(∅,i)-√do/behave This phrase works for "what are you doing (generally)," but could be interpreted that you are doing something culturally wrong and someone is letting you know by asking you this.

progressive imperfective (+)

yaa nx̱agút.	i am walking along.
	<ÿaa= na>-x̱a-∅-√gút <along= progressive>-i.(1s.S)-cl.(∅)-√walk/go.(singular)

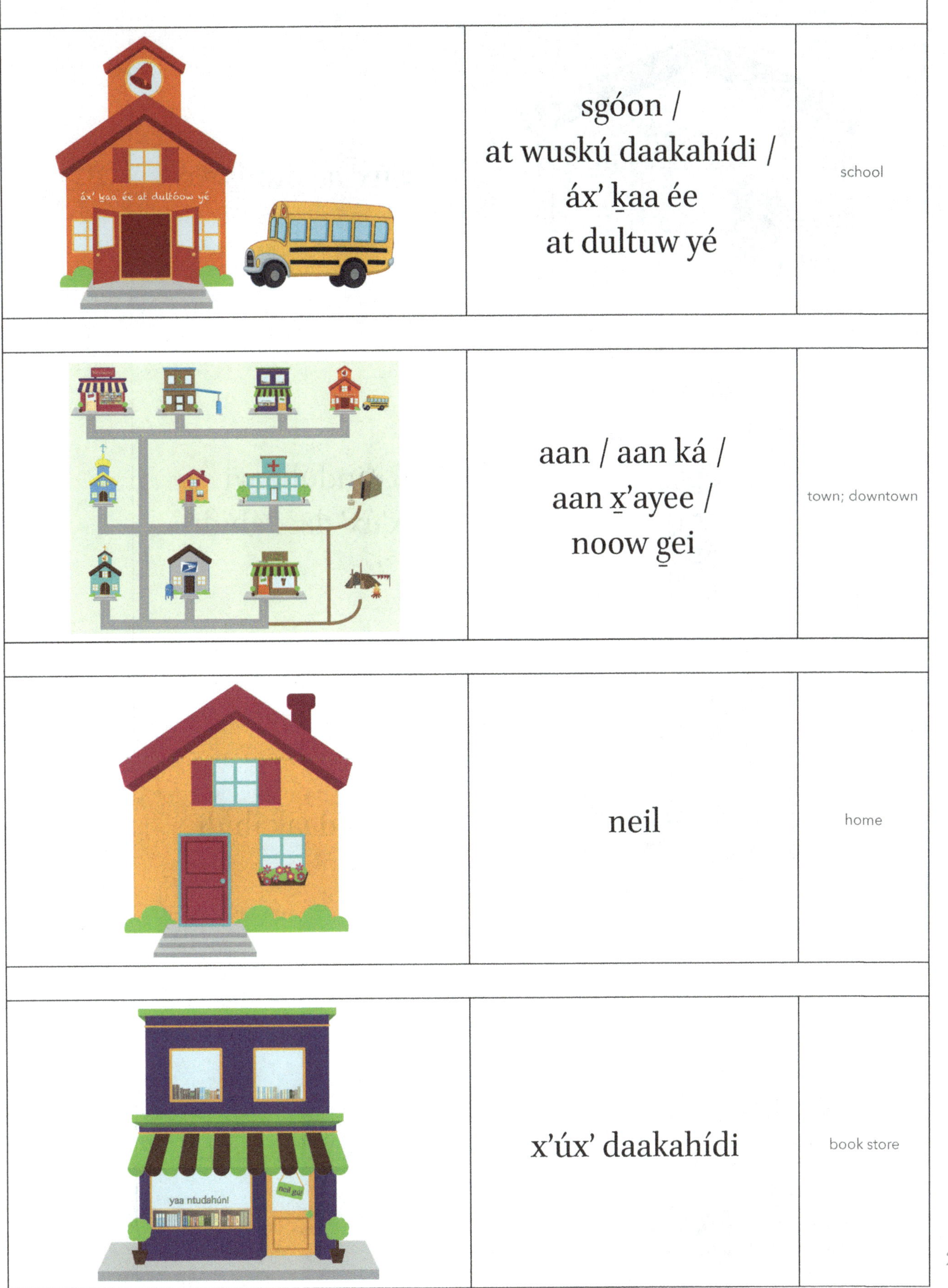

	sgóon / at wuskú daakahídi / áx’ ḵaa ée at dultuw yé	school
	aan / aan ká / aan x̱’ayee / noow g̱ei	town; downtown
	neil	home
	x’úx’ daakahídi	book store

x'úx' áa duhís' yé	library (lit. place where people borrow books)
jinduháayi x'úx' daakahídi	post office
atx̱á daakahídi	restaurant; cafe; cafeteria
dáanaa daakahídi	bank

	k̲unáakw daakahídi	hospital; clinic
	at x'aan hídi / s'eik̲ daakahídi / s'eik̲ hít	smokehouse
	hoon daakahídi	store
	x̲'agáax' daakahídi; chéch / cháach	church

kanéisdi hít

church (often Orthodox)

Towards

progressive imperfective (+)

goodé sá yaa nagút?

where are they going?

goo-dé =sá
where-towards =name

<ÿaa= na>-∅-∅-√gút
<along= progressive>-they.(3.S)-cl.(∅)-√walk/go.(singular)

Most open noun suffixes (ends with a vowel) have a vowel that has the opposite tone of the vowel before it, for example: hítde (high-low), neildé (low-high).

progressive imperfective (+)

____-de/-dé yaa nagút.

they are going to ____.

____-de
{noun}-towards

<ÿaa= na>-∅-∅-√gút
<along= progressive>-they.(3.S)-cl.(∅)-√walk/go.(singular)

progressive imperfective (+)

goodé sá yaa neegút?

where are you going?

goo-dé =sá
where-towards =name

<ÿaa= na>-i-∅-√gút
<along= progressive>-you.(2s.S)-cl.(∅)-√walk/go.(singular)

progressive imperfective (+)

____-de/-dé yaa nx̱agút.

i am going to ____.

____-de
{noun}-towards

<ÿaa= na>-x̱a-∅-√gút
<along= progressive>-i.(1s.S)-cl.(∅)-√walk/go.(singular)

progressive imperfective (+)

goodé sá yaa nagut i éesh?

where is your father going?

goo-dé =sá
where-towards =name

<ÿaa= na>-∅-∅-√gút
<along= progressive>-they.(3.S)-cl.(∅)-√walk/go.(singular)

i= éesh
your.(2s.P) father

progressive imperfective (+)

____-de/-dé yaa nagút ax̱ éesh.

my father is going to ____.

____-dé =sá
{noun}-towards =name

<ÿaa= na>-∅-∅-√gút
<along= progressive>-they.(3.S)-cl.(∅)-√walk/go.(singular)

ax̱= éesh
my.(1s.P) father

progressive imperfective (+)

ax̱ aat x̱ánde yaa nx̱agut.

i am going to see my paternal aunt.

ax̱= aat x̱án-de
my.(1s.P)= paternal.aunt proximity-towards

<ÿaa= na>-x̱a-∅-√gút
<along= progressive>-i.(1s.S)-cl.(∅)-√walk/go.(singular)

progressive imperfective (+)

ax̱ ____ x̱ánde yaa nx̱agut.

i am going to see my ____.

ax̱= ____ x̱án-de
my.(1s.P)= {kinship.term} proximity-towards

<ÿaa= na>-x̱a-∅-√gut
<along= progressive>-i.(1s.S)-cl.(∅)-√walk/go.(singular)

Away From

progressive imperfective (+)

goodáx̱ sá yaa nagút?

where are they coming from?

goo-dáx̱ =sá
where-from =name

<ÿaa= na>-∅-∅-√gút
<along= progressive>-they.(3.S)-cl.(∅)-√walk/go.(singular)

Closed noun suffixes (ends with a consonant) have a short and high vowel, for example: hítdáx̱, neildáx̱.

progressive imperfective (+)

____-dáx̱ yaa nagút.

they are coming from ____.

____-dáx̱
{noun}-from

<ÿaa= na>-∅-∅-√gút
<along= progressive>-they.(3.S)-cl.(∅)-√walk/go.(singular)

progressive imperfective (+)

goodáx̱ sá yaa neegút?

where are you coming from?

goo-dáx̱ =sá
where-from =name

<ÿaa= na>-i-∅-√gút
<along= progressive>-you.(2s.S)-cl.(∅)-√walk/go.(singular)

progressive imperfective (+)

____-dáx̱ yaa nx̱agút.

i am coming from ____.

____-dáx̱
{noun}-from

<ÿaa= na>-x̱a-∅-√gút
<along= progressive>-i.(1s.S)-cl.(∅)-√walk/go.(singular)

progressive imperfective (+)

goodáx̱ sá yaa nagut i tláa?

where is your mothing coming from?

goo-dáx̱ =sá
where-from =name

<ÿaa= na>-∅-∅-√gút
<along= progressive>-they.(3.S)-cl.(∅)-√walk/go.(singular)

i= tláa
your.(2s.P) mother

progressive imperfective (+)

____-dáx̱ yaa nagút ax̱ tláa.

my mother is coming from ____.

____-dáx̱ =sá
{noun}-from =name

<ÿaa= na>-∅-∅-√gút
<along= progressive>-they.(3.S)-cl.(∅)-√walk/go.(singular)

ax̱= tláa
my.(1s.P) mother

progressive imperfective (+)

ax̱ aat x̱ándáx̱ yaa nx̱agut.

i am coming from seeing my paternal aunt.

ax̱= aat x̱án-dáx̱
my.(1s.P)= paternal.aunt proximity-from

<ÿaa= na>-x̱a-∅-√gút
<along= progressive>-i.(1s.S)-cl.(∅)-√walk/go.(singular)

progressive imperfective (+)

ax̱ ____ x̱ándáx̱ yaa nx̱agut.

i am coming from seeing my ____.

ax̱=	____	x̱án-dáx̱
my.(1s.P)=	{kinship.term}	proximity-from

<ÿaa= na>-x̱a-∅-√gút
<along= progressive>-i.(1s.S)-cl.(∅)-√walk/go.(singular)

Types of Motion

progressive imperfective (+)

yaa naḵúx̱

they are going by boat or car

<ÿaa= na>-∅-∅-√ḵúx̱
<along= progressive>-they.(3.S)-cl.(∅)-√go.by.boat/car

progressive imperfective (+)

yaa neeḵúx̱

you are going by boat or car

<ÿaa= na>-i-∅-√ḵúx̱
<along= progressive>-you.(2s.S)-cl.(∅)-√go.by.boat/car

progressive imperfective (+)

yaa nx̱aḵúx̱

i am going by boat or car

<ÿaa= na>-x̱a-∅-√ḵúx̱
<along= progressive>-i.(1s.S)-cl.(∅)-√go.by.boat/car

progressive imperfective (+)

yaa ndaḵín	they are flying
	<ÿaa= na>-∅-da-√ḵín <along= progressive>-they.(3.S)-cl.(d,∅)-√fly.singular

progressive imperfective (+)

yaa nidaḵín	you are flying
	<ÿaa= na>-i-da-√ḵín <along= progressive>-you.(2s.S)-cl.(d,∅)-√fly.singular

progressive imperfective (+)

yaa nax̱daḵín	i am flying
	<ÿaa= na>-x̱a-da-√ḵín <along= progressive>-i.(1s.S)-cl.(d,∅)-√fly.singular

progressive imperfective (+)

yaa ḵunatín	they are traveling
	<ÿaa= ḵu-na>-∅-∅-√tín <along= areal.progressive>-they.(3.S)-cl.(∅)-√see

progressive imperfective (+)

yaa k̲ineetín	you are traveling
	<ÿaa= k̲u-na>-i-∅-√tín <along= areal.progressive>-you.(2s.S)-cl.(∅)-√see

progressive imperfective (+)

yaa k̲unx̲atín	i am traveling
	<ÿaa= k̲u-na>-x̲a-∅-√tín <along= areal.progressive>-i.(1s.S)-cl.(∅)-√see

progressive imperfective (+)

yaa nashíx / yaa nashxíx	they are running; they are hurrying
	<ÿaa= na>-∅-sh-√xíx <along= progressive>-they.(3.S)-cl.(d,sh)-√run

progressive imperfective (+)

yaa neeshíx / yaa neeshxíx	you are running; you are hurrying
	<ÿaa= na>-i-sh-√xíx <along= progressive>-you.(2s.S)-cl.(d,sh)-√run

progressive imperfective (+)

yaa nx̱ashíx / yaa nx̱ashxíx

i am running; i am hurrying

<ÿaa=	na>-x̱a-sh-√xíx
<along=	progressive>-i.(1s.S)-cl.(d,sh)-√run

yaa sh kanaltséx̱ / yaa sh kanaltsíx̱

they are riding a bicycle

<ÿaa=	sh=	ka-na>-∅-l-√tséx̱
<along=	rflx=	surface.progressive>-they.(3.S)-cl.(d,l)-√kick

progressive imperfective (+)

yaa sh kaneeltséx̱ / yaa sh kaneeltsíx̱

you are riding a bicycle

<ÿaa=	sh	ka-na>-i-l-√tséx̱
<along=	rflx	surface.progressive>-you.(2s.S)-cl.(d,l)-√kick

progressive imperfective (+)

yaa sh kanx̱altséx̱ / yaa sh kanx̱altsíx̱

i am riding a bicycle

<ÿaa=	sh	ka-na>-x̱a-l-√tséx̱
<along=	rflx	surface.progressive>-i.(1s.S)-cl.(d,l)-√kick

Lingít preverbs and motion verbs

A í is a word or set of words that appear before the **verb** and alter its meaning. Sometimes these can create a whole new verb, such as:

yéi yatee (is that way)
yáx̠ yatee (is like that)
a eetéenáx yatee (they need it)

Sometimes the **preverb** is needed to change the **verb mode**, which is one of the things we will be looking at in the final chapter of this workbook. Other times, the **preverb** shows the motion, which can affect the verb and the way we use it. Here are some **preverbs** that are common in Lingít.

preverbs	
yéi	thus
yan / yax̠	finishing or completion
The preverbs above can be used to alter meaning, and the preverbs below are often used for verb modes, such as *progressive imperfective* and *future*.	
yaa	along; down; obliquely. also progressive for ∅- and na- verbs
yei	down; downward. also progressive for g̱a- verbs
kei	up; upward. also progressive for ga- verbs
yoo	to and fro; back and forth
directional preverbs	
yeik̠ / yeek̠	down to shore; beachward
k̠ut	astray; lost

The following direction preverbs can take a suffix, which will often change the vowel within them. They are shown here with two variations, the first with no suffix and the second with the suffix *-de* (towards)	
daak̲ | dak̲dé	inland from shore; back from open; off of fire
daak | dakdé	out to sea; out into the open; falling from sky; onto fire
yan / yax̲ | yánde	ashore; onto ground; resting; to completion
haa(n) | haadé	hither; this vicinity; this area
neil | neildé	inside; homeward; into building
k̲ux̲ | k̲úx̲de	aback; reversed direction; return (+**d**)
Some direction preverbs will cause the classifier to add the d-component, which is marked here as +d.	

	progressive imperfective (+)
yei nagút	they are going down; they are getting aboard (a boat or car)
	<yei= na>-∅-∅-√gút <down.conj= progressive>-they.(3.S)-cl.(∅)-√walk/go.(singular)

	progressive imperfective (+)
kei nagút	they are going up
	<kei= na->∅-∅-√gút <up.conj progressive>-they.(3.S)-cl.(∅)-√walk/go.(singular)

progressive imperfective (+)	
yeik̲ nagút	they are going down to the shore (from the forest)
	<ÿeik̲ na->∅-∅-√gút <shoreward progressive>-they.(3.S)-cl.(∅)-√walk/go.(singular)

progressive imperfective (+)	
daak̲ nagút	they are going up from the shore (into the forest)
	<daak̲ na->∅-∅-√gút <inland progressive>-they.(3.S)-cl.(∅)-√walk/go.(singular)

progressive imperfective (+)	
daak nak̲úx̲	they are going out (to sea)
	<daak na->∅-∅-√gút <seaward progressive>-they.(3.S)-cl.(∅)-√go.by.boat/car

progressive imperfective (+)	
daak nahéin / daak nahwéin	they are wading out (to sea)
	<daak <seaward na->∅-∅-√hóo-n progressive>-they.(3.S)-cl.(∅)-√swim.mammal/wade-<progressive>

progressive imperfective (+)

ḵut kei nagút	they are getting lost

ḵut	<kei=	na->∅-∅-√gút
astray	<up.conj	progressive>-they.(3.S)-cl.(∅)-√walk/go.(singular)

progressive imperfective (+)

haandé yaa nagút / haadé yaa nagút	they are walking this way

haa(n)-dé	yaa	na->∅-∅-√gút
hither-towards	<along=	progressive>-they.(3.S)-cl.(∅)-√walk/go.(singular)

progressive imperfective (+)

ḵúx̱de yaa ndagút	they are returning; they are walking back

ḵux̱-dé
return/revert-towards

<ÿaa=	na>-i-∅-√gút
<along=	progressive>-they.(3.S)-cl.(d,∅)-√walk/go.(singular)

More question particles

In our first lesson we learned about question particles. These also have special uses when preceded with the particles *ch'a* (the very; just) or *tlél* (not), as in the following tables:

daa(t) sá	what
daak̲w.aa sá	which one
wáa sá	how
aadóo sá / aa sá	who
goosá	where
x'oon sá	how many
gwátgeen sá / gútgeen sá (Y)	when (in future)
gwátk sá / gútk sá (Y)	when (in the past)
daat yís sá	for what (benefit)
daatgáa sá	for what (purpose)
wáanáx̲ sá	why
wáa kuwáat' sá	for how long
wáa yateeyi aa sá?	what kind?

CH'A	
ch'a daa(t) sá	whatever
ch'a daak̲w.aa sá	which ever one (of a set)
ch'a wáa sá	however
ch'a aadóo sá / ch'a aa sá	whoever
ch'a goo sá	wherever
ch'a x'oon sá	how ever much/many
ch'a gwátgeen sá / ch'a gútgeen sá (Y)	whenever (in future)
ch'a gwátk sá / ch'a gútk sá (Y)	whenever (in the past)

TLÉL	
tlél daa sá	nothing
tlél wáa sá	okay (lit. no particular way)
tlél aadóo sá / tlél aa sá	no one

The *tlél* particle has special meaning with *wáa sá* and generally translates to 'okay' so it does not follow the same grammatical patterns as the others. Also, once either of these particles are added then the function of the question particle changes, as in the follwing:

daa sá i tuwáa sigoo?	what do you want?
ch'a daa sá i tuwáa sagoowú.	whatever you want.
wáa sá k̲ukgwatée?	how is the weather going to be?
ch'a wáa sá k̲ukgwateeyí.	however the weather is going to be.
aadóo sá i tláa?	who is your mother?
ch'a aadóo sá yisateení.	whoever you see.

Direction / Location Suffixes

Once we start talking about motion in Lingít, then directional suffixes should be talked about. You will see later how these affect the verbs, but for now just focus on learning the basic meaning of these common directional suffixes. These can refer to physical directions and also time. Like most other things you learn, you should be committing them to memory by listening and looking for them, and also by trying to incorporate them into your daily speech.

-dáx̲ ~ -tx̲	from, out of; since
-de	to, toward; until; in the manner of
-náx̲	through; along, via; including the time of
-t	coming to, arriving at; moving about; at a point
-wu ~ -u	is/are at
-x' ~ -∅	residing at; at (the scene of); at (the time of)
-x̲	(in prolonged contact) at; (repeatedly arriving) at; being, in the form of

There will much to learn about how these suffixes interact with nouns, verbs, and relational nouns. Also, the suffix -dáx̲ ~ -tx̲ (from; out of; since) has three irregular forms that you will see and hear:

aax̲	from it
kaax̲	off (the surface of) it
–yaax̲	off the face of

10B

Ḵaa X̱'akaneek Kawdu.aagú 10

Translation Exercises 10

Lingít → English

Ax̱ aat x̱ánde yaa nx̱agút.	
Wáa sá ḵeeyanóok / Máa sá ḵeeyanóok?	
Neildé yaa nx̱agút.	
Goodé sá yaa nagút i éesh?	
Goodáx̱ sá yaa nagút?	
Yaa nidaḵín.	
Goodáx̱ sá ḵineetín?	
Dáanaa daakahídidé yaa nagút.	
Haandé yaa nagút / Haadé yaa nagút.	

English → Lingít

They are walking back.	
You are riding a bicycle.	
I am traveling to Sitka.	
They are walking to the store.	
My mother is coming from visiting her mother.	
I am walking down to the beach.	
You are running home.	
They are walking from the store.	

11A

Wáa sá k̲ukg̲watée?

How will the weather be?

«Ch'a yá lingit'aaní kát igux̲latéet.
Tléil wáa sá ikg̲wanei,» yóo ayawsik̲aa.
«Ch'a yá lingit'aaní kát igux̲latéet.
Tléil wáa sá ikg̲wanei.»

— Kaasgéiy

"You'll just float over the world.
Nothing will happen to you," he said to her.
"You'll just float over the world.
Nothing will happen to you."

– Susie James, Chookanshāa

(recorded by K̲aat'éix̲' Mary Pelayo
and translated by K̲eixwnéi Nora Dauenhauer)

ch'a	yá	lingit'aaní	ká-t	i-<ga-u-g̲a>-la-√téet
just	right.here	world	on-at.(arriving)	you.(2s.O)-<future>-cl.(l)-√wave

tléil	wáa	=sá	i-<ga-u-g̲a>-∅-√nei
not	how	=name	you.(2s.O)-<future>-cl.(∅)-√do/happen

yóo=	a-<yú>-∅-si-√k̲aa
as.precedes=	them.(3.O)-<perfective>-they.(3.S)-cl.(s,i)-√say

Wáa sá ḵukg̱watée?

Dialogue Practice

A	1	Seigánin áwé gwál Aangóondé gax̱tooḵóox̱	Maybe tomorrow seig̱án-in á-wé gwál tomorrow-future focus-there maybe We will go to Angoon (by boat) Aangóon-dé <ga-u-g̱a>-tu-Ø-√ḵóox̱ Angoon-towards <future>-we.(1p.S)-cl.(Ø)-√go.by.boat/car
B	2	Wáa sá ḵukg̱watée?	How is the weather going to be? wáa =sá ḵu-<ga-u-g̱a>-Ø-√tee how =name areal-<future>-cl.(Ø)-√be
	3	Tlél ax̱ tuwáa ushgú k'ccljáa haa hat wuxeexí.	I don't want tlél ax̱= tu-ÿá Ø-<u>-sh-√gú not my.(1s.P)= inside-face them/it.(3.O)-<not>-cl.(sh)-√happy a storm to come upon us. k'eeljáa haa= ká-t storm our.(1p.P)= on-at.(arriving) Ø-<ÿu>-Ø-√xeex-i it/them.(3.O)-<perfective>-cl.(Ø)-√fall.singular-subordinate
	4	Hél x̱wasakú.	I don't know. hél <u-ÿu>-x̱a-sa-√kú not <not-perfective>-me.(1s.S)-cl.(s)-√know
A	5	Séew daak nastán yeedát, seigánin ḵu.aa akg̱wadáaḵ shákdéi.	It's raining right now, séew daak <na>-sa-√tán yeedát rain out.into.open <progessive>-cl.(s)-√long.object.moves now but it might clear up tomorrow. seig̱án-in ḵu.aa a-<ga-u-g̱a>-Ø-√dáaḵ shákdéi tomorrow-future though a.theme-<future>-cl.(Ø)-√clear-up i.guess

A	6	Ax̱ éesh áwé kayáash kát a.án; yéi oowajée kei ḵukg̱wak'éi.	my father ax̱= éesh á-wé my.(1s.P)= father focus-there is sitting on the porch watching the weather kayáash ká-t platform/porch on.at.(arrived) a-Ø-Ø-√.án a.theme-they.(3.S)-cl.(Ø)-√sit.watching/meditating he thinks it is going to be good weather. yéi= a-<u>-Ø-ÿa-√jée thus= it(3.O)-<not>-they.(3.S)-cl.(Ø,i)-√opine kei= ḵu-<ga-u-g̱a>-Ø-√k'éi up.conj= areal-<future>-cl.(Ø)-√good
B	7	Yaa ḵudzigéi áwé i éesh.	Your father is intelligent. yaa= ḵu-Ø-dzi-géi i= éesh mental= areal-they.(3.S)-cl(d,s,i).√intelligent your-(2s.P)= father
	8	At gaxoon!	Get ready (for a trip)! at= <ga>-Ø-√xoon thing.(4n.O)= <command>-cl.(Ø)-√prepare-(for travel)
	9	Aadé gax̱tooḵóox̱.	we're going to go there. á-de <ga-u-g̱a>-tu-Ø-√ḵóox̱ there-towards <future>-we-(1p.S)-cl.(Ø)-√go.by.boat/car
A	10	Yak'éi!	good! Ø-ÿa-√k'éi them/it.(3.O)-cl.(Ø,i)-√good
	11	Ax̱ éesh een kakḵwanéek.	i will tell my dad. Ax̱= éesh ee-n my.(1s.P)= father empty.base-with Ø-ka-<ga-u-g̱a>-x̱a-Ø-√néek it.(3.O).surface.<future>-i.(1s.S)-cl.(Ø)-√tell
B		Kakḵwacháak; gunalchéesh.	i will pack; thank you. Ø-ka-<ga-u-g̱a>-x̱a-Ø-√cháak it.(3.O).surface.<future>-i.(1s.S)-cl.(Ø)-√pack gunalchéesh thank.you

Lingít verb modes

As mentioned earlier, Lingít does not change verbs for time, but does so for event. What that means is that the language has ways of noting time, but that is not one of the main reasons for changing a verb. When we change a verb, sometimes it is called **conjugating** the verb.

The reasons we might **conjugate** a verb is to note whom the verb is happening to (**object**) and who is doing the verb (**subject**). The next thing to learn about them is that they might change to note what we are saying is happening with the verb. Lingít does this using what we call **verb modes** which is going to introduce some new terms to you.

When learning terms about Lingít grammar, remember that it is more important to know what these things do than to memorize what these things are called. These things have names, which makes it easier to talk about them, but do not feel worried if the names are not sticking with you. We will take a look at what some of the parts of the verb change in order to change **mode**, but for now we will start with a few time references to show that we might be talking about things that happened yesterday, are happening now, and might or will happen tomorrow.

You will learn a lot about the way that the Lingít thought world views time, but for starters keep in mind that time and space work in a lot of the same ways in Lingít. You can place a directional suffix onto a noun for a place (hítde – towards the house) or for a time reference (yeedádidé – up until now). Also, generally speaking the future is in front of you, but so are your ancestors. The concepts will come to you through more listening, speaking, and talking about these things.

Time References	
yeedát	now
yáa yakyee (S) / yáa yagiyee (N) / yáa yagee (T)	today yáa yakyee this day
tatgé	yesterday
seig̱ánin / seig̱án	tomorrow

Perfective

When we look closer at the Lingít verb, we will see that there are distinctive parts, and these parts all play a role in how we understand and speak the language. We have looked at the **preverb** when looking at **motion verbs**, have changed the **object** to show whom the verb impacts, and changed the **subject** to show who is doing the verb. The next two things we will look at are the **conjugation** and the **classifier**.

The **conjugation** prefixes are activated when we need to change how the verb is working. For example, look at the examples below and see where they changes are taking place within both the **conjugation prefixes** and the **classifier**. As you continue your study in Lingít, you will learn how to use complex combinations naturally, and we take them apart a bit here to show what is happening as a verb changes.

preverb + object | thematic | conjugation | subject | classifier | stem

NEGATION	PREVERB	OBJECT	CONJUGATION	SUBJECT	CLASSIFIER	STEM	COMPLETE VERB	TRANSLATION
	—	i-	—	x̱a-	si-	√x̱an	ix̱six̱án	i love you
tlél	—	i-	u-	x̱a-	sa-	√x̱an	tlél eex̱sax̱án	i don't love you
	kei	i-	<ga-u-g̱a>-	x̱a-	sa-	√x̱an	kei ikḵwasax̱án	i will love you
	kei	i-	<ga-u-g̱a>-	x̱a-	sa-	√x̱an	tlél kei ikḵwasax̱án	i won't love you
	—	i-	ÿu	x̱a-	si-	√teen	ix̱wsiteen	i see you; i saw you
tlél	—	i-	<ÿu>-u-	x̱a-	sa-	√teen	tlél ix̱wsateen	i don't see you; i didn't see you
	yei	i-	<ga-u-g̱a>-	x̱a-	sa-	√téen	yei ikḵwasatéen	i will see you
tlél	yei	i-	<ga-u-g̱a>-	x̱a-	sa-	√teen	tlél yei ikḵwasateen	i won't see you

Teaching and learning and using Lingít involves a series of interconnected pieces. If you are learning Lingít, then you should continue to keep yourself motivated and inspired to keep going. There are lots of concepts coming at you simultaneously, and these reveal the genius of Haa Léelk'u Hás (Our Ancestors) and Haa Tlagu Ḵwáanx'i (Our Eternal Ones; Our Ancient Ones).

Do not be afraid of this material. Everyone learns at different paces and in different ways. The reality we face is often discouraging. If everyone who, for whatever reason, quit learning and using the language, was still going today we would have hundreds and hundreds of speakers. But our numbers are falling. Because of this, you need to keep yourself on the path that was cleared for you.

Our next step is to look at the **perfective** mode of the Lingít verb. These would be used to talk about the way the weather was yesterday, but in many verbs it also refers to something that has already happened or became a certain way. Again, this is not about time but is more about event: whether or not the verb has happened or become a certain way.

In later lessons you are going to learn the names, functions, and meanings of all of these prefixes. For now, you are going to learn how to start moving the verb around and look for patterns. You are encouraged to memorize these phrases through use and to analyze them by thinking about what you are hearing and seeing and letting your subconscious and your active mind put the pieces together.

	perfective
wáa sá ḵoowatee?	how was the weather?
	wáa =sá ḵu-<ÿu>-ÿa-√tee how =name areal-<perfective>-cl.(∅,i)-√be The perfective can appear as *wu- w-* or *-y-*. When expanding the grammar (segmenting), we write this as *ÿu-*. The *ÿ* means that the letter will be a *y* unless preceded by a rounded vowel (*u* or *oo*), in which case it will be *w*.

	perfective
ḵoowak'éi	the weather was good
	ḵu-<ÿu>-ÿa-√k'éi areal-<perfective>.cl.(∅,i)-√good

	perfective
ḵuwligóos'	the weather was cloudy
	ḵu-<ÿu>-li-√góos' areal-<perfective>-cl.(l,i)-√cloud

	perfective
ḵoowat'áa	the weather was warm/hot
	ḵu-<ÿu>-ÿa-√t'áa areal-<perfective>-cl.(∅,i)-√warm/hot

perfective

k̲uwsi.áat’

the weather was cold

k̲u-<ÿu>-si-√.áat’
areal-<perfective>-cl.(s,i)-√cold

perfective

k̲uwdigwás’

the weather was foggy

k̲u-<ÿu>-di-√gwás’
areal-<perfective>-cl.(d,∅,i)-√foggy

perfective

tlél k̲uwushk’éi

the weather was bad

tlél	k̲u-<u-ÿu>-sh-√k’éi
not	areal-<not-perfective>-cl.(sh)-√good

The u- prefix here is called *irrealis* and has to do with disagreement with the actual world. It often marks the verb as “not happening” or “not being that way,” and is used in negative modes, future modes, comparisons, and more.

perfective

aawadaak̲

the weather cleared up;
it stopped precipitating

a-<ÿu>-ÿa-√daak̲
a.theme-<perfective>-cl.()-√weather.clears.up

imperfective

wáa sá yatee gáan?	how is it outside?
	wáa =sá ÿa-√tee gáan how =name cl.(∅,i)-√be outisde

future

aadéi akk̲walg̲éin / aadéi akk̲walg̲éen	i will look there
	aa-déi a-<ga-u-g̲a>-x̲a-l-√g̲éin it-towards a.theme-<future>-i.(1s.S)-cl.(d,l)-√look.at

a daa yakk̲was.áa	i will look it over; i will examine it
	a= daa its.(3n.P)= aorund/about ÿa-<ga-u-g̲a>-x̲a-s-√.áa face-<future>-i.(1s.S)-cl.(d,s)-√examine

perfective / imperfective

___ tatgé, k̲a yáa yagiyee tsú ___.	it was ___ yesterday, and ___ today too.
	___ tatgé k̲a {perfective} yesterday and yáa yagiyee tsú ___ right.here day also {imperfective}

perfective / imperfective

___ tatgé, yáa yagiyee k̲u.aa ___.	it was ___ yesterday, though today it is ___.
	___ tatgé {perfective} yesterday yáa yagiyee k̲u.aa ___ right.here day though {imperfective}

ch’u tatgéidá<u>x</u> áyá.	it has been since yesterday. ch’u — still tatgé-dá<u>x</u> — yesterday-from á-yá — focus-right.here
seig̱ánin / seig̱án	tomorrow
<u>k</u>u.aa ~ <u>k</u>wa	however; though This word does not start a sentence or clause, and is not a conjunction, but instead refers to the word before it. If it appears at the beginning of a sentence, it is preceded by the *á* (it) or *ch’a aan* (nevertheless). It creates a slight turn in logic, or points out who might be talked about, and sometimes will appear as *<u>k</u>wá*.
shákdéi	i guess; perhaps Indicates possibility and is usually placed after the first phrase in a sentence. *Shákdéi* is a somewhat non-judgmental way to say ‘perhaps, or ‘I guess’, and *gwál* usually signals some doubt.

Future

	future
kei k̲ukg̲wak’éi	the weather will be fine
	kei= k̲u-<ga-u-g̲a>-Ø-√k’éi up.conj= areal.<future>-cl.(Ø)-√good

	future
yei agux̲dagáan	it will be sunny
	ÿei= a-<ga-u-g̲a>-da-gáan down.conj= a-mode.<future>-cl.(d,Ø)-√burn/light

	future
kei k̲ugux̲lagóos’	it will be cloudy
	kei= k̲u-<ga-u-g̲a>-la-√góos’ up.conj= areal.<future>-cl.(l)-√cloud

	future
k̲ukg̲wat’áa	the weather will be hot
	kei= k̲u-<ga-u-g̲a>-Ø-t’áa up.conj areal.<future>-cl.(Ø)-√hot

future

kei ḵugux̱sa.áat'

the weather will be cold

kei=	ḵu-<ga-u-g̱a>-sa-√.áat'
up.conj=	areal.<future>-cl.(s)-√cold

future

{séew, dleit} daak gux̱satáan

it will rain/snow.

{séew, dleit}	daak	<ga-u-g̱a>-sa-táan
{rain, snow}	out.to.open	<future>-cl.(s)-√long.object.moves

This verb is used for rain or snow, but if one were to say *daak gux̱satáan* without specifying, a speaker would likely interpret that as 'it is going to rain.'

future

ḵugux̱dagwáas'

the weather will be foggy

ḵu-<ga-u-g̱a>-da-√gwáas'
areal.<future>-cl.(d,∅)-√foggy

future

yei ayagux̱datée

it will be stormy/windy

ÿei=	a-ya-<ga-u-g̱a>-da-√tée
down.conj=	a.theme-face-<future>-cl.(d,∅)-√windy/stormy

	future
akg̱wadáaḵ	it will clear up; it will stop (precipitating) a-<ga-u-g̱a>-∅-√dáaḵ a.theme-<future>-cl.(∅)-√weather.clears.up
gwál	perhaps Indicates doubt and is usually placed at the beginning of the sentence.
gwál yé	maybe so
seig̱ánin ___ shákdéi.	tomorrow ___ gwál.
seig̱ánin gwál ___.	tomorrow maybe ___.

Progressive imperfective

yei ḵunak’éin	progressive imperfective
	the weather is getting better
	ÿei= ḵu-<na>-∅-√k’éi-n down.conj= areal-<progressive>-cl.(∅)-√good.<progressive>

yei andagán	progressive imperfective
	it is getting sunny
	ÿei= a-<na>-da-√gán up= a.theme-<progressive>-cl.(d,∅)-√burn/light

kei ḵunalgóos’	progressive imperfective
	the weather is getting cloudy
	kei= ḵu-<na>-l-√góos’ up.conj= areal-<progressive>-cl.(l)-√cloud

yaa ḵunat’éin	progressive imperfective
	the weather is getting hot
	ÿaa= ḵu-<na>-∅-√t’áa-n along= areal-<progressive>-cl.(∅)-√hot-<progressive>

progressive imperfective

kei ḵunas.áat’

the weather is getting cold

kei=	ḵu-<na>-s-√.áat’
up.conj=	areal-<progressive>-cl.(s)-cold

progressive imperfective

{séew, dleit} daak nastán

it is beginning to rain/snow

{séew,dleit}	daak	na-s-√tán
{rain, snow}	out.to.open	<progressive>-cl.(s)-√long.object.moves

progressive imperfective

yaa ḵundagwás’

the weather is getting foggy

ÿaa=	ḵu-<na>-da-√gwás’
along=	areal-<progressive>-cl.(d,∅)-√foggy

progressive imperfective

yei ayandatéen

the weather is getting windy

ÿei=	a-ya-<na>-da-√tée-n
down.conj=	areal-<progressive>-cl.(d,∅)-√windy/stormy.<progressive>

tlél kei ḵoonashk’éin

the weather is getting worse

tlél	kei=	ḵu-<u-na>-sh-√k’éi-n
not	up.conj=	areal-<not-progressive>-cl.(sh)-√good.<progressive>

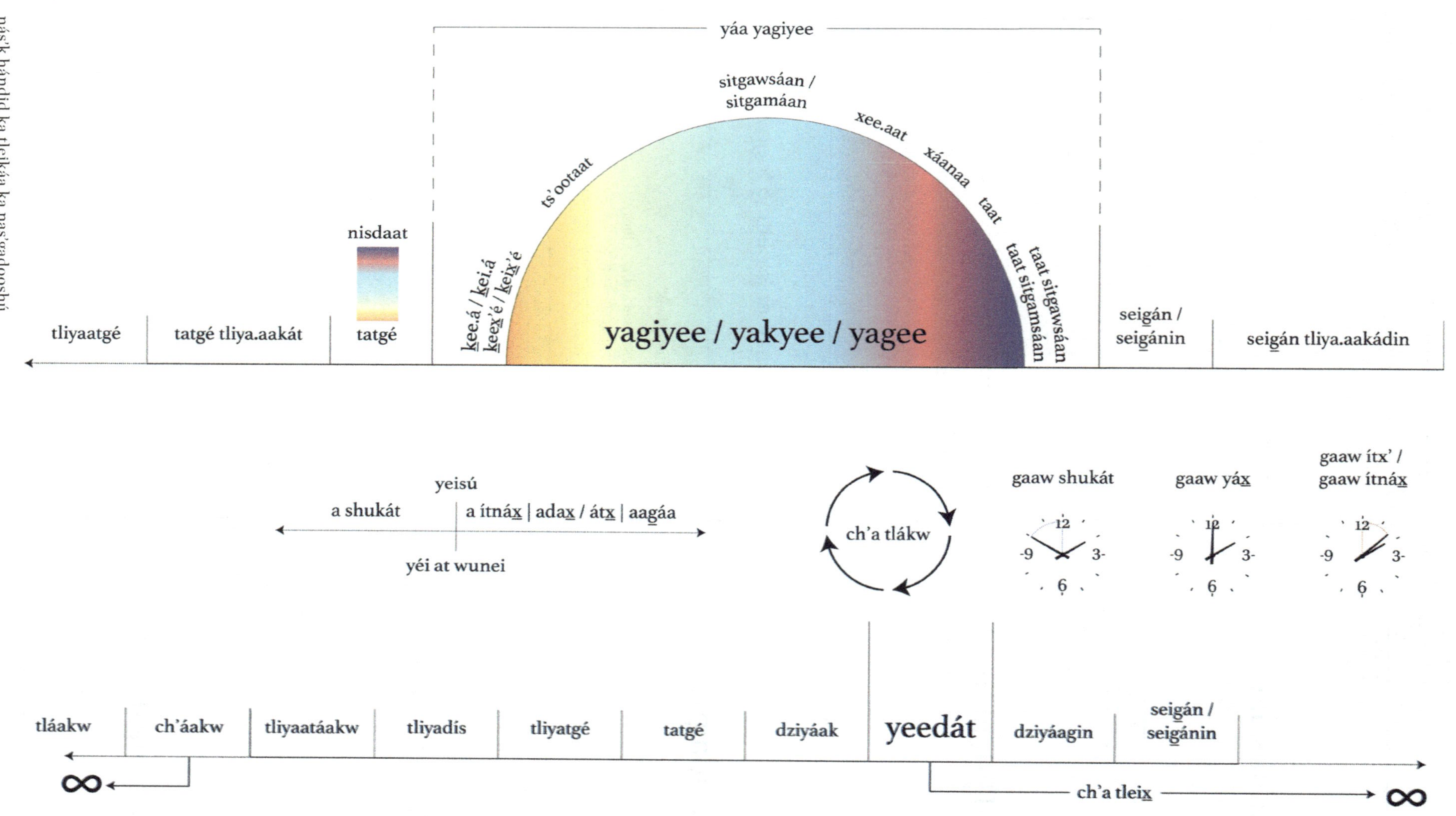
yáa yagiyee
sitgawsáan /
sitgamáan
xee.aat
xáanaa
taat
taat sitgawsáan
taat sitgamsáan
ts'ootaat
ḵee.á / ḵei.á
ḵeex̱'é / ḵeix̱'é
yagiyee / yakyee / yagee
nisdaat
tliyaatgé
tatgé tliya.aakát
tatgé
seig̱án /
seig̱ánin
seig̱án tliya.aakádin
yeisú
a shukát
a ítnáx̱ | adax̱ / átx̱ | aag̱áa
yéi at wunei
ch'a tlákw
gaaw shukát
gaaw yáx̱
gaaw ítx' /
gaaw ítnáx̱
12
3
6
9
tláakw
ch'áakw
tliyaatáakw
tliyadís
tliyatgé
tatgé
dziyáak
yeedát
dziyáagin
seig̱án /
seig̱ánin
ch'a tleix̱
∞

11B

K̲aa X̲'akaneek Kawdu.aag̲ú 11

Translation Exercises 11

Lingít → English

Wáa sá k̲oowatee?	
Wáa sá k̲ukg̲watée?	
K̲ugux̲dagwáas'.	
Akg̲wadáak̲	
Yei andagán	
Kei k̲ugux̲lagóos'	
Awdigaan tatgé, yáa yagiyee, k̲u.aa séew daak wusitán.	
Ch'u tatgéidáx̲ áyá.	
Aadéi akk̲walg̲éin	

English → Lingít

It is starting to rain.	
Maybe it will be sunny.	
It was warm weather.	
The weather is getting better.	
The weather was foggy.	
It was snowing yesterday, but it is sunny today.	
How is it outside?	
It will be warm weather.	

Made in the USA
Las Vegas, NV
27 August 2023